Foreword

Wherever the WEA was established in Britain at the beginning of the last century it seemed destined to start with a flourish and make itself quickly indispensable. The North-East of England, where the WEA has maintained its presence now for a hundred years, was no exception, once the Association got underway.

It's doubly encouraging that the burst of energy which characterised the WEA's early years in the North-East is again to the fore in the first decade of the twenty-first century. Over the last five years the WEA has become rejuvenated, rediscovering its mission and purpose and very effectively extending its connections with the North-East. Its recent partnerships with the Open University, the Co-operative Movement and UNISON in particular have also enhanced the work and reputation of the Association as a whole.

Perhaps the Pitmen Painters provide a fitting theme for the history of the WEA in the North-East. They developed their art and reputation through WEA classes in Ashington in the early decades of the WEA's existence, and they provided one of the more vivid images of the WEA's relevance into the twenty-first century.

It is inconceivable now for the WEA not to be part of the warp and weft of the North-East of England. Now that Lee Hall's remarkable play, The Pitman Painters, has successfully crossed the Atlantic to Broadway, should we expect a first base for the WEA in New York?

Richard Bolsin
General Secretary
Workers' Educational Association

Preface

This volume celebrates the centenary of the Workers' Educational Association (WEA) in the North and North-East. Whereas the WEA nationally was created in 1903, the inaugural meeting of what is now formally known as WEA North-East Region was held at the King's Hall of Armstrong College (later to become the University of Newcastle-upon-Tyne) on 29 October 1910. From early 2009 the WEA North-East Region started to think of ways of celebrating its hundreth birthday. Among many suggestions was the idea of writing a history. Could it be done in time? How would it differ from the two prior histories (Corbett, 1980 and Standen, 2003) of the Northern District? Starting from a meeting in April 2009, the Centenary Book Working Group decided to attempt the task. There were three early decisions which guided our work. The first was that the book would be multi-authored with chapters written by a variety of contributors. The second was our choice of title: *The Right to Learn.* At a very late stage we added to this title the explanation: *'the WEA in the North of England 1910-2010'.* The third decision was to develop the centenary book from earlier histories, using them to locate materials and ideas. In particular, the Group felt that in addition to chronicling the work of the WEA over the last hundred years, colour and depth should be incorporated wherever possible in the shape of people and events. Thus, we have linked the work of the WEA in this region to national events and also to the activities of students, tutors and affiliated organisations. This decision gave a structure which is reflected in the two broad sections of the new volume. The first is an 'Outline History' of the WEA in the North of England, and the second is called 'Themes, Vignettes and People'.

Our plan based on these early decisions was to persuade many people to become involved in the project as authors and 'witnesses'. Originally the intention was that all the chapters would be specially commissioned new work, but as the book developed the Group identified existing material that deserved re-publication. In the end *The Right to Learn* has fourteen specially written chapters and four which are reprinted from earlier work. Authors of the fourteen chapters were set firm deadlines and the task of identifying copyright holders for the four other chapters (8, 10, 13 and 17) was undertaken. The voices of student and tutor 'witnesses' are clearly deployed in Chapters 7 and 9. Anecdotes from many periods adorn the text. For instance, in Chapter 1, Nigel Todd relates the saga of District Secretary Jack Trevena who was a conscientious objector in the First World War. At a much later date Victor Cadaxa remembers in Chapter 15 a WEA Study Group visit to Kiev in 1989 which witnessed open conflict at a meeting with Ukraine's TUC Executive, presaging the break-up later that year of the old Soviet Empire. The chapters are written in differing styles and based on a variety of sources. In putting together a hybrid multi-authored work of this kind the Centenary Book Working Group is aware that its coverage is necessarily uneven, in that some periods are covered in much greater detail than others. Indeed, some years are scarcely mentioned. For example, the final fifteen years of our hundred receive scant attention, as does the period from 1940 to 1945. There is also little mention of the summer schools which played a major role up until at least the 1960s. With WEA histories perhaps there is an imperative to leave some of the story blank to allow for later interpretation!

Despite these gaps the volume well illustrates both continuity and change in the WEA North-East Region story. There is continuity in demanding the right to learn, in democratic structures right down to branch and class levels, and the necessary interaction between volunteers and professionals. At times both at branch and at the District or Regional levels there are tensions which surface. The essential democracy and the need for involved members is reflected in the words of Phyllis Heatley (1995) in her record of the Newcastle Branch:

> A WEA branch consists only of the energy and commitment of its members, and never achieves a separate existence. If active branch members withdraw, the branch goes into abeyance, but can be resuscitated by a fresh infusion of physical and mental energy. Newcastle Branch is fortunate in that for more than eighty years there has been a constant supply of people on whom it has existed, the written records now only whisper what was once discussed and decided with fervour and vision, and the dusty attic of memory holds only a few of the many branch activities of the branch, but the long series of committee and branch meetings has never stopped. (Heatley 1995: 2)

Our book looks in detail at two very different branches in Chapter 5, where Ian Roberts writes about Bellingham and Ruth Tanner about Darlington. The tensions at District level during the 1973-76 period are discussed by Jonathan Brown in Chapter 6. There is continuity also in the partnerships formed by the WEA particularly with the trade unions throughout the century. Tom Nesbit recalls his own work as a Trade Union Education Officer in Chapter 12. Another much later partnership with the Pre-School Playgroups Association (PPA) is the subject of Chapter 7. Up to relatively recent times there were almost umbilical partnerships and joint working with what were originally called the Extra-Mural Departments of the Universities of Durham and Newcastle-upon-Tyne. There is continuity also in student aspirations and progress. This is illustrated in many chapters in the second part of the book but particularly so in Chapters 7, 9, 12 and 15. The impact of the WEA on his life's journey is the subject, among so many other things, identified by Sid Chaplin in Chapter 17. Finally, there is the continuity of never having enough money in relation to all that needs to be done. Being hard up is a constant for the WEA. This is well articulated by Ian Roberts in Chapters 2 and 4 and by Michael Standen in Chapter 13. Penury is an ever-present sub-plot in the WEA story and is reflected in most of the chapters of this book.

Change is also reflected throughout the WEA Northern District's one hundred years. Changes in national government and its educational policies are the backcloth to Ruth Tanner's Chapter 3. At a later stage changes brought in after the Report of the Russell Committee (Russell, 1973) had a profound effect as Michael Standen recounts in Chapter 13, but see also Chapters 4, 6 and 11. Changes also occur over time to the curriculum. In the early days the social sciences were the WEA staple, but increasingly the humanities came to the fore. The challenges of introducing more science to the WEA programme are the subject of Nigel Todd's account of the WEA Science Project of the 1960s in Chapter 14.

In preparing the book for publication members of the Centenary Working Group have learned much about the development of the WEA Northern District: learned much about principles, practices, organisation, people and places. It has not been a dull process. We hope that this book reflects the spirit and the times of the WEA in the hundred years from 1910. We think it is readable and we hope you, the reader, will also agree.

The WEA is grateful to the following copyright holders: Messrs Jasper Lyon, P. W. Pickles, Mrs Irene Chaplin and Val and Guy Standen, for permission to reprint works by Robert Lyon, Hilda Pickles, Sid Chaplin and Michael Standen. Every effort has been made to obtain permission to reproduce extracts where appropriate and all other source materials have been acknowledged in the text.

Thanks are due also to Dr Máire West and Dr Jonathan West for editorial and proof reading services; Dr Ian Roberts and Dr Jonathan West for the Index; Liz Langdown; Ivan Corbett; the many WEA students and tutors who contributed to the book either directly or indirectly; Minna Ireland for initiating the concept of the centenary book; David Neville for additional information about Lisbeth Simm, and Tom Kelly for sharing his research into the life of Hilda Trevena (nee Johnson); Brenda Flynn and Kate Singlehurst for access to the Darlington branch archives; Andrew Palmer of Inspired Design for our book's cover design. Last but not least, we record our debt to the librarians and keepers at Tyne and Wear Records, which houses the WEA Northern District archives; London Metropolitan University, which houses the WEA National Archives; The National Archives at Kew and Newcastle City Library.

During the preparation of this book we were saddened to hear of the death of Peter Kaim Caudle, Professor Emeritus at the University of Durham. Peter was a keen supporter of the WEA from his early years at the then Durham Extra Mural Department (see Chapter 16); he became District Chair in 1975 to assist the District through a significant crisis (see Chapter 6), and was later our Vice-President. We also recently heard of the death of George Flynn, a stalwart of the Darlington Branch and a local history tutor. Both George and his wife Brenda are mentioned in Chapter 5.

The Centenary Book Working Group consisted of Jonathan Brown, Ian Roberts, Ruth Tanner and Nigel Todd. Their individual and collective enthusiasm and hard work has made this volume possible.

The WEA acknowledges funding to assist with publication from the Trusthouse Charitable Foundation, the History Workshop Trust, and Lord Jeremy Beecham.

Jonathan Brown
July 2010

SOURCES CITED

Corbett, Ivan, 2003. '"So noble an institution": A History of the Workers' Educational Association Northern District 1910-80'. In: Standen (2003a:5-81). [Originally published 1980.]

Heatley, Phyllis, 1995. *Something Sustained — The Newcastle upon Tyne WEA Branch (1912—)*. Newcastle upon Tyne, WEA Northern District.

Russell, Edward Lionel, 1973. *Adult education: a plan for development. Report by a Committee of Inquiry appointed by the Secretary of State for Education and Science under the Chairmanship of Sir Lionel Russell C.B.E.* London: HMSO.

Standen, Michael (ed.), 2003a. *A hunger to be more serious ...: The Story of the WEA Northern District.* Newcastle upon Tyne: WEA Northern District.

A Working-class Hero is Something to Be: the Origins of the Workers' Educational Association in the North-East to 1920

Nigel Todd

According to folklore, the movement that became known as the Workers' Educational Association (WEA) was formed in 1903 by Francis and Albert Mansbridge in the kitchen of their London home. Albert Mansbridge, a Co-operative Wholesale Society clerk by day, and an evening class teacher after office hours, was elected 'Honorary Secretary (*pro tem*)' by Francis, who lent 2*s*. 6*d* to get going. Within six months, the new secretary proved himself by convening a national conference at Toynbee Hall that elected a provisional organising committee of co-operators and trade unionists to take the movement forward.

It was a very ordinary beginning for an extraordinary story. As it happened, the Mansbridges had already prepared the ground and, as always, Albert Mansbridge had paid attention to detail before calling the conference. One fact was certain. The North-East of England was there at the beginning. According to Albert Mansbridge, 'the first organisation to enter its affiliation with the provisional body was the Co-operative Society at Annfield Plain, Co. Durham' (Mansbridge 1920:12). A month later, representatives of most of England's six universities gave their endorsement, following a conference with the provisional committee at Oxford chaired by George Kitchin, Dean of Durham and Chancellor of the University of Durham.

Schools — bad and better

Most people would have been completely unaware of the Mansbridges' ambitions for them. Among the majority was five-year-old Harold Heslop, son of a colliery overman, living at New Hunwick, Bishop Auckland. Attending 'the council school at the top of the street', Heslop recalled:

> We suffered the stinging lashes of the cane of the master […] wept over our sore hands […] and yet he thumped the permitted lessons into our heads […] Whatever knowledge I came to possess passed over the beginnings inculcated by him. (Heslop 1994:82-3)

Victorian and Edwardian schooling could be a poor inducement to lifelong learning. Of course, not everyone shared Heslop's grim experience. Jack Lawson, another miner's son, went to an elementary school in the 'interminable unpicturesque streets' of the great industrial and social melting pot of Boldon Colliery in the 1890s. Lawson

> […] liked that school at Boldon, and have very grateful memories of the headmaster and teachers — especially one George Grey […] He was an artist of getting a lesson home, and one who could secure discipline. He was an uncertificated teacher, but divinely endowed to teach, and many there are in all parts of the world who think of him with gratitude and affection.

But at twelve, Lawson was off to work at the pit and 'freedom from school' (Lawson 1944:43).

Harold Heslop, despite everything, wanted to stay at school, and passed a scholarship examination in 1911 enabling him to attend 'the most down-at-heel establishment in the British Isles' at Bishop Auckland's James I Grammar School: 'There were better facilities in a wayside pub.' It didn't last long. In just a few months Heslop's father had taken a better job at a remote ironstone mine near Boulby Head on the Cleveland coast and the family moved with him. Without a grammar school in walking distance, Heslop too went down the mine, if less keenly than Lawson, starting 'my servitude in the underworld' (Heslop 1994:88-9).

For girls, education was generally rigidly prescribed. They were less likely to work outside the home than in any other part of the country due to the prevalence of male-dominated heavy industries such as mining, shipbuilding and engineering, together with the custom of early marriage and consequent high birth rates.

Elementary schools institutionalised these social expectations in ways signalled by the new higher elementary school at Atkinson Road, Benwell, Newcastle-upon-Tyne, in 1910:

> To a great extent distinctive instruction will be given to boys and girls, so that each may be fitted for the duties

of adult life. For boys […] who intend to enter the engineering and allied trades […] a course of instruction in the elements of machine drawing, physics and mechanics; while for those intended for commercial life a course in book-keeping, shorthand and commercial practice will be given. The girls, as a rule, will receive training in needlework, dressmaking, cookery and laundry, and be instructed in domestic science and hygiene; but the other courses will also be open to them should it be desired. (Callcott 1999:85)

Conditions could be more limiting in the countryside. Children's education in Northumberland was often disrupted when agricultural workers moved between farms at the annual 'hiring fairs', low wages made it impossible to afford secondary education fees, and 'clever girls fared even less well than their brothers partly because of the prevailing belief that education was likely to be wasted on a girl who would get married, rather than pursuing a career' (Brook 2005:30). Cycles of harvesting and lambing interrupted schools' work, buildings could be below standard, and attracting and retaining teachers, particularly female teachers, in remote areas where local farmers were school managers was hard (Roberts *et al.* 2008). Nevertheless, as Jack Lawson noted, those teachers who were committed and professional still managed to convey a passion for learning.

Lawson, having joined the miners' union, found his horizons broadened by reading labour newspapers. He joined a branch of the Independent Labour Party (ILP) at Boldon in 1904, and began visiting a socialist bookseller in Newcastle market: 'To them I would go on pay Saturdays to buy books and pamphlets, and there I met kindred souls from other parts of Northumberland and Durham' (Lawson 1944:75). Gripped by the belief that education was essential to 'breaking the serf-status to which the manual worker is condemned', Lawson launched into 'organising adolescent classes' at his mother's home, soon extending his scope:

> We had great times and I was much encouraged. A group of us, including some school teachers, started an adult school, with lectures and a gymnasium. There was also a very good art class. This went on for years in a building made by knocking two colliery houses into one […] This, it must be reported, was long before the Workers' Educational classes, or any such organisations, had been heard of. (Lawson 1944:75)

It was a road that led Lawson in 1907 to a year's study at Ruskin College, Oxford, then emerging as a residential centre for working men with trade union and socialist leanings. Only a minor miracle of family fund-raising and help from a county councillor made it possible to meet the proportion of the costs not covered by a scholarship. Several years later, Harold Heslop, now a miner at Harton Colliery, South Shields, attended Ruskin's rival, the Central Labour College (CLC) in London, on a Durham miners' union grant. Both returned to the pits to pursue political, trade union and adult education aims.

Women challenging the barriers

Meanwhile, women were building their own fragmented access to education. The Women's Co-operative Guild, whose first North-East branch was formed in 1884 at Wallsend, arranged lectures and classes on domestic, co-operative and 'citizenship' topics, sometimes linked with seeking improved maternity, health and education services.

From the turn of the century, Labour and other socialist organisations with membership open to women and female suffrage movements grew rapidly. One of the most spirited was the Women's Labour League (WLL) whose North-East secretary, Lisbeth Simm (1870-1952), had grown up in the Northumberland coalfield. A brilliant organiser and a fluent writer for Labour newspapers on social and economic equality for women, Simm helped set up over twenty League branches in the North-East between 1906 and 1914, providing a platform for political education in working class neighbourhoods from Blyth and North Shields to Stanley, Shildon and Hebburn. She could function equally well as a member of the national executive of the WLL and as a speaker at open air market place meetings when this was rare for women. Married to Matt Simm, the ILP's North-East organiser, she was told to stay at home and look after her husband during elections by opponents, but she fought her way on to a Board of Guardians at Gosforth, campaigning for free school meals (Collette 1989:121-122; see also Neville 1997).

Above all, as someone who had become a school teacher using the pupil teacher pathway, she saw education as a liberating force, brushing aside those who claimed that women would neglect the home if they were educated:

> In schools we contrive that each lesson shall encourage the reasoning powers of our girls, but when they put these same powers into practice, and ask why life is such a burden to the poor […] then they are subjected to foolish criticism. I do not think that any woman's brain was meant to exert itself wholly on cooking food, but I think if

she is capable of grasping the meaning of the great social problem [...] surely she will manage the other thing. (Neville 2007:47)

Connecting education and social reform flowed from deep sources. Under the leadership of Joseph Cowen, the North-East's dominant radical throughout the second half of the nineteenth century, popular education had been championed through large circulation newspapers, theatre, political campaigns, and the Co-operative Movement as the foundation for a 'militant democracy' based on universal suffrage. Cowen had opened up the mechanics' institutes to women as well as men, introduced discussion circles and 'liberal' subjects, and made reading rooms available on Sundays as early as the 1840s and 1850s. The Cowenite institutes even provided children's playgrounds so that the whole family could take part in learning (Allen 2007:51-58, 116-8; Todd 1991:27-29).

The universities' false start

During the 1870s, Cowen called for a university in Newcastle, registering partial success when the University of Durham agreed to create Armstrong College. An initial bonus was the launch of Durham's University extension lectures at Newcastle in 1879 with help from the Newcastle Literary and Philosophical Society. Approximately 3,500 people attended the first lecture series and a students' association was formed.

At its height, the North-East led the way in university extension, notably among the miners. Over 1,300 working miners attended extension lectures, chiefly in political economy and mining technology, science and literature at five centres on Tyneside in 1880, with colliery owners subsidising the scheme. Welbourne, in his history of the Northumberland and Durham miners summarised how the scheme unfolded:

> [...] there was an unprecedented and perhaps unequalled awakening of interest in education [...] In 1883 the University Extension Lectures were given the official support of the Durham Miners' Association. At union meetings, in the union circulars the advantages of study were urged upon the miners. Over a thousand men attended the lectures given that winter, losing wages and paying fines for shifts missed to learn elementary science, history, and political economy. The local secretary of the movement paid a high tribute to the intelligence of his new pupils, to their straightforwardness of speech and their appreciative attention. (Welbourne 1923 cited in Simon 1974:89)

It was a 'thrilling chapter' in adult education, though one that closed as suddenly as it opened. The death knell was a four-month miners' strike against wage reductions that gripped the northern coalfield in 1887, 'reduced the miners to penury' but undermined the extension movement ideologically. This was because the university approach to political economy implied the supposed common interests of miners and colliery owners, justifying the 'sliding scale' that increased wages when trade was buoyant but failed to guarantee a living wage at other times. The system was finally discredited on the back of a twelve-and-a half-per-cent cut in wages. During the consequent bitter industrial struggle, new views of political economy, spread by socialists such as William Morris and Tom Mann, attracted the miners and reshaped their unions' politics. Here, then, was a foretaste of subsequent debates about what should be taught in adult education (Simon 1974:90).

The impressive numbers attending lectures meant that the extension experiment came to be regarded as 'the glory days' by adult educators after 1900 (*The Highway,* April 1911, p. 98). These included Dr. F. B. Jevons, Principal of Durham's Hatfield College, who had held 'working men's classes [...] in his younger days above a shop on Framwellgate Bridge, Durham', and became Treasurer and then Chair of the WEA in the North-East continuously from 1910 to 1927 (Whiting 1932:257).

The arrival of the WEA

Against a background of interest in education, the North-East should have been ready ground for the WEA. Yet the seeds sprouted hesitantly. Although the North-East shared in the foundation of the WEA nationally, the Association struggled initially to put down roots in the area as other parts of England raced ahead in forming branches and districts.

At first, the signs had been promising. Numbers of people from the North-East joined the Association, including the Bishop of Newcastle and the first miners' MP, Thomas Burt. Darlington stood out as keen to pioneer the WEA, but not until three years after the national launch. Mansbridge reported moves to form a Darlington Branch in May 1906 (see Chapter 5), and a 'town conference' the following September conjured a 'federation' of trade unionists, co-operators, benefit societies, a prominent councillor and the Mechanics' Institute — a model of the Mansbridge concept of a WEA 'federal' Branch. Even better, the secretary,

R. Murray, agreed to act as voluntary District Secretary, and a Durham Branch, with Dean Kitchin as President, and support from three unions and the city's education committee, took shape in December.

It all came to very little. The Durham Branch faltered, and Darlington seems to have closed by 1909, though Murray remained as notional District Secretary. Why the movement remained so tenuous is unclear, but one of Association's pioneers, Tom Metcalfe, a miner at Bishop Auckland, later pointed to 'prejudice and jealousy' that harked back to the experience of the 1880s:

> [...] the Miners' Lodges generally were distrustful of the aims of coalowners and other employers who it was believed were financing the Association. Although the Association was avowedly un-sectarian and non-party there were fears that the movement might become a channel for the propagation of unorthodox and dangerous ideas in industrial and economic fields. What an atmosphere in which to evoke support for a scheme of adult education for the ordinary worker. (Metcalfe 1953:8)

Mansbridge and his allies

Luckily for Mansbridge, more sympathetic interest gradually made itself known from three sources. Firstly, Tom Metcalfe recalled that he and 'a small group of young colleagues in our lodge decided on a plan of campaign'. Tramping around the miners' lodges, they finally generated interest in the WEA within the Durham Miners' Association.

Coincidentally, the co-operative societies' education committees put up their own plan of campaign. Those societies whose members elected education committees, and voted funds for education, began to affiliate to the WEA. Annfield Plain and Darlington have already been mentioned but in 1909 the larger Jarrow and Hebburn Society which, along with the Sunderland, Wallsend and Blaydon Co-operative Societies, was a leader in the co-operative commitment to education in the North-East, affiliated as well.

Mansbridge's friend, W. R. Rae, a Sunderland head teacher who chaired the Co-operative Movement's Central Education Committee got involved and so too did Wilson Clayton, a cashier at the Consett Iron Company and an influential co-operator. Clayton, another friend of Mansbridge, was secretary to the region's Co-operative Education Committees' Association and in that role took over from Murray as *pro tem* WEA District Secretary.

Rae and Clayton lent their considerable weight to aiding the WEA, marshalling and organising resources that were beyond Mansbridge's dreams in the cash-strapped national Association. They were motivated partly by a strong commitment to the value of education generally, a belief embedded in the origins of the Co operative Movement. On the other hand, they recognised the limitations of what small co-operatives could provide. And not all co-operators agreed with spending money on education, preferring higher dividends. Even the Annfield Plain Society was gently criticised by its official historians:

> But when we look into the [...] ways in which a Co-operative society can be used to the benefit of those who form its membership, we cannot but conclude that the Annfield Plain Society might have done considerably better than it has done. The educational and social possibilities of the Society might have had more attention. It has, of course, had its occasional Co-operative classes and made modest attempts to inaugurate reading rooms here and there, but a Society of such trading proportions, situated in an area and with a membership so full of potency, has had wonderful possibilities of educational and social uplift, other than those which are purely material, and one cannot but conclude that with a wider vision and a slightly higher interpretation of what the Co-operative idea means a much larger contribution might have been possible. (Ross and Stoddart 1921:83-4)

Rae saw a need for more training in co-operation and in the skills required by staff to manage co-operative societies, and among lay members and committees to properly assess performance. The WEA could fit the bill.

The third ingredient was the National Union of Teachers (NUT). Edwardian England was turbulent for an NUT that saw itself as opposing an 'undemocratic' and 'caste ridden' government Board of Education whose civil servants were 'haughtily prejudiced' and conniving to impose 'public school men from Whitehall' on local education authorities as inspectors. The point was emphasised at the NUT's national conference in 1911 by a delegate named Mr. Pickles:

> The old liberal policy [...] was to provide an open road with no unbridged moat for every scholar able and willing to continue his education. The policy of some of the [Board of Education] permanent officials was the medieval plan which barred the road to the masses, picked up here and there a clever lad of lowly birth, took him out of his order, fitted him with the education of the ruling classes, and made him one of them — a system which had been described as providing a handful of prigs and an army of serfs. (Tropp 1957:193)

Pickles's colourful caricature was not out of place in the explosive labour militancy of the period. But NUT thinking had its own distinctive dimension, noted by Beatrice Webb in a very Fabian eulogy:

> The leaders of the NUT [...] had a vision of an all-embracing system of public education from the infant school to the modernized university, administered by one ad hoc elected local authority, regulated by one central Government Department. (cited by Tropp 1957:174)

Underpinning the structure, there would be appointments on merit in education and administration, schooling at no cost to parents, and an end to class distinction. Sensing that Mansbridge and his colleagues were allies, County Durham's teachers' association and two Newcastle NUT associations declared for the WEA, and other local associations soon followed.

The WEA adventure begins

In this context, Mansbridge carefully built support for launching the WEA in the North-East. He reported in June 1909 that he had 'interviewed representatives of various activities', enlisting their help for a conference at Newcastle. The soundings were sufficiently positive for Mansbridge to confirm:

> our intention to convene a large Conference at Newcastle [...] The reconstruction of the University of Durham, which will become the University of Newcastle and Durham, will increase the facilities open to workpeople in those parts. We shall have a hearty welcome from the University and the movements of workpeople. (WEA Central Executive *Minutes* 15 June 1909 and WEA *Annual Report* 1909)

The conference took place on 31 October 1909 at the King's Hall, Armstrong College, Newcastle, with much of the organisation provided by Rae and the co-operators, supplemented by personal invitations from Mansbridge to people who might help. Dean Kitchin chaired and Dr Hadow, Principal of Armstrong College, was also present. Representatives of the Northumberland, Newcastle and County Durham education committees were there, as were those of 119 societies including co-operatives and their women's guilds, the North-East Federation of Trades and Labour Councils, the Club and Institute Union (CIU), the Durham Miners' Association, the Newcastle and County Durham NUT associations, along with other unions.

Whilst it was an impressive gathering, there was still an argument to win. Tom Tilley, who was present and much later became Chair of the WEA in the North-East, remembered the conference as one of :

> great enthusiasm, mixed with not a little suspicion on the part of the advanced Trade Unionists on the one hand, and the old fashioned Tories on the other, each doubting the goodwill of the other in the spirit of the times.

Dean Kitchin, whose 'widely accepted impartiality and social work made him an admirable chairman of what might easily have proved a difficult meeting', defused antipathies. Mansbridge 'spoke for nearly an hour':

> His gift of exposition, his social appeal, his religiously based visions of a future England, and his prophetic eloquence all combined to hold his difficult audience spell-bound. (Tilley 1953:4)

Apparently, Mansbridge didn't hold back on the radical aims of the Association:

> They were out to make a great highway of education. They did not want any ladder from the primary school to the universities. A ladder was the most pernicious educational instrument ever invented. A few working men get into university and then promptly forget their old association with the people. They wanted a highway so broad and so free that brains and character would open the door to the highest and best educational fare that England had to offer. (*The Journal,* Newcastle-upon-Tyne, 1 November 1909)

Rae, an eloquent public speaker, and many other 'skilled debaters' added their views, culminating in endorsement of a proposal from the Durham miners to elect a provisional committee charged with planning a further conference in a year's time to formally launch a 'Northern Section' of the WEA.

The 'powerful provisional committee', composed of members of the co-operatives' education committees and boards, Armstrong College, the local authority education committees, the CIU, and the NUT set to work on preparing a constitution. Places were left open for any further affiliates and within a few months co-operatives, teachers' associations, and other societies joined, including the boilermakers', enginemen's, postmen's, pattern makers' and typographical unions, as well as several trades councils, many as a result of local conferences held at West Stanley, Sunderland, Jarrow, Ashington, Blyth, Gateshead and Bedlington. Wilson Clayton acted as secretary and organiser.

The committee did its job well, and when the founding conference met at the King's Hall on 29 October 1910, there was a prepared air of expectation. Dean Kitchin once more chaired and over a hundred societies sent representatives. Mansbridge spoke but this time to call the new North-East District of the WEA into existence. Dr. Hadow was elected District Chairman, and Jevons became Treasurer. A District Executive Committee and a wider District Council were established, and their memberships populated from trade unions, clubs, the co-operatives, political and other societies and a growing list of individual members. (Tilley 1953:4; WEA NE District Executive, *Minutes,* 19 November 1910)

Interestingly, those who framed the constitution made sure that women could be elected to the District Executive by reserving places for them if other routes were blocked. This probably reflected the influence of Independent Labour Party women like Lisbeth Simm who joined the Executive, together with Florence Harrison Bell from the Newcastle Women's Co-operative Guild. Both were active in the women's suffrage campaign, and Florence Bell had been the first secretary of the Newcastle Labour Representation Committee.

The John Lee years: 1910-1914

The 1910 Newcastle conference was the turning point. It consolidated a framework of organisational alliances, and brought together that core of activism essential in advancing the Association. And it created a basis for at least some consistency of funding through affiliation and individual membership fees (at 2s. 6d.). Key to making progress was the appointment of a full-time District Secretary, John Lee (1874-1953). Forced out of his living as a Baptist minister at Jarrow by chapel elders who objected to his support for striking dockers, Lee had not been paid for his last six months as minister (Wilson 1979). With the WEA he was to be paid £2 a week, working from his Dunston home but, when this proved impractical, Wilson Clayton arranged an office free of charge in the Co-operative Wholesale Society's building at 84 Westmoreland Road, Newcastle (Corbett 2003:14; Tilley 1953:4-5; WEA NE District Executive, *Minutes,* 2 May 1911).

Lee conducted the job with little concern for his own comforts. His weekly diary entries reveal a punishing schedule of meetings, interviews and, in a commonplace of the times, a willingness to walk as when he visited Ashington in December 1910: 'to save expense I walked 4 or 5 miles to Blyth and stayed overnight with my brother' (Corbett 2003:11). Lee's role was to act as a class and branch organiser, an advocate for the WEA, the secretariat for the new District, and for much of the time a fund raiser since the £2 a week salary was always precarious. Durham University made a contribution of £10 early in 1911, and £50 a year later, but this by no means covered the expenses. As local authority financial support was not forthcoming, Lee spent many evenings and Saturdays visiting trade union and importantly, club committees, gathering affiliation fees.

The Highway, the WEA's monthly national magazine, in a regular column on the working men's clubs, noted that Jevons and 'the ever-energetic' Lee managed to enlist the support of the Durham and Northumberland Club and Institute Unions with help from Thomas Burt MP. The County Durham CIU was represented on the WEA District Council by T. Bland, one of the Association's North-East founding members. Galvanising the clubs took a great deal of Lee's time, but with Bland's assistance it was possible to arrange conferences and meetings at Darlington, South Shields, Hebburn Quay, Felling, Brandon, Langley Moor, Spennymoor, and Middlestone Moor in 1911. At Hebburn Quay club, the WEA ran Sunday evening lectures on topics spanning child care, Robert Burns, labour and art, and the ideals of education (*The Highway,* August 1911, p. 176).

The work flourished. WEA branches were set up at West Stanley, Jarrow, Sunderland, and Gateshead in 1911, followed by Newcastle, South Shields, Easington, Carlisle and Spennymoor in 1912, and Darlington and Stockton in 1913. Some of these branches were 'federal' which meant, in Newcastle's case, that 'almost half the members were representatives of other organisations' including trade unions, co-operative guilds and adult schools, (Heatley 1995:2) Sunderland, under Rae's leadership, assumed a similar profile. The records are incomplete, but there are reports of WEA activity at Wallsend, Whitley Bay, Blyth, Bishop Auckland, Jarrow, Consett, Langley Moor (a meeting of 300 people), Middlesbrough and Stockton that produced branches, in several cases prior to 1914.

A detailed account of the meeting to form the West Stanley Branch appeared in *The Highway* in April 1911, highlighting the almost 'missionary' appeal projected by the WEA along with careful recruiting of local support. Held at the Co-operative Hall, the conference:

> foregathered the delegate from the Miners' Lodge, the ILP member, the co-operator, the schoolmaster, the trade

unionist of every type, together with the members of the women's guilds. Here, in fact, one could almost say, was a representative of every type of organised democracy of the 20th century. What were they there for? Not to vie with each other [...] but to further so far as possible the common cause of education on behalf of the working classes of this district.

Alderman Henry Curry Wood, who chaired the Durham County Council Education Committee, presided and other speakers included the Rev. W. E. Moll (a well known ILP-er) and George Hyden from the NUT's local executive. John Lee outlined the WEA and answered many questions, making the point:

There is to be nothing formal or stereotyped about the teaching, but, on the contrary, the classes are to be something in the nature of a round table conference, with the teacher in the middle, who holds himself open to be questioned at any point.

The meeting voted unanimously to set up a provisional committee and elected an interim Secretary before dispersing with no regrets about missing a major football cup match at Newcastle (*The Highway,* April 1911, pp. 106-07). Later in the year, the Stanley WEA had seventeen affiliates, including miners' lodges, the ILP, social clubs, co-operatives and the Amalgamated Union of Co-operative Employees.

Branches invented a variety of interests, with women's education frequently seen as a high priority. These ranged from Dr Lilian Macgregor's 'experimental' classes on 'Constitutional and Industrial History' for women at Newcastle and Jarrow in 1911 ('Pioneering Women of the Nineteenth Century'), which had a connection with women's suffrage campaigns (Aird 1982), to the West Stanley Branch's tutorial classes in literature and economics, together with the creation of a choir and a drama society and a 'women's section' class on 'Health and the Home' (Corbett 2003:7). As an insight into the kind of disadvantage the WEA sought to rectify, *The Highway* applauded the South Shields Branch in January 1913 when 'the wife of one of its most active members — a platelayer — has lately learned to read, at the age of 65'.

Public conferences on education reform were another branch province, serving as a meeting point with the NUT and sometimes the co-operators. Newcastle arranged a series of conferences in 1913-14 on 'The Next Step for Educational Reform', covering universities, secondary and primary schools, and with Margaret Bondfield, WLL national secretary, on 'The Higher Education of Working Women' (in 1929 Margaret was to become the first woman member of a British Cabinet). Similar efforts were made at Middlesbrough, where a joint conference on primary education with the NUT was held in April 1914. Jevons supported the branches with a speaking tour (*The Highway,* November 1913, p. 38 and April 1914, p. 136).

The tutorial classes

Alongside the broad growth, Lee embedded the WEA's 'gold standard', a programme of 'University Tutorial Classes' held as weekly two-hour sessions over three years. The tutorial classes, constructed in partnership with universities, were the basis of Mansbridge's appeal for university funding. But it was essential that the students' work matched university expectations, so a good deal of evidence and monitoring had to be marshalled by the WEA to confirm that industrial workers could function at the same level as undergraduates. Students pledged to attend the tutorial classes regularly and submit written essays. It was a challenging scheme, not because the worker students lacked ability but they had to study in very unfavourable circumstances, not least for women, and remain intellectually alert after their shifts. Most of them had to learn how to express themselves in writing and in an essay format.

The tutorial classes created an unusual institution, the Joint Committees for Tutorial Classes, composed of equal representation from universities and labour organisations. Lee, Hadow and Jevons helped to form a Joint Committee with Durham University in 1911 and the WEA recruited the nine labour representatives from trade unions, the CIU, Labour councillors, adult schools and the co-operatives. A target of four tutorial classes was agreed though this was exceeded. Eight were operating by June 1912 when the first summer school was convened at Hatfield College (Mansbridge, 1913; Stevenson 1918: 293-294 and Munby 2003: 212-218).

Greater ambitions followed, articulated by Jevons following a conference of Durham tutorial class summer school students in January 1914:

It is from the WEA that the students in the tutorial classes have come; but the classes must not provide a means of exit from the WEA or a temptation to desert it. The WEA wants the students back again after their three years' course is over. It wants them to be the centres of its study circles, the leaders in its discussions, the lecturers, both to its short-course classes and to its tutorial classes. For all these purposes the WEA should be or become sufficient in itself. (The Highway, February 1914, p. 92)

The WEA tradition of 'growing your own tutor' was born.

Committing to a tutorial class was a big step for most miners, shipyard and shop workers, and Lee's task was to make sure that they understood the pressures. In this he could draw on an emerging pattern of branch courses:

> Most Branches held short lecture courses. These were seen as a stimulus to the establishment of fully fledged Tutorial Classes and not as an alternative. Easington Branch, for instance, had organised a course of six lectures on the 'Growth of English literature' given (in the Temperance Hall, Haswell) by Mr. A. B. Harsley of West Hartlepool. In the village school at Easington, Mr. J. W. Ramsbottom BA, 'the newly appointed lecturer in Economics at Armstrong College' gave six lectures on 'Economic Developments in the 19th Century'. A further half-dozen single lectures were given at South Easington and Haswell, one of the lecturers being a Mr G. D. H. Cole, MA from Oxford. Meanwhile [...] starting on the 9th January 1914 a class for the study of 'Plato's Republic' will commence in The Rectory. (Corbett 2003:7)

Additionally, branches developed one-year 'preparatory' courses that could be taken as either self-contained programmes or as stepping stones into tutorial classes.

WEA tutors

Lee could also count on keen tutors, some of whom were volunteers simply 'pleased to get their tram fare' and others, like Lilian MacGregor, donated their fees to the WEA (Corbett 2003:13). A few were employed by either the WEA or the Tutorial Classes Committee and three of these were Meredith Atkinson, Philip Brown and Harry Hallsworth.

Meredith Atkinson (1883-1929), the son of a Hartlepool blacksmith, had followed a scholarship route through elementary school, became an assistant school teacher in Hartlepool, and gained a degree at Keble College, Oxford, in 1908. Introduced to the WEA by the co-operator, Muriel Madams, who tutored his correspondence class on Co-operation, Atkinson became 'a disciple of Albert Mansbridge', returning to the North-East as an extension lecturer for Durham University. He spoke in favour of establishing the WEA at the 1909 King's Hall conference, and was seen by those who knew him as

> a man of wide sympathy and deep culture, singularly fortunate in attracting to himself and the work he was supporting very large numbers of friends. His passion for the welfare of others always led him to overwork.

Atkinson was tireless in promoting the WEA — he helped to start the Carlisle Branch — as well as tutoring on economic history and his favourite subject, 'Social Problems'. Always keen on innovation, he would be one of the first to use the 'wireless' as a tool for adult education (The Times, 16 May 1929; The Highway, February 1912, p. 80; March 1914, pp. 111-112; Tilley 1953:4; Osmond 1979.121-2).

Atkinson's WEA journey was slightly more 'home-grown' than the journey that brought Philip Brown to the North-East. Born at Beckenham, Kent, in 1886 to middle class parents, Brown attended Malvern and New College, Oxford, where he took a First Class Honours degree in History in 1909. He spent a couple of terms acting as private secretary to Gilbert Murray, Oxford's Regius Professor of Greek, a man of Liberal politics and anti-imperialist internationalism. But sharing Atkinson's interest in the WEA (Brown had started to tutor for the Association in Oxford), he moved to the North-East in 1911 as the first full-time Tutorial Classes Committee lecturer. From 1912, he combined his Durham post with a similar lectureship at the London School of Economics, assuming an 'enormous' amount of work and travelling, but when offered a post at Newcastle 'which would have halved his work and doubled his salary' he turned it down: 'It was not teaching working men; and the teaching of working men was what he liked' (Brown 1965:Introduction). Brown, in common with numbers of his contemporaries, put his social conscience above his own privileges and advantages.

Atkinson and Brown joined the slightly older Harry Hallsworth (born 1876), an Oldham economist who had graduated from Manchester University in 1901. Hallsworth co-authored an influential study of unemployment in Lancashire, where he tutored university tutorial classes, and was appointed a lecturer in Economic History at Armstrong College in 1910, with a strong expectation that he should work closely with John Lee. A fairly orthodox economist, Hallsworth was capable of apparent liberalism, as he confirmed in one of his early lectures on the distribution of wealth:

> But very great inequality is not inevitable. Nor is it desirable. It brings grave social dangers. Less inequality would render society more stable and more united. It would also greatly increase the sum of human happiness.

Hallsworth's preference, however, was to allow 'natural economic forces' to bring about change (*The Highway,* December 1910, p. 35; Hallsworth 1913:17-18).

Hallsworth brought a connection between teaching and influencing public policy towards industry and employment. Atkinson echoed this with a fascination for pushing back the boundaries of economic history and exploring the new discipline of sociology. And Brown collaborated with R. H. Tawney and Alfred Bland on producing a collection of economic history primary source documents for use in WEA classes. He began work too on his own book (Brown 1965), *The French Revolution in English History*, tracking the reception for democratic ideas and reflecting the kind of historical writing subsequently associated with his WEA contemporary, G. D. H. Cole.

Atkinson and Brown wanted to make learning accessible for their students. This drove Brown, Tawney and Bland (Bland, Brown and Tawney 1914) to publish their well-regarded *English Economic History: Select Documents* for use in tutorial classes, allowing the students to explore interpreting original texts. Atkinson dealt with a chief barrier facing adult students, namely how to produce essays, read effectively and take relevant notes. Invariably persuasive, he got Lee and the District executive to print vast numbers of his booklet, *First Aid in Essay Writing,* price 3*d.*, in November 1913. These were sold throughout the WEA, but there were still four hundred copies taking up space in the Newcastle office by 1917. *First Aid in Essay Writing* was an exemplar guide for explaining study skills. Written in a modern, crisp style, with none of the flowery language typical of the period, it contained a 'model' essay on trade union history. Atkinson based the booklet on his experience of WEA classes, and spoke directly to adult students, emphasising clear communication and 'natural' writing styles expressing 'independence' of thought.

This powerful combination of youthful enthusiasm and academic talent brought energy and intellectual credibility to the WEA. By the 1912-13 session, the numbers of tutorial classes had sharply risen to seventeen with all but two tutored by Hallsworth, Brown, and Atkinson (*The Highway,* November 1912, p. 26; Atkinson 1913:4).

For Lee, building the new movement took a personal toll. Mansbridge suggested that Rae offer 'a word of cheer' to the District Secretary in August 1911 as he was 'I think, a bit depressed because the harvest in the North-East has not ripened as quickly as he hoped'. Lee had a troubling time with Dr. Hadow who rewrote Lee's circulars, and he complained about being regarded as a 'servant'. Early in 1913, he was 'unwell' and off work for about two months and the District Executive set aside money for 'help for Mr. Lee' whom they believed was overworked. Unfortunately, the District had financial problems that must have worried Lee, and Mansbridge asked G. D. H. Cole, who was lecturing on 'Syndicalism' for WEA branches in the North-East, to make enquiries. Cole found an 'apparent catastrophe' in the making due to a 'misunderstanding' that had led to subscriptions being made to the District by mistake (Mansbridge Papers: letter to W. R. Rae, 30 August 1911; Corbett 2003:10, 12; WEA NE Executive, *Minutes,* 15 February 1913; Mansbridge Papers: letter to G. D. H. Cole, 11 March 1914).

By the early autumn of 1914, Lee had called it a day, returning to religion as a Unitarian minister in Sheffield.

Jack Trevena

The District Executive acted speedily, and without advertising, to fill Lee's post. They had a very willing volunteer. Jack Trevena had been a tutorial class student at Stanley where he was a miner. The District Council had given financial support in 1913-14 for him to attend the new adult residential Fircroft College opened by George Cadbury at Selly Oak, Birmingham, and he was soon hoping to work for the WEA. Trevena had heard Mansbridge tell a WEA conference in Derby that the WEA was 'under-staffed' and promptly wrote offering his services. Mansbridge replied in May 1914 that the movement was 'really under-staffed because we have no money'. Undaunted, Trevena asked again in June, and Lee's departure soon afterwards as war broke out in Europe probably placed Trevena in the right place at the right time. Trevena was just as zealous about the WEA as Lee, but had a personal reason for returning to the North-East. He wanted to marry Hilda Johnson, the dynamic Secretary of the West Stanley WEA, and the object of his daily letters from Fircroft. The early WEA was not without its love stories (Mansbridge Papers: letter to Trevena, 22 May 1914 and letters from Trevena, 21 May and 8 June 1914).

Trevena wasted no time getting into the job and grappling with war-time conditions. His approach was summed up in lengthy and 'newsy' letters designed partly to encourage Mansbridge who was recovering from a severe illness:

> I am sitting in my diggings now, just returned from Sunderland, and ruminating on the WEA […] it has occurred to me to write you a cheery sort of letter. Well, in the first place, how are you both keeping?

> I give you a letter which might cheer your spirits. I expect you are getting anxious about me & wondering how I am getting on, so to relieve your anxiety I am going to give you a somewhat spry account of how the Movement is faring up here. The Movement is sound and there are no cases of absolute breakdown.

> [Two Branches are] slack but Mr. Lee says they have always been slack. Well, they are not going to slack any longer than the length of the War! It may mean in one or two cases getting the old secretaries to resign but that will be quite easy as I have got new energetic secretaries ready.

> I am going to make this a rule as far as possible to get the girls to take on the secretaries work. They are keener, are full of optimism and generally succeed in getting their own way.

> Since I came to Newcastle I called the women together of the Newcastle Branch; got them to appoint a Lady Secretary & now we have a women's class of 40 meeting regularly each week studying 'First Aid'. Then take Stanley, although perhaps I shouldn't speak of it for Miss Johnson the secretary is my promised wife; but still I'll just give you a short account of what they are doing.

Trevena went on to describe the Stanley Branch's tutorial and women's classes, dramatic society and even a Morris Dancing troupe. He added references to the Wallsend Branch, led by Miss McMurson the new secretary, a new women's section at the Sunderland Branch and prospects of branches at Howdon, Eppleton, Consett and Bishop Auckland.

Finally, Trevena wrote:

> I am certain if this War was over that the Movement would spread like wildfire […] Mr. Mansbridge please don't think this letter cocky. It is quite true every word of it & if this War was settled & we had an inspiring visit from you   why we should have 'a walk-over'!

> How does this make you feel? Cheer up. Well now I should say Goodnight & Goodbye. I hope you have a very Happy Xmas & that the New Year will find you well and starting again ready for the Fray. May this next year be the most Useful & consequently the happiest one you have ever spent! With kindest regards. Sincerely yours, Jack Trevena. (Mansbridge Papers: letter from Trevena, 18 December 1914)

Women take the lead

The openness of the North-East WEA towards women was a strength that Trevena grasped, but it was a virtue that now dovetailed with necessity. The Association was losing active members to the armed forces and male industrial workers found that longer shifts curbed their chances of attending meetings and classes. Women helped to fill the gaps. By 1915 four branches had female secretaries — Newcastle, West Stanley, Carlisle and South Shields — and at least twenty-seven classes were arranged for women with enrolments of between fifteen and thirty-five. Subjects covered included Literature, Hygiene, Home Nursing, First Aid, and at West Stanley 'The Economic Position of Women'. By 1916, eight out of twenty-six preparatory, or one-year, courses were for women and Trevena had gained District Executive approval to set up a women's advisory committee. This eighteen-strong committee included five branch nominees with the rest from the wider membership, including Lisbeth Simm, Hilda Trevena (formerly Johnson), and Dr Ethel Williams (WEA NE Executive *Minutes,* 29 July 1916).

Ethel Williams was the first female doctor to open a general practice in the North-East. Arriving in Newcastle in 1896, she was shunned by male GPs, but with Dr Ethel Bentham, she gradually built up a practice on the edge of Newcastle city centre, and with an emphasis on women's health. Williams and Bentham shared a house complete with Edwardian middle class social attributes of cook/servant, dressing for dinner and entertaining. But their guests were generally other female doctors and women involved variously in Socialist and Labour organisations, supported by Ethel Bentham, and women's suffrage campaigns in which Ethel Williams avidly took part.

Before the war, Williams had campaigned for the National Union of Women's Suffrage Societies and for improved child health services and school meals. She had moved away from the Liberals by 1914, being pro-Labour but not joining the Labour Party and on the outbreak of war worked with Lisbeth Simm providing material support for mothers when their men volunteered for the army. Extending her concern for women's health, she found the WEA.

The women kept the WEA afloat, but wartime pressures still reduced class attendances, finance was more restricted, and the numbers of tutorial classes fell to nine in 1914-15, reaching a low point of only four in 1916-17. On the other hand, the one-year preparatory classes were reported as 'much in demand by women' (WEA North East District, *Annual Report,* 1916, p. 17). Ethel Williams and Lisbeth Simm went into overdrive to promote and provide classes for women. Simm built a considerable following for her sewing classes at Newcastle, whilst Williams recruited new tutors from the Durham University Women's Graduates' Union which she chaired. Having her own car, Williams was able to tour the North-East assisting branches in setting up courses with female tutors on 'Famous Englishwomen', and women's health and problems. She played a leading part in arranging a programme of WEA lectures when the British Association for the Advancement of Science met at Newcastle in September 1916.

The challenge of the Labour Colleges

The women kept the WEA moderately vibrant as Trevena faced new threats. One of these was rivalry from supporters of the Central Labour College. Stemming from a 'strike' at Ruskin College in 1909, when the college staff and students divided over whether working class adult education should be influenced by the universities or fashioned around a Marxist agenda, Ruskin rebels formed their own 'Labour College', with local 'Plebs League' groups delivering an alternative to the WEA's liberal education. There was goodwill for the CLC in the North-East and Denis Hird, the former Ruskin College Principal, and then Warden of the break-away Central Labour College, was in Newcastle promoting the Labour College movement just prior to Mansbridge's 1909 conference (*North Mail,* 4 October 1909).

The Plebs League attracted support among younger Durham and Northumberland miners. Ebby Edwards had been a Ruskin student in 1908 and on his return to Northumberland took up the cause of the Central Labour College, immediately

> promoting independent working class education, first in his own lodge at Ashington, the largest in the union, starting and directing tutorial classes throughout the coalfield, and ultimately recruiting in the lodges a force of young and enthusiastic miners. (Craik 1964:115-116)

A collision with the WEA was inevitable. It hardly helped that the Association had found it impossible to establish a foothold in Ashington — 'the largest mining village in the world' — probably because the town already had its own well-developed adult education institution. Chester Armstrong, in his penetrating account of life and education in Ashington from 1889 to 1914, described the critical importance of the Ashington Debating and Literary Society as a centre for discussion, lectures and classes run by local miners. Rather like Lawther's adult school at Boldon, they felt that they had no need of the WEA. Once Edwards and the Plebs League got moving as well, things became much tougher and included a challenge in 1916 from the Ashington miners' lodge to the WEA to debate 'the Question of Partisan Education being best for the workers'. The invitation was declined, but the Plebs League campaign continued, prompting James McTavish, Mansbridge's successor as WEA General Secretary, to ask the North-East District Executive to 'discuss fully the subject of propaganda in Northumberland in order to counter the attacks of the CLC advocates'. A special 'propaganda committee' was formed and a conference with the miners' lodges was held (WEA NE Executive, *Minutes,* 17 July 1916 and 11 June 1917; Armstrong, 1938).

A similar process occurred in the Durham coalfield led by Will Lawther, a member of a Socialist mining family at Chopwell. Lawther reportedly described the WEA as the 'Wasted Effort Association' for many years (Hocking, n. d.). He had studied at the Central Labour College, and then set up the Chopwell Anarchist Club in 1912. Taking part in a national Anarchist-Communist conference at the Socialist Club in Newcastle in 1914 — a meeting described by a local newspaper reporter as resembling 'members of a young men's mutual improvement society […] extremists of an inoffensive kind' — he called for rejection of the 'doss house of Westminster' in favour of workers' control of industry. In Durham, Will Lawther 'pursued the same course that Ebby Edwards had already begun to take in Northumberland, organising tutorial classes in increasing number in the coalfield', including classes on Economics at Consett and Chopwell in 1915, and causing the DMA to create scholarships at the Central Labour College (*Newcastle Daily Chronicle,* 13 and 14 April 1914; Craik 1964:116; Simon 1974:336).

The struggle intensified in 1916 when Lawther and Edwards held a Trade Union Conference at Newcastle followed by an Open Letter from Lawther to the Durham miners calling for support for the Labour College and its local classes. When the WEA secured a £50 grant from the Durham miners and sought a similar amount from the Northumberland Miners' Union, Lawther and Edwards set up a regional Labour College organisation and Edwards challenged McTavish to a debate. The exchange subsequently took place at a great meeting in Newcastle convened by the WEA, sparking a lively pamphlet war nationally between the two movements. By 1917, 'the Labour College movement had taken firm roots among the miners of the North-East', boasting fifty trade union affiliated branches, sixteen classes, and money from the miners' unions (Simon 1974:336; see also McIlroy 1996).

Tensions and problems

Considerable sympathy for the WEA was also evident among the miners' unions, but Trevena had his work cut out dealing with Lawther and related issues nearer home. The problem was apparent at the meeting of the Durham Miners' Executive when the £50 was voted to the WEA. Trevena wrote to Mansbridge:

> When I came across the C.L.C. people last week in working for the Grant from the D.M.A. I was always taunted with our Capitalist Economist, Prof H. M. Hallsworth. And speaking quite frankly I think there is something in what they say about him teaching his ideas — apologist and pro-capitalist ones — to his students in the Tutorial Classes. I have met some of his ex-students and they are full of the Hallsworth doctrines about lack of thrift amongst the workers; need for big salaries to the organisers of labour, etc., etc. (Mansbridge Papers: letter from Trevena, 11 February 1916)

Hallsworth's free market economics had always been obvious. He maintained that 'the antagonism of labour and capital is less than is commonly supposed' and he was strongly against a introducing a state minimum wage, believing that wages should reflect the market. These ideas distanced him from a trend in labour opinion that saw the enhanced regulatory role of the war-time state in managing the economy as a vehicle for social justice in a post-war society (Hallsworth 1913:13). Trevena was blunt about Hallsworth:

> I wish to goodness he was away — I am sure the movement would be considerably stronger in consequence. I find his connection with us one of the biggest obstacles I have in furthering our work amongst men who have Labour sympathies.

And he had further concerns:

> I don't want him as a tutor & I hope to goodness I may be able to prevent him being one again. He has his eye on another class or, rather, the £60 a year, for he wrote to me last week saying that he thought it was time he had another class at Newcastle […] it will be a struggle to prevent Hallsworth from being a tutor but it will be done.

It wasn't just Hallsworth whom Trevena suspected of doubtful ethics. Another tutorial classes tutor named Wilson ('on the look out for No.1'), came into Trevena's sights when told that someone else had enquired about tutoring: 'When I told Wilson about it he walked about spluttering & weeping because he thought he was going to be done out of a class'.

Trevena found this shocking, telling Mansbridge:

> I am a little bit disgusted with all the self seeking that I come in contact with. I used to imagine when I was younger that the middle & upper class had none of the failings of the workers but now I find that they have all the failings without the virtues. Were it not that one had faith in the goodness at least among the workers, the work would be hardly worthwhile. I get more joy in going to address a Workmen's Club or Trade Union than in any other part of the work almost. (Mansbridge Papers: letter from Trevena, 11 February 1916)

Possibly the ex-miner Trevena was sensitive to the tensions inherent in a cross-class movement that had prompted Lee to note: 'There is a class distinction too marked, and a patronising air, which the workers notice and don't like' (Corbett 2003:12). An awkward issue to discuss at the best of times, Trevena kept his feelings confidential with Edwards and Lawther at the gates.

War takes its toll

The fracture with Hallsworth was a reminder that the creative triumvirate with Atkinson and Brown was over. Atkinson had left for Australia in March 1914, having been recommended as a tutorial classes tutor by Mansbridge. His primary job was to help build up the WEA in New South Wales, which he did impressively, if not without local controversy due to his pro-conscription advocacy. Atkinson was not forgotten and, in February 1916, Mansbridge wrote to tell him 'how pleased the North-East people were when I told them about your work'. Trevena might even have welcomed Atkinson as an ally, if only because of Atkinson's willingness to openly challenge contemporary pretensions as when he argued that 'correct English is not necessarily best English'. Australia's academic establishment was treated to his 'great charm and stormy temperament and intellect', his crusade for sociology and his ultimately successful bid to be a professor. They rewarded him by ensuring that he 'remained an outsider in academic circles' (Mansbridge Papers: Mansbridge to Meredith Atkinson, 1 February 1916; Atkinson 1913:24; Osmond 1979:121-122; Cole 1918:335-337; Mansbridge 1920:49).

More tragically, Philip Brown was dead. Along with several college friends, he had volunteered for the army in 1914, typically enlisting as a private, having no wish to be an officer. Persuaded eventually to accept a Second Lieutenancy in the Durham Light Infantry, he led men whom he had taught in his WEA classes. Conducting a night patrol in France on 4 November 1915, he was severely wounded. It took more than an hour under heavy fire for Durham miner, Private Thomas Kenny, to carry Brown back to the British lines, ignoring Brown's repeated suggestion that Kenny should save himself. Kenny earned the Victoria Cross (and the WEA's thanks) for his selfless bravery, but Brown died soon after being returned to safety. His Colonel wrote:

> He was the most popular officer with both men and officers in the regiment, and his platoon were so angry that they could with difficulty be restrained from going out there and then to avenge his death. (Ruvigny 2003:43)

The Highway recorded that 'the whole District is profoundly shocked and saddened at the news' and that Philip Brown's death had come as a fearful blow. Brown had been revered and John Lee and his wife even named their youngest son after him. To mark his passing a memorial service was held attended by many from the WEA, and a P. A. Brown bursary was set up to assist summer school students; the first £200 coming from a bequest made by Brown (he left a further £200 to the WEA national office). Brown's mother presented the North-East District with a picture of her son and a memorial plaque to be placed in the District office where it remained for many years.

The loss weighed heavily because the WEA was still a young people's movement. Behind the formality of the Edwardian fashion statements in numerous photographs of summer schools, meetings and outings, there were men and women often in their twenties. They had come together to learn new things, and in doing so they found 'fellowship'. It was part of Mansbridge's great 'adventure', a free, democratic horizon to cross and explore and enjoy in each others' company without intellectual restriction. Their movement was novel and growing, their entire lives and hopes stretched before them and, as with Jack and Hilda Trevena, they sometimes met their lifelong partners in the WEA. No one expected these young people's lives to end suddenly and viciously, and the twenty-nine-year-old Philip Brown's death was keenly felt. It was not just Brown, of course. Of the three authors of *English Economic History*, both Brown and Alfred Bland were killed and Tawney was wounded. Grimly, each monthly issue of *The Highway* lengthened the list of the WEA's own 'lost generation' among students and tutors.

The rising death toll was not the only difficulty. The Association still had to manage disagreements between members holding different positions on the war. By and large, members' cohesion was eased by circulating a book written by WEA tutors, including Alfred Zimmern and Arthur Greenwood, and generated by discussions among WEA summer school students as war broke out in August 1914. *The War and Democracy,* published in 1915, argued that 'all that is worth living for depends upon the outcome of this war — for ourselves the future of the democratic ideal, for the peoples of Europe deliverance from competing armaments and the yoke of racial tyranny' (Seton-Watson 1915:Preface). The authors presented a background to the war, and posed many questions, believing that education was the path to finding solutions. In so far as the book offered a prescription, it called for foreign policy to be made transparent and accountable to democratic arrangements, incorporating points set out by the emerging Union of Democratic Control. (Seton-Watson 1914:Chapter VI; *The Highway,* May 1915, p. 128)

For some WEA people, the book was seen as endorsing the war, while others felt that it offered scope for discussing various interpretations of the war's causes. Trevena used *The War and Democracy* as the basis for study circles in which divergent opinions could be considered. Overall, the book probably helped the WEA to accommodate diverse opinions and keep faith with those of its members who took part in the war like the President of the Middlesbrough Branch:

> The Branch is suffering greatly through the temporary loss of Mr. G. R. Bowes, who has joined the colours. He has been President of the Branch for two years [...] starting the series of excursions to places of historical interest, which has become such a feature of the Branch's work. He himself acted as a guide for the majority of these

excursions, and by means of them the interest in the W.E.A. was maintained among classes from session to session. At a meeting, held a few days before he left the town, he said, in answer to the farewell speech made to him, that the Association is needed more than ever now. (*The Highway,* April 1916, p. 124)

The situation worsened when married men were made liable for military conscription in May 1916. Several District Secretaries were now at risk and the Association's Central Executive resolved to support District Councils if they lodged objections with military appeal tribunals on the grounds that WEA officials were engaged on 'work of national importance'. The decision received a slightly mixed response in the North-East. Both the District Executive and the Council welcomed the national offer, though there was dissent by a delegate from the Newcastle Branch. In July, Trevena was called up but, as a firm pacifist, declared himself a conscientious objector and unwilling to take part in any aspect of the war. The District Executive supported his case for exemption using the national argument, knowing that three other District Secretaries had been excused, and one of their members, William Straker from the Co-operative Printing Society, agreed to speak at the tribunal on the WEA's behalf.

Ominously, Percy Corder, the District Treasurer, distanced himself from the decision stating that he was 'uncertain' about its wisdom. Corder, a partner in a prominent Newcastle solicitors' firm and on the governing body of Armstrong College, was influential locally, and by September he was joined by six more District Council members critical of WEA participation in Trevena's appeal. But Straker, who was associated with the Union of Democratic Control, was still able to put a case to the tribunal in September. It was rejected, and Trevena went to prison (WEA Central Executive, *Minutes*, 29 April 1916; WEA NE District Executive, *Minutes*, 27 May 1916 and 17 July 1916; WEA NE District Council, *Minutes*, 16 September 1916; Newcastle *Evening Chronicle*, 4 November, 1915).

Trevena's choice to be a conscientious objector took courage. Feelings ran exceptionally high in the North-East where there was sparse public regard for conscientious objectors, although the Tyneside Quakers gave unstinting aid. The army had learned that the area responded strongly to the concept of 'Pals' Battalions' in which men from the same parts of the coalfields, or with Scottish or Irish backgrounds, could serve alongside their neighbours, workmates and relatives. In military terms, the 'Pals' Battalions' cultivated immense solidarity under extreme conditions, but for families and friends at home the emotional impact of the slaughter in France could be magnified to a terrible degree by these units. This was not a good place to take Trevena's stand.

Hilda Trevena

The District's leaders moved swiftly to cover Trevena's absence. They had already agreed that Hilda Trevena should take over the job with the proviso that her husband's post would be kept open for him on his return 'after the cessation of the war' (WEA NE District Executive, *Minutes*, 9 September 1916 and 17 November 1916; WEA NE District Council, *Minutes*, 16 December 1916). Hilda, already a respected WEA stalwart, at the age of twenty-three became the Association's first full-time female District Secretary. A product of unusual circumstances and curious appointment procedures, the decision underscored the centrality of women in the WEA in the North-East.

Hilda Trevena spent the next twenty months stabilising the Association, protecting its course provision and turning it outwards as a campaigning movement. Together with Ethel Williams, she went to numerous branch meetings and launched new classes at West Stanley, Newcastle, South Shields, Easington, Gateshead, North Shields, Seghill, Wheatley Hill, and Middlesbrough where a well planned women's programme was created in partnership with the Women's Co-operative Guilds. Contact was made with the Belgian refugees at their Elisabethville settlement at Birtley, near Gateshead, and the possibility of holding English classes for them was discussed. When the Joint Tutorial Classes Committee separated into two committees (Durham and Armstrong College) in September 1916, she took on the secretaryship of both Committees. Liaising with allies in the Durham Miners' Union, she was able to canvass two hundred lodges, winning a vote to give a further £50 to the WEA, writing:

This year, owing to the generosity of the miners, we have been able to run fifteen classes in the county — an increase of nine upon the year preceding and we are hopeful of doubling this number during the next session. (The Highway, March 1917, p. 110)

Hilda put the WEA into reasonable shape as thoughts turned to social reconstruction after the war. Affiliations rose to one hundred and seven by 1918 (they were forty-eight in 1914), and a hundred individual members and nineteen branches now formed the foundations of the WEA community.

Big successes were registered by organising regional conferences pressing the case for post-war educational reform as part of a national WEA and NUT campaign. A WEA conference on 'What Labour Wants from Education', highlighting a reduction in school class sizes and extending the school age from six to sixteen, was attended by five hundred people at the Newcastle Literary and Philosophical Society in October 1916, and addressed by William Straker, General Secretary of the Northumberland miners, and McTavish. This prepared the ground for a conference on 'The Place of Education in Social Reconstruction' attended by three hundred and forty delegates from one hundred and seventy teachers' associations, trade unions, co-operatives, working men's clubs, adult schools, ILP branches and other organisations in March 1918, leading to a further high profile conference on 'The Value and Need of Education' at Newcastle in October. The October conference, chaired by Jevons, brought three hundred and twenty delegates together to consider democracy, education and the scope of the coming Education Act with Viscount Haldane, George Lansbury and Rev. William Temple, the WEA's national president and future Archbishop of York and Canterbury: 'altogether it has made the W.E.A. movement much more widely known'; Lisbeth Simm helped reinforce the campaign by joining a WEA and National Amalgamated Union of Labour (she had become the union's Chief Women's Officer) deputation that lobbied the Prime Minister in 1917 (National Amalgamated Union of Labour, *Executive Committee Minutes*, 19 March 1917; *The Highway*, November 1918, p. 16, May 1918, p. 115 and November 1916, p. 37; Cole 1918:355-56).

With Hilda Trevena at the helm, the WEA enlarged the coalition of organisations that had brought it into existence and focused on local educational activity. But the war relentlessly stimulated frictions, notably between Lisbeth Simm and Ethel Williams. The two women appear to have worked well together in the WEA, despite their different social backgrounds, until the war finally drove them apart. Both wanted the conflict to end, but when the National Union of Women's Suffrage Societies divided over whether to support the war, Williams joined the pacifist wing that formed the Women's International League for Peace and Freedom. Lisbeth Simm, contrastingly, held that victory in a just war was more important. For Lisbeth and Matt Simm, this stance was to lead to her severing all links with the Labour Party and to his short-lived career as a Coalition 'National Democratic' MP at Wallsend from 1918, following an election campaign in which the Simms raged against anti-war socialists and conscientious objectors. Lisbeth then threw herself into persuading women to emigrate to Australia from 1919, and became warden of Newcastle's Orchard House, a residential training centre for domestic service, in 1928. She died at Los Angeles in 1952 having followed her son to America in 1946 (Collette 1989: 187-88; *Newcastle Illustrated Chronicle*, 9 December 1918; Neville 1997:101-02).

Ethel Williams dramatically took her anti-war efforts to fresh heights. In July 1917 she acted as secretary of the Newcastle Soldiers' and Workers' Council that tried to arrange one of a country wide series of public meetings welcoming the overthrow of the Russian Tsar. The aim was a negotiated peace and friendship with the revolutionary government in Russia. Special Branch intervention prevented all the planned meetings from taking place and at Newcastle the meeting was wrecked by soldiers in plain clothes singing 'Rule Britannia', whilst other people responded with 'The Red Flag'. As chairs and fists flew, Williams was lucky to escape unscathed. It could also have meant the end of her medical career in the City but her reputation seems to have protected her (Todd 1996:20-21).

Reaction, survival and change

The Trevenas may have found Ethel Williams supportive, yet others were less disposed to tolerate pacifism. The Hebburn miners' lodge had already questioned Hilda Trevena's appointment and, in March 1918, they withheld their subscription to the WEA 'until the present secretary is removed from office'. The District Executive refused the demand (North East District Council, *Minutes*, 15 December 1917; WEA NE District Executive, *Minutes*, 9 March 1917). These clashing attitudes took on a new lease of life from June 1918 when Jack Trevena was released from prison. The District Executive asked him to return to work immediately, gave Hilda their appreciation, and invited her to stay as secretary to the Tutorial Classes Committees (WEA NE District Executive, *Minutes*, 22 and 27 June 1918). Bursting with anger, Percy Corder called on the November Executive meeting to agree:

> that J. G. Trevena having as a Conscientious Objector refused to perform work of National importance as an alternative to Military Service is unfitted to act as District Secretary [… and that the District council should …]

forthwith determine his appointment. (WEA NE District Executive, *Minutes*, 30 October 1918)

Jack Trevena had read a statement as part of the debate, and the motion was defeated by seven votes to four. Corder was not ready to give up, particularly as Jevons seconded the motion. He wrote to McTavish confirming an intention to table the same motion at the December meeting of the WEA's North East District Council. The response may have surprised him. Believing that Corder's proposal was a breach of the constitution, the Association's Central Executive felt that dismissing an official because of his 'personal views' would be 'foreign to the spirit of the Movement'. The President, Vice-President and General Secretary were all authorised to go to the Newcastle District Council meeting to lay down the law (WEA Central Executive, *Minutes*, 22 November 1918).

The 21 December meeting of the District Council must have been a 'high noon' moment. Jevons was already annoyed with the national Association for publishing an *Education Year Book* that opened with a direct swipe at him by George Bernard Shaw disparaging Jevons's interest in regulating school teaching (almost half of the District Council seem to have agreed with Shaw). The General Secretary was present and Jevons duly ruled Corder's motion out of order ('after careful consideration'), but caused uproar by inviting Corder ('out of courtesy') to explain why he had brought the motion. Several members objected, and then Corder tried to propose a further motion, which Jevons would not allow as no notice had been given. A furious Corder promptly resigned and 'immediately afterwards left the meeting', storming out of the Burt Hall and out of the WEA (WEA NE District Council, *Minutes*, 21 September 1918 and 21 December 1918; Corbett 2003:17; Cole 1918:15).

The episode could have been worse but for the moderating presence of a long-standing WEA member, Harry Barnes, who had defended Jack Trevena at each meeting. Barnes, a major in the Northumberland Fusiliers who had lost a son in the war, was well known as a WEA occasional lecturer and respected for his work as an architect designing good public buildings, including schools. Despite being in the midst of a general election campaign as a Coalition Liberal candidate, Barnes set aside the political risks from appearing to support a conscientious objector. He did what he thought was right. And after being elected as a Coalition MP for Newcastle East in 1918, he took on the role of deputy Treasurer of the North-East District in January 1919 when Corder refused to draw cheques. Barnes left the Coalition in November 1919 and went on to write two well-researched books arguing that the problems of slums and poor housing could only be solved by state intervention. He was elected as a Labour Councillor in London in 1934, but died at the age of sixty-four in 1935 (*The Times*, 14 October 1935; WEA NE Executive, *Minutes*, 11 January 1919; *Newcastle Illustrated Chronicle*, 13 December 1918; Corbett 2003:17; WEA NE District Council, *Minutes*, 21 December 1918).

If Barnes was able to prevent the crisis spinning out of control and its public perception was well-managed, the controversy still refused to go away. The Tynemouth branches of the NUT and the WEA, together with the North Shields Co-operative Society's Education Committee, called for a special District Council meeting to consider Corder's resignation and Jevon's ruling on his motion. As the District Executive refused to call a meeting, the Sunderland NUT and the Newcastle Co-operative Education Committee announced they were 'seceding from membership' (WEA NE District Executive, *Minutes*, 8 February 1919).

Other decisions threatened to prolong the wounds. Early in 1918, and before the row over Jack Trevena's return, the Co-operative Union had given notice that they would need the office they had provided free and then at a nominal rent to the WEA at Westmoreland Road. Towards the end of the year, the Association found a new office at Newcastle's Royal Arcade. But the furnishing of the office was to be met out of the Philip Brown legacy and Brown's picture and memorial plaque were to be displayed in the rooms where Trevena worked. Juggling these day-to-day items was bound to be emotionally fraught.

In the end, McTavish and the national leadership came up with a compromise to resolve the 'important split'. In September 1919 the Trevenas were helped to move to the newly created WEA South-West District, based at Plymouth, where Jack Trevena served as District Secretary for the next thirty-five years. The North-East District was left free to move on (Turner 1986; WEA Central Executive, *Minutes*, 25 July 1919).

So what of the balance sheet? From hesitant beginnings, the WEA had matured quickly. Proving its educational value on very little money, dealing with an all-consuming war, coping with rivals, overcoming difficult working relationships without completely falling apart, reaching out both to universities and trade unions in a class-divided culture, cultivating at least a fragile space for women, mobilising others in campaigning for a better world, all demonstrated real strengths. It had been hard but the Association's pioneers in the North-East could look back on their first ten years — *it had only been ten years!* — with a degree of pride. They had achieved a great deal, and they did it themselves. Now, looking forward to uncertain times, they set off confidently to do more.

SOURCE MATERIALS

Aird, Eileen, 1982. *A Gift in Our Hand*. Newcastle upon Tyne: WEA Northern District.

Allen, Joan, 2007. *Joseph Cowen and Popular Radicalism on Tyneside, 1829-1900*. Monmouth: Merlin Press.

Armstrong, Chester, 1938. *Pilgrimage from Nenthead: An Autobiography*. London: Methuen.

Atkinson, M., 1913. *First Aid in Essay Writing*. Newcastle upon Tyne: WEA North East District.

Brook, Maureen, 2005. *Herring Girls and Hiring Fairs: Memories of Northumberland Coast and Countryside*. Newcastle upon Tyne: Tyne Bridge Publishing.

Brown, Philip Anthony, 1965. *The French Revolution in English History*, London: Cass. [Introduction to the new edition by G. Murray. Originally published 1918.]

Brown, Philip Anthony, Richard Henry Tawney and Alfred Edward Bland, 1914. *English economic history: select documents*. London: Bell.

Callcott, M., 1999. 'A Woman's Place'. In: Anna Flowers and Vanessa Histon (eds), *Water Under the Bridges: Newcastle's Twentieth Century*. Newcastle upon Tyne: Tyne Bridge Publishing.

Cole, G. D. H. et al., 1918. *The W.E.A. Education Year Book 1918*. London: Workers' Educational Association.

Collette, Christine, 1989. *For Labour and For Women: The Women's Labour League, 1906-1918*. Manchester: Manchester University Press.

Corbett, Ivan, 2003. '"So noble an institution": A History of the Workers' Educational Association Northern District 1910-80'. In: Standen (2003a:5-81). [Originally published 1980.]

Craik, William White, 1964. *The Central Labour College 1909-29: a chapter in the history of adult working-class education*. London: Lawrence & Wishart.

Hallsworth, Harry Mainwaring, 1913. *Syllabus of a Course of Twelve Lectures on The Production and Distribution of National Income*. Cambridge: Cambridge University Press.

Heatley, Phyllis, 1995. *Something Sustained — The Newcastle upon Tyne WEA Branch (1912—)*. Newcastle upon Tyne, WEA Northern District.

Heslop, Harold, 1994. *Out of the Old Earth*, Newcastle upon Tyne: Bloodaxe.

Hocking, C., n. d. WEA Collection, Tyne & Wear Museums and Archives, E.WEA1/16/34.

Lawson, J., 1944. *A Man's Life*. London: Hodder and Stoughton.

Mansbridge Papers. Correspondence and papers of Albert Mansbridge (1876-1952) founder and first organising secretary of the Workers' Educational Association at the British Library. Location and Catalogue: 65195-65368.

Mansbridge, Albert, 1913. *University Tutorial Classes: a study in the development of higher education among working men and women*. London: Longmans.

Mansbridge, Albert, 1920. *An Adventure in Working-Class Education: Being the story of the Workers' Educational Association 1903-1915*. London: Longmans.

McIlroy, John, 1996. 'Independent Working Class Education and Trade Union Education and Training'. In: Fieldhouse, Roger (ed.), *A History of Modern British Adult Education*. Leicester: NIACE.

Metcalfe, T., 1953. 'Education and Social Responsibility'. In: *Workers' Educational Association, Northern District, 1903-1953, Jubilee Brochure*. Newcastle upon Tyne: WEA.

Munby, Zoë, 2003. 'Women's Involvement in the WEA and Women's Participation'. In: Roberts 2003:212-18.

Neville, David, 1997. *To Make Their Mark: The Women's Suffrage Movement in the North East of England, 1900-1914*. Newcastle upon Tyne: Centre for Northern Studies, University of Northumbria.

Neville, David, 2007. 'Hope Springs Eternal: The Life of Labour Pioneer Lisbeth Simm'. In: *North East History* 38.43-66.

Osmond, Warren, 1979. 'Meredith Atkinson (1883-1929)' In: *Australian Dictionary of Biography*, Vol. 7, pp. 121-22. Melbourne: Melbourne University Press.

Roberts, Stephen K. (ed.), 2003. *A Ministry of Enthusiasm: Centenary Essays on the Workers' Educational Association*. London: Pluto Press.

Roberts, Ian and Bellingham WEA Group, 2008. *Telling Tales Out of School: A History of Education and School Life in North Tynedale and Redesdale from 1870 to 1944*, Seaton Burn: Northern Heritage.

Ross, Thomas, and A. Stoddart, 1921. *Jubilee History of the Annfield Plain Co-operative Society Ltd: 1870-1920*. Manchester: CWS.

Ruvigny et Raineval, Melville Henry Massue, marquis de, 2003. *De Ruvigny's roll of honour 1914-18: a biographical record of members of His Majesty's naval and military forces who fell in the Great War 1914-1918*. Uckfield: Naval and Military Press.

Seton-Watson, Robert William, et al., 1914. *The War and Democracy*. London: Macmillan.

Simon, Brian, 1974. *Education and the Labour Movement, 1870-1920*, London: Lawrence and Wishart. [First published 1965.]

Standen, Michael (ed.), 2003a. *A hunger to be more serious …: The Story of the WEA Northern District*. Newcastle upon Tyne: WEA Northern District.

Stevenson, Miss, 1918. 'The University of Durham Joint Committee, 1911-1916'. In: Cole (1918:293-94).

Tilley, T. B., 1953. 'Retrospect' In: *Workers' Educational Association, Northern District, 1903-1953, Jubilee Brochure*. Newcastle upon Tyne: WEA.

Todd, Nigel, 1991. *The Militant Democracy: Joseph Cowen and Victorian Radicalism,* Whitley Bay: Bewick Press.

Todd, Nigel, 1996. 'Ethel Williams: Medical and Suffrage Pioneer'. In: *North East Labour History* 30:20-21.

Tropp, Asher, 1957. *The School Teachers: The Growth of the Teaching Profession in England and Wales From 1800 to the Present Day*. London: Heinemann.

Turner, Michael, 1986. *A History of the Workers' Educational Association Western District*, 1911-86. Plymouth: WEA.

Welbourne, Edward, 1923. *The Miners' Unions of Northumberland and Durham*. Cambridge: Cambridge University Press.

Whiting, Charles Edwin, 1932. *The University of Durham*, 1831-1932. London: Sheldon Press.

Wilson, Dora, 1979. Letter to Ivan Corbett, 11 January 1979. Tyne & Wear Museums and Archives, E.WEA1/16/34.

The Northern District of the WEA from 1920 to 2010 — an Overview

Ian Roberts

An overview of the fortunes of the Northern Region of the WEA must, by its very nature, be selective in terms of content. In attempting to present an outline of the Northern District's history between 1920 and 2010, broad generalisations may obscure many events and activities which are well known and widely cherished by members and branches in the District. However, the purpose of this chapter is to present a picture of the District and the national arenas in which many of those events and activities, some of which are chronicled elsewhere in this book, took place. Prior to 1920, the first decade of the Northern District's life was one of pioneering endeavour in which local enthusiasts built up an organisation inspired by Albert Mansbridge and others that was designed to provide an educational service for people in the north of England who had previously been ignored by other educational initiatives. In the latter years of that decade these same pioneers had piloted the new WEA District through the problems created by the First World War and emerged into a peacetime world determined to expand on the success it already enjoyed.

Ivan Corbett (2003) described the first dozen years between 1919 and 1931 in this post-war world as *'The Smith Years'* when reviewing the work of Alderman W. N. Smith, who was appointed District Secretary in the wake of the departure of Jack Trevena for the West Country. While recognising Smith's ability and the wide range of his contacts, Corbett made no attempt to conceal his misgiving about the appointment. He describes the period as 'Smith's reign' in which 'Smith ruled, the Committee followed', while 'either by intent or accident, Smith functioned as an executive'. Following his appointment as Chair of Durham County Council in 1926, where he was also Chair of the Education Committee, Smith consolidated his position by proposing and obtaining the appointment of an Assistant Secretary of the WEA District, one J. B. Hall, to relieve him of some of the work of the secretaryship. Smith paid half of Hall's salary for the first three years of his appointment and Hall succeeded Smith as District Secretary. Thus, when Smith finally stepped down in 1931, Corbett comments:

> Personal recollections are of a dominant personality, commandeering meetings with little of the common touch. Whether the District was right in choosing an autocrat like Smith is highly debatable.

For further details of Smith's term of office and a slightly different, but essentially sympathetic, view of the man, see Ruth Tanner's analysis in Chapter 3 of this book.

From the standpoint of the pre-war pioneers, it is possible to understand Corbett's misgivings and his criticism of Smith as an autocrat governing the Northern District on the basis of personal whim. Corbett knew that the field of candidates from which Smith had been selected was very large and contained a number with proven WEA credentials, so that the appointment of an outsider appeared a betrayal of WEA loyalists. However, in the context of the period, there is much to be said in Smith's favour. The end of the war brought great relief but it also revealed that the District was not well endowed from a financial point of view. The office premises, now located in the Royal Arcade in Newcastle, were more costly than the previous ones, subscriptions and voluntary contributions had not increased with the times and some of the miners' associations were unable to continue their support. All of these local problems were set against a background of deteriorating national economic conditions.

Smith's answer to these difficulties, which by the time of the Annual General Meeting in 1919 had brought about a loss of £94, was to shift the source of income from individual contributions to grants from Local Education Authorities (LEAs) and elsewhere. This policy diminished the role of individuals and branches but created an increasingly healthy income which enabled the District to expand the number and variety of its classes. Perhaps the high point in all of this was the creation of the 'Responsible Bodies' by the government in 1924 which enabled the Northern, along with the other WEA Districts, to access a larger measure of state finance. This had to be for academic work — finance for practical and vocational studies was not forthcoming. Thus, in contrast to other sectors of education where there were savage economies such as the Geddes' axe on salaries, the Northern District continued throughout the 1920s to increase its number of classes and students. When Smith retired from office in 1931, he was able to assert in the *Annual Report*:

> we practically had to commence re-building our movement in 1919 after peace was declared, and this rebuilding had to be done in the midst of the most appalling commercial and industrial dislocation and depression ever experienced within living memory, but in spite of these conditions our work has gone on and developments have taken place.

In support of these claims, he was able to show that in 1919:

> the total number of Classes of all types was 41 and the total number of students slightly over 800. For the same year the total Income from all sources amounted to £608. The total number of classes for the present year is 171. Total number of students 3046. Total Income this year £1877.

What Smith omitted to mention here was that the total grant money within this income amounted to £1122 11s. 5d. — approximately 60% of the sum — whereas before 1919 almost all of the £608 would have been raised from individuals, branches, trades unions and the Club and Institute Union (CIU).

In the first chapter of this book, Nigel Todd has explained something of the administrative organisation of the Northern District and the type of classes that the WEA was providing for its students before the First World War. Encouraged by Trevena and members of the District Committee as well as by university supporters, these classes had flourished in spite of the war and under Smith had been developed into a full-scale system of courses that could take the student through to a university degree. This was the central structure of the educational work of the WEA which lasted until the Russell report of 1973, when some elements of that work were refocused by the government of the day as part of its response to the recommendations of the report. The most demanding studies in the WEA's traditional programme took place in the tutorial courses, which were three-year courses with a standard of work comparable to a university degree. Indeed, a number of the most successful students went on to take university courses at Durham, King's College in Newcastle, Ruskin College at Oxford or Fircroft College and qualified with degrees. These courses were supported by a number of other classes. There were advanced tutorial courses that extended the work of the three-year course, sessional courses which lasted two terms and met weekly for twenty to twenty-four meetings and terminal courses that lasted one term and met ten to twelve times weekly. There were also lecture courses that met anything from one to five times, where a lecture was delivered to the students but where no tutorial support was provided.

In addition there were day schools, week-end schools and highly organised and much esteemed summer schools, many of which were held at Hatfield College in Durham. All of these classes were grant-earning, but some non-grant-aided classes were offered for those who wished to pursue adult education not related directly to a university-type course and, as in the case of courses such as those taken by the Pitmen Painters described in Chapter 8, there had to be a degree of flexibility in the approach of the tutors to allow their acceptance by the authorities. Throughout the 1930s, over 4,000 students attended the university classes while several hundred more were enrolled in the WEA non-grant-aided classes. Teaching of the university-type classes was shared between tutors recruited by the WEA and the staffs of the two Extra-Mural Divisions of Durham University's Extra-Mural Board. One of these served the Durham Colleges, while the other was at King's College, the Durham College located in Newcastle which ultimately gained its own charter to become the University of Newcastle-upon-Tyne in 1963.

At the same time a Northern District administration of some complexity had emerged to guide and support this work. Given the pride with which Alderman Smith relinquished his role of District Secretary and the differences between the WEA he had administered and that of the present time, it would seem appropriate to describe the structure of the District's administration at that time and explore some of the ways in which it has changed. At the centre of the day-to-day administration were the District Secretary and the office staff whose precise size was not determined, but seemed to fluctuate depending on the requirements of the Secretary and the money available to pay salaries. The body which oversaw the staff most closely and was involved most frequently with the problems of students, tutors and branches was the District Committee. This committee was headed by three elected officers: a Chairman, a Vice-Chair and an Honorary Treasurer, supported by an Executive Committee of approximately twenty members drawn from the branches and affiliated bodies. There was also an Honorary Auditor, but it is likely he did not attend meetings. In those early days, there were six voluntary area organisers within the District who assisted the paid staff, in particular the newly appointed Tutor Organiser David Wiseman, whose salary was drawn from a recently awarded grant in support of the post. In addition, there was an Extra-Mural Board formed into two divisions for Durham and Newcastle, which had over twenty members as well two Tutor Organisers.

It would be appropriate at this juncture to explain that the District Committee did not only represent the North-East District as, from 1921 to 1937, the counties of Cumberland and Westmorland formed a Sub-District with its own committee and officers, linked with the North-East District. This status ended in 1938 and from then until 2001 there was one WEA Northern District. Re-organisation in 2001 relocated Cumbria, which had united Cumberland and Westmorland in 1974, within the North-West Region to which the counties of the Sub-District had been attached between 1916 and 1921, while the Northern District then became the WEA North-East Region. In addition to all of these changes in the west of the Region, over the last century the WEA's northern territory also had a fluctuating southern boundary. From the District's inception until the 1930s the North-East also included Middlesbrough and Wensleydale until their transfer to Yorkshire North. However, in 1989 the transfer was partially reversed when Middlesbrough and Redcar were returned to the Northern District.[1]

In addition to the Executive Committee which had responsibility for this elastic District, there was a District Council with a much larger membership and broader representation. This body met three or four times each year and one of their meetings constituted the District Annual General Meeting. The Annual Report and Financial Statement was presented to this meeting and officers were elected. At this distance in time, the extent to which the Council had control over the District is not clear. Gradually, its power eroded and its only current form is as the Annual General Meeting of the District. From the late 1960s until the late 1990s, the offices of President and up to three Vice-Presidents were also in existence for the District. Carrying on the tradition of the Church of England's connection with the WEA, the last person to hold the position of President was the Bishop of Jarrow. These largely honorary offices have now been discontinued and any authority which they may have had has been transferred to the District Committee and its Chair, while the day-to-day running of the organisation has, since the appointment of Nigel Todd, been the responsibility of the Regional Director.

The structure of the organisation that existed in the 1930s was the one under which the Northern District entered the Second World War in 1939, with two important changes. One of these was the creation of the Tutor Organisers who played an important part in managing the branches and organising classes throughout the District. These roles, which were permanent and salaried, were established by District Secretary Abrahart who was appointed in 1936, following Mr Hall's death in 1935. These officers replaced the voluntary organisers and brought a new measure of efficiency to the organisation, although sometimes the circumstances of their appointment may have been somewhat unorthodox, as Hilda Pickles describes in Chapter 10. The other change that took place with the coming of war concerned the culture of the organisation rather than its formal structure. It is clear from the *Annual Reports* that in the 1920s and 1930s there was a social side to the WEA. Rambles, visits to places of interest and dramatic presentations formed part of the life of many branches. During the chaos of war and the post-war era of austerity, these aspects of life in the WEA disappeared and were often never revived. Other features of the pre-war era such as classes for the unemployed and youth initiatives did surface from time to time, but others which gave a more personal approach to learning seldom survived.

One pre-war development worth noting was the removal in 1937 of the District office from the Royal Arcade, Newcastle, apparently following a row with the landlord, to 51 Grainger Street in Newcastle's city centre. The Grainger Street address, with its rabbit-warren features, cramped accommodation, idiosyncratic heating and occasional water-filled lift shaft, gradually became an iconic venue for WEA classes and meetings over the next six decades.

As explained more fully in Chapter 4 of this book, we have no reports for the war years and there is much less extant information than for other periods of the Northern District's history. Corbett (2003:42-53) provides a brief overview of what transpired but the most thorough account of the WEA during the war has been provided by John Field (2003), whose detailed account on this period redresses the slight treatment given to this topic in earlier studies. Suffice it to say that the Northern District policies were similar to the other Districts and an adapted service was retained during the period of hostilities. In Newcastle, for example, only one tutorial class continued to run during the war and the energies of the branch became focused on providing courses mostly for women who engaged in war work (Heatley 1995:11-12).

With the end of the war, the Northern District began to return to the type of work that had been undertaken

---

[1] I am grateful to Jonathan Brown who clarified this situation in a personal communication.

during the 1930s. A spirit of optimism was initially generated by the passage of the 1944 Education Act and further encouraged by the results of the 1945 General Election. Although the WEA was apolitical, it was hoped that the new Labour government would be favourable to adult education in particular as the Cabinet contained fourteen ministers with previous WEA connections and another fifty members of the Commons had previously taken part in various aspects of the organisation's work (Doyle 2003:50-51). In the Northern District, programmes of classes of all types began to be offered and by the end of 1947 over 6,000 students were enrolled. During the next few years, numbers continued to grow so that by 1950 the number of tutorial classes had grown from seventy-five to one hundred and two and there were nearly 10,000 students taking part in classes of various types. Although less money was forthcoming from central government than had been hoped for, a growing desire was evident on the part of many who joined the classes to make up for time lost during the war and to prepare themselves better for the future by gaining educational qualifications.

Perhaps this was no better illustrated than through one of the key areas of growth in adult education during the 1950s — the Trade Union Movement. The Workers' Education Trade Union Committee (WETUC) had been founded in 1919 and had led to the growth of a partnership in which the trade unions provided financial support for the WEA towards organisational and teaching expertise. During the inter-war period trade union educational activities fluctuated in response to the economic climate and, instead of training courses for workers, classes for the unemployed were often offered. The collaboration of the unions and the WEA was revived after the Second World War through the WETUC, and with the encouragement of the new District Secretary, Charles Hocking and the District Committee, became an important feature of the Northern District's work. Commencing in Northumberland, by 1948 trade union classes had been extended to County Durham. By 1951, there was a special Trade Union Advisory Committee with a full-time officer working on behalf of WETUC in the District. Moreover, the Advisory Committee also had a permanent representative on the District Committee.

The steady growth of trade union courses and classes resulting from these developments was paralleled by a growing awareness by the unions and the TUC that more could and should be done for specialist studies in this field. As a result of many meetings and negotiations (Doyle 2003:60-65; WEA Northern District 1957), the WEA set up special schemes in three pilot areas in 1954, one of which was on Tyneside in the Northern District, to explore the future of trade union education. The study was conducted through three years 1955-57, and was reported on extensively and with HMI assistance in 1958 and 1959. Many conclusions were drawn from the reports, including showing that both practical training and liberal education can be run together as two sides of the same educational process (WEA 2003:12). In consequence, this heralded a major expansion of trade union education in the 1960s and 1970s in which the WEA played a large part, acting both as an advisory body and delivering some 20% of the courses. These two aspects of the WEA's response to the report and to the unions were particularly strong in the Northern District. As a result, the success of the pilot study helped cement a strong relationship between the trade unions and the Northern District Committee that has continued to the present day. On the way, it has survived the Miners' Strike and the problems of the 1980s, but the fact that it is still in place in the form of workplace learning and other activities designed to help and empower the employee is a testimony to the lasting ideals built into the original WETUC agreement that still find expression in the WEA North-East Region. Further reflections on this relationship can be found in Chapter 12 of this book.

The Northern District continued to flourish in the 1950s and 1960s. The original three-year tutorial classes continued, though perhaps slightly fewer in number, but still delivering courses that could lead to a university degree. Charles Hocking managed to prevent the new Director of Extra-Mural studies in Newcastle, the former District Secretary Abrahart, from taking most advanced courses under his control and thus the number of students under WEA auspices was maintained. In this respect the Northern District was more fortunate than WEA groups elsewhere. In Leicester, for example, the authorities at the university pursued a vigorous campaign in the late 1940s and early 1950s in which they managed not only to dispossess that WEA branch of its more advanced academic classes, but also to secure some of the premises which the Association had formerly occupied (Brown 2008:22-24).

By contrast, with the assistance of the Extra-Mural Departments and in association with the tutorial classes and other courses, the WEA's very popular summer schools, week-end courses and day schools were revived in the late 1940s and continued into the mid-1970s when they appear to have become a casualty of the financial crisis of that time (Corbett 2003:73-78; Heatley 1995:13). Another important venture in this period was the Science Project which forms the subject of Chapter 14 in this book. Although it might not have been extended as widely as some members of the WEA would have wished, it was nevertheless an important and innovative venture which demonstrated that the association, and the Northern District in particular, were capable of embracing and delivering new course types based on curricular matters that had previously been neglected. District Secretary Hocking was able to maintain firm links in other areas as well. The relationship with the Co-operative Movement, for example, has endured the test of time, in addition to a positive, although not so long-lived, relationship with the Club and Institute Union (CIU), all of which helped to strengthen the role played by the Northern District in adult education in the north of England.

Charles Hocking was awarded an Honorary MEd by Durham University in 1968 and retired in March 1969. He famously described his service to the District as one of twenty years hard labour, but if that had been the case it had had a very successful outcome, as the District during his term of office had recovered from the war and progressed by the mid-1960s to have some of the largest numbers of classes and students ever. Hocking's labours also demonstrated the key role played by the District Secretary in the management of all aspects of the Northern District's activities. His retirement took place just before the District was forced through a major re-appraisal, not just of its educational role but also of its organisational efficiency.

One aspect of the disruption that took place in the 1970s is the financial crisis through which the District went and which resulted in the DES having to provide a special grant of nearly £10,000 to re-finance it. Because of the difficulties involved in reconstructing events, previous works have only dealt with these events in a limited fashion (e.g. Corbett 2003:76), but it is now possible to provide a more thorough explanation of the problem and this has been done by Jonathan Brown in Chapter 6 of this book. The effects of the crisis were far-reaching. For many WEA members and for some of the general public, it undermined the credibility of the organisation and many years of hard work were required to recover the goodwill established by Charles Hocking and others. It is a tribute to the hard work of Michael Standen that he accomplished so much in his time as District Secretary, and an equally powerful tribute to the modesty of the man that in describing his work in that office, reprinted here as Chapter 13, he made so little of the efforts required of him to rebuild the reputation and effectiveness of the Northern District.

One major change that took place in the 1970s which was to have a powerful influence on the work of Michael Standen and the District Committee was the outcome of the report of the Russell Committee of Enquiry into Adult Education. The Committee of Enquiry had actually been convened in 1969 and in order to understand the nature of its work and subsequent recommendations, it must be understood in the context in which it was established. As shown above, the Northern District had itself undergone a period of growth and diversity of courses in the 1960s. Elsewhere there had also been a considerable reappraisal of the whole educational structure in Britain through government-inspired reports such as those of Crowther, Newsom, Robbins and Plowden, which had been accompanied by smaller but no less important enquiries into aspects of Welsh, Scottish and Northern Irish education. Higher education had expanded in the form of the New Universities, some of which had a highly technological remit, while Teacher Training Colleges had become Colleges of Education under university supervision. In the North-East, Durham was separated from Newcastle which had now become a university in its own right. In 1969 the Wilson government inaugurated the Open University (OU) which was to have particular importance for the WEA. This represented a challenge to the WEA for some members, while others saw in it a great opportunity to work with another provider of advanced adult education. More ominous than the opening of the OU was the formal dissolution of the link between the University Extra-Mural Department in Northern Ireland and the WEA, so that their courses were no longer produced in co-operation. The relationship between these two bodies was to become one in which the WEA was seen as a provider of pre-university education and no longer a participant in graduate studies.

The Russell enquiry was undertaken by government as a logical step in which adult education could be reformulated to take account of other changes taking place in the field of education and encourage providers to move into a new era offering different types of courses for new audiences. The WEA took the stance of giving priority to 'the educationally deprived and socially disadvantaged' as a 'logical extension of the WEA's long-standing commitment to working-class education (Corbett 2003:76). Consequently, the report's authors identified four areas for development by the WEA in the future. These were: (i) education for the socially and culturally deprived in urban areas; (ii) work in factories arranged with the TUC or individual unions; (iii) political and social education, and (iv) courses of liberal and academic study below the level of university work (Corbett 2003:77).

Although there were critics, these recommendations were found to be very workable by most of the WEA. The Northern District, like other Districts, was already engaged in many of these activities and could see good opportunities for future developmental work. Examples of the types of work that grew out of the Russell recommendations can be found in Chapters 7 and 9 and illustrate the new spirit of educational adventure unleashed by the adoption of the report. One drawback for the Northern District in all of this was that it coincided with its financial crisis and these new initiatives required funding. The fact that it was 1976 before government funding was provided for the new requirements and by that time the District needed to be bailed out as well made for added difficulties. It is, therefore, a remarkable testament to the energies and endeavour of the staff and volunteers that the 1979 *Annual Report* speaks enthusiastically of work in a whole variety of new courses and workplace initiatives that were being delivered, including Women's Studies.

However:

> … the momentum was broken by the election of the Conservative Government in 1979, which almost immediately withdrew the funding agreed by the Labour Government to support new staff appointments in trade union education. In 1983, the Department of Education and Science (DES) announced its intention to claw back grant from Districts' surpluses and to impose an 8.3% reduction in grant aid phased over the following three years.

> The end of the 1980s were financially difficult for the WEA. Relations with the DES were conditioned by the recognition that there would be no fundamental improvement in grant support, and that consequently the WEA's interests might be best served through jointly reworking labyrinthine funding formulas. (Doyle 2003:35)

Under these circumstances, it was hardly surprising when the government moved towards the notion of paying for specified work delivered and also decided to deal with the WEA as a single body rather than through the individual Districts. Thus, in 1988, the 'Responsible Body' status was withdrawn and in future finance was to be provided to a central point where it would be divided up by the Association among its Districts.

Between 1979 and 1988, the Northern District soldiered on. Freda Tallentyre's account in Chapter 11 demonstrates that it was possible to organise new classes and to sustain branch activity during the hardest of times. Her work in Ashington brought success and also proved that there were still large bodies of people seeking education which they could gain through no other medium than the WEA. It also showed that it was possible to fulfil the 'Russell conditions' so that the work of the District could continue to be financed. Michael Standen found the tasks of balancing the budget and providing worthwhile courses difficult but his greatest problem was the loss of branches and volunteers. Always the great strength of the WEA, he now witnessed the loss of some 20% of its branches between 1977 and 1987, as 'the quiet erosion of the old structures', the sound of their demise being drowned by the pressures of an integrated WEA, the need for increased accountability, the demands to fulfil criteria and the clamour required of the Women's Institutes to persuade government to permit the WEA to be financed through the Further Education Funding Council (FEFC), (Corbett 2003;90-92)

Michael's early retirement in 1995 prevented him being exposed to the problems of the Learning and Skills Council (LSC) — the body that replaced the FEFC in 2000 — and the debate over whether WEA should be funded by the local LSCs or by the central body in London. Somehow, other than in the *Annual Reports*, the actual courses, students, tutors, branches and volunteers which had formed such a critical part of the old WEA disappeared beneath considerations of funding, balancing the budget, meeting targets and achieving the best grade possible in the assessments. In many ways, the WEA's national centenary year in 2003 proved to be the nemesis of the movement. Financial problems and an initial bruising encounter with the Government's standards watchdog, Ofsted — a culture shock for both sides, as inspectors and the WEA struggled to understand each other — brought about radical changes at both national and District levels. The Association became 'Incorporated', producing a new constitution with a body of Trustees at its pinnacle, and reorganised its Districts into Regions coterminus with government office boundaries. Cumbria was 'lost' from the Northern District, which now became the North-East Region. However, the new Region still retained considerable functional autonomy and locally accountable governance. Following a staffing restructure, it was possible to deploy staff to support members throughout the whole of the area, and a robust approach to quality assurance ensured favourable external judgements, including those delivered by Ofsted.[2]

Despite the problems posed by funding systems, the North-East Region set out to revitalise the values of the WEA as a democratic voluntary association. With a generous grant from the Co-operative Fund, a *Without*

---

[2] I am grateful to Nigel Todd for information which he provided for the final part of this chapter.

Boundaries voluntary membership development project was implemented. This contributed to a revival of some branches, the updating of volunteer support policies and a closer relationship with co-operatives, leading to a national partnership agreement between the Association and the Co-operative Movement, and assisted in the growth of WEA individual membership in the North-East from about four hundred people to over two thousand in just two years.

The Region's successful broad adult learning programme, largely informed by its branches and by an elected Regional Committee strengthened with co-options from the OU, the Open College Network, the Co-operative, and the Angelou Centre, has been augmented by engaging with new topics such as tackling climate change. WEA courses in the arts and humanities continue to achieve, publishing books and holding impressive exhibitions, whilst a substantial emphasis is placed on recruiting students whose previous experience of education and employment has been slight, in keeping with the traditional aims of the WEA. In 2008-09, some 48% of WEA students in the North-East Region came from postcode districts defined as areas of social and economic disadvantage; over half held either no previous qualifications or none above Level Two; more than a third declared a disability of one kind or another, and participation by members of ethnic minority communities (6%) was higher than the regional population.

Finally in 2007, the WEA North-East Region achieved its own home! After a century of renting and leasing properties, the Trustees bought 21 Portland Terrace in Newcastle to serve as the Regional headquarters. Newcastle University kindly agreed to allow the WEA to use the title 'Joseph Cowen House' for the building, carrying forward a great regional tradition already mentioned in Chapter 1, and the ground floor meeting and teaching area has been named after Michael Standen in tribute to his excellent work for the WEA. Here in Portland Terrace and in the streets beyond, the North-East Region continues to answer the cry for education and strives to fulfil the needs of those who see the WEA as the champion of THE RIGHT TO LEARN!

SOURCES CITED

Brown, C., (ed.), 2008. *Still Learning — 100 Years of the Workers' Educational Association in Leicester. Leicester:* WEA Leicester Branch.

Corbett, Ivan, 2003. '"So noble an institution": A History of the Workers' Educational Association Northern District 1910-80'. In: Standen (2003a:5-81). [Originally published 1980.]

Doyle, Mel, 2003. *A Very Special Adventure — The Illustrated History of the Workers' Educational Association.* London: Workers' Educational Association.

Field, John 2003. 'Survival, Growth and Retreat: The WEA in Wartime, 1939-45'. In: Roberts 2003:131-52.

Heatley, Phyllis, 1995. *Something Sustained — The Newcastle upon Tyne WEA Branch (1912—)*. Newcastle upon Tyne, WEA Northern District.

Roberts, Stephen K. (ed.), 2003. *A Ministry of Enthusiasm: Centenary Essays on the Workers' Educational Association.* London: Pluto Press.

Standen, Michael (ed.), 2003a. *A hunger to be more serious …: The Story of the WEA Northern District.* Newcastle upon Tyne: WEA Northern District.

WEA, 2003. *A Century of Learning — The Workers' Educational Association 1903-2003.* London: Workers' Educational Association.

The WEA and the Impact of the Twentieth-Century World

Ruth Tanner

By its very nature as an educational organisation, the WEA could not be but affected by events in the world around it. The economic situation and world events, from wars to the weather, all created the backdrop against which students chose the topics they wished to study, and the Association chose both the particular target groups it wished to work with and the causes for which it would campaign.

The early twentieth century was a tumultuous period for any organisation to be born into and to find its feet. Alderman William N. Smith, Northern District Secretary from 1919 to 1931, notes in the twenty-first *Annual Report* (1930-31) that:

> it should be borne in mind that during our 21 years of life more than 15 of these were lived during the actual conduct of the greatest war in world history and the effects which followed [...] we practically had to commence re-building our movement in 1919, and this rebuilding had to be done in the midst of the most appalling commercial and industrial dislocation and depression ever experienced within living memory.

In the previous year, Smith had noted:

> the continued and widespread industrial depression which prevails throughout the greater part of the District, especially in the coal and iron trades which form the basic industries in these northern counties. Yet, although industrial conditions retard progress to a certain extent [...] we are pleased to report progress in most branches and Centres.

Indeed, despite the continuing social and economic pressures during the 1920s and 1930s, the truth is that the Northern District continued to grow by whatever measure one may care to choose — classes, students, or branches. One can only imagine how large the organisation might have become in quieter and less troubled times.

This was a credit to Alderman Smith and his small band of staff and to his zeal for two particular aspects of the WEA's work, that of campaigning on national educational issues and making important strategic links locally. He also recognised, when recording the number of summer and day schools, rambles, socials and dramatic productions 'in which our branches are engaging more and more', that the WEA 'differs from other educational institutions in that it is more than an educational machine — it is an educational fellowship of men and women who have a common aim'. Future secretaries also emphasised the important role of the social activities engaged in by branches as a supplement to attendance at classes, something which is considered in more detail in Chapter 5 on the Darlington Branch.

Alderman Smith, however, moved into more demanding territory, in that he was a redoubtable campaigner for educational causes on the national stage and responded vigorously to the Association's campaign in support of the Fisher Education Act of 1918, and the drive to raise the school-leaving age and establish a regular structure of secondary schools from the age of eleven as defined by the Hadow Report of 1926. Smith was, as Ivan Corbett (2003) described him, a 'political animal'. During his time in office he was Chair of Durham County Council's Education Committee, ending as Chair of the County Council itself. He also held several national posts including membership of the Burnham Committee, the body which determined the pay of school teachers. Indeed, one wonders how he managed to fulfil the responsibilities of District Secretary in addition to these other duties. It is recorded that he spent several Saturday mornings at the District Office, then located in Newcastle's Royal Arcade, dealing with correspondence. Corbett notes that by 1926, after a period of illness, he secured the services of James B. Hall as Assistant Secretary, and shared the cost of Hall's salary of £210 with the District.

Smith was obviously impatient at the way educational policy was, 'blown this way and that by the icy blasts of the 1920s economic situation'. He reserved particular scorn for those who:

> overlook the educational interests of the child [...] by placing the emphasis too much on their own secretarial (sic) interests. Too often in the past has the child been made the victim of warring and contending factions. The children are our greatest national asset and any investment on their behalf is a sound investment for the nation as a whole.

The following year, however, Alderman Smith had to report the failure of the Bill to Raise the School Leaving Age, despite the support of the WEA, the trade unions and the National Union of Teachers (NUT). Once again he castigated 'the petty prejudices of party politicians and the wretched wranglings of self-seeking sectarians'. Another comment on 'dull, depressing dead-as-dodo dogmas' confirms not only his frustration at the lack of progress but also his considerable rhetorical skills.

Alderman Smith's retirement is recorded in the 1932 *Annual Report* with a fulsome tribute to his contribution to the Northern District's expansion since the end of the First World War: 'a period of rapid growth and surprising activity'. Particular mention is made of his work to change the WEA from 'an association little known' and 'of slight suspicion as to its aims and objectives', to one 'at the forefront of voluntary bodies … with active practical working relations' with Local Education Authorities, the Trade Union Movement, the Club and Institute Union, Miners' Welfare Committee, the Women's Institute, the Co-operative Movement and so on. He is credited with 'taking his share in making a broad highway of educational and social advancement smooth for the generations who will follow'.

On Smith's recommendation, James B. Hall was appointed his successor. Hall had been Assistant Secretary since 1926 and the District Executive Committee did not think it necessary to advertise the post. Central Office had other ideas and challenged the appointment as being unconstitutional. So strongly did they feel that both Firth, the General Secretary, and Green, his assistant, came up to state the case. The Executive Committee rallied its forces and at the Council Meeting in April 1932, got a reasonable vote of confidence (53 to 37). Firth and Green swallowed their pride, no doubt caught the next train back to London and notified the District Executive that Central Office 'ratified Mr. Hall's appointment, on the understanding that in future […] Hall got £300', whereas Smith had received £425, which perhaps reflects the opinion the Committee had of their respective merits (Corbett 2003:30-31).

Hall engaged in a campaign against the 'unsettled state of the people'. The National Government had been elected in the summer of 1931, with a second election in the autumn, and the terms of the (Adult Education) Amending Regulations Circular 1471, which, after the promise of increased grants, had actually cut back on grants for tutor fees, thus hindering the delivery of the planned programme. It is recorded that the District Council carried a resolution of protest against 'these economy proposals', with the complaint that education was generally the first to suffer, and that the price paid would far outweigh any so-called savings. Following three conferences across the district on the topic of Circular 1421 which sought to withdraw free places at secondary schools and impose a means test, several branches, including Ferryhill, were also recorded as holding their own public protest meetings. On this occasion the WEA's campaigning zeal fell on deaf ears, the economic situation being far worse than anyone at the time suspected. It was not until the passing of the Butler Education Act in 1944 that something approximating to the desired programme of educational reform was finally achieved. Mary Stocks notes a complaint registered at the 1943 National Conference from the rank and file that National Officers and Executive were 'so obsessed with the progress of the Education Bill that insufficient attention was devoted to the advance of Adult Education which is the primary concern of the WEA' (Stocks 1953:131-2). It was only after the Executive noted the rebuke that the emergency resolution on the government's White Paper was passed. It may have been the comprehensive nature of the Act, or perhaps the complaints of members, that virtually halted further campaigning for some years, so that it did not figure in the second half of the century to anything like the extent it had done earlier.

Perhaps even more important in the long term than his political campaigning was William Smith's legacy in building what we would today call partnerships with the many outside bodies mentioned above, making opportunities available for educational experiments, sometimes in response to directives from the National Executive, but also on local initiative alone. After his retirement as District Secretary, Smith remained on the District Council. Through his good offices as Chair of the Executive Committee of Durham County Community Service Council, a grant was made to the WEA in 1935 and 1936. This grant was to offer six-week courses for the unemployed 'who have in the past been reluctant to enter into our ordinary class work'. These shorter, non-grant earning courses were seen as breaking new ground in the hope that they would 'create a desire for more serious work of a higher standard'. Interestingly, a similar concern was voiced in the 1960s, when afternoon classes were introduced with the specific intention of attracting housewives.

A study of the topics studied in these 1935 and 1936 classes shows an interesting spread between those which addressed issues then current such as 'The Great Nations of Europe' and 'Elementary Survey of Main Economic Factors' and those of more general interest, including 'The History of Durham', 'Six Famous

Women' 'Esperanto' and 'Literature'. In addition two one-day schools for the unemployed were held in Durham. In November 1935, the topics were 'Where is civilisation taking us?' and 'Where should we make civilisation take us?' In January 1936, the topic was 'The League of Nations' and the audience of two hundred and fifteen comprised a hundred and ninety-five men and twenty women.

Work with the trade unions proceeded under the Workers' Education Trade Union Committee (WETUC) banner, as did schemes with the Northumberland and Durham branches of the Working Men's Club and Institute Union (CIU). In Durham branch from 1935 to 1936, it was recorded that eighty-nine members were in tutorial classes and a further two hundred and five in one-year and terminal classes across the two branches.

In 1953 the WEA Northern District published a Jubilee Brochure from which the following extracts from two of the papers are taken. The first is from Jim Boyden, then Director of Extra-Mural Studies at Durham and later MP for Bishop Auckland:

> In the early days Durham Division was one of the most flourishing parts of the country for the Tutorial Class Movement. The demand came largely from working class students [...] In Durham the Miners were the backbone of the Movement, both as students (exactly one-third of tutorial class students in 1924 were colliery workers) and as County Council representatives in helping to finance classes when they were organised [...]
>
> A special Tutorial Class for the Durham Miners' Association was established to be held on Saturday morning. This class is now in its third year and at one stage comprised seven local Councillors, all elected during the year of study and all still continuing with their studies, despite heavy Lodge and Local Government calls on their time.

The second extract is from Tom Metcalfe JP who attended a tutorial class in Bishop Auckland in Industrial History and later became a tutor. In addition to fellow miners, his classmates included two schoolmasters and the principal of the Girls' Grammar School, a sanitary inspector and the local medical officer of health.

> Think for one moment what the discussions of such an enlightened cross section of people meant to us four miners, and it will be appreciated why we walked five miles each way to the class every week, rain, snow or blow, often after a hard day's work, and once every fortnight knowing that we had to rise at 3 a.m. next day for the early shift. Think of the unselfish devotion of our tutor who on many occasions walked from Bishop Auckland to Durham, because there was no late train!
>
> [Imagine] the undisguised amazement, and amusement, of H.M. Inspector who on dropping in to a class at Browney School, beheld a student clad in pitman's clothes, replete with lamp and stick. It was explained that the class would finish at 9 p.m. and Jim was due to go down the pit at 9.10 p.m.

The broad spread of interests of working men, as they mostly were, can be seen most easily by comparing the Easter weekend schools held by the CIU and the WETUC, where the subjects were mostly of direct interest to their working lives, though not what would be termed 'practical subjects' today, such as Economics, Local Government, or World Affairs. The summer schools, on the other hand, tended more towards what we would call traditional liberal studies such as History, Philosophy, Geology and Literature. Yet, of the ninety-one participants at the 1933 Summer School, eighty-three were working men, including forty-six miners and twenty-seven in manual or distributive trades.

One of these weekend schools was held in the Lake District from 28 April 28 to 1 May 1932. Extracts from the 1931-32 *Annual Report* for the Cumberland and Westmorland Sub-District, written by John Carmichael, Honorary Secretary, give a flavour of the proceedings:

> This, the fourth since 1927, was again held at the Holiday Fellowship guest House, Stair, Newlands Valley. Including the lecturers, school officers and the students, there were 52 persons in residence for varying periods [...] These came from all parts of Cumberland and a few from the Counties of Durham and Northumberland.
>
> They travelled by train or bus to Keswick and then by taxi or on foot. Others journeyed direct by means of private cars, hired cars, motor cycle or even by push bike. In singles, couples and parties of three or more they came and ultimately departed. Workers of all kinds they were, from those who juggle with words and phrases, administrators and supervisors of officialdom, traders, housewives and wielders of the pen, pencil, brush, cane, pick and shovel. From quarry, steelworks, engineering and shipbuilding, also home, shop, office, school or university, were drawn those who met together for intellectual and social intercourse. All enjoyed their experience, which to some was a new one. (It is due to the energy of our District Secretary, Mr. J. B. Hall, who acted as treasurer of the School, that some students, manual workers, were able to attend. He negotiated for and secured, scholarships awarded by Trade Unions affiliated to the WEA [...] (through WETUC). On the Saturday afternoon, many of the students took advantage of a ramble up Catbells. On reaching a suitable position commanding a view of the country around Lake

Derwentwater, they enjoyed an instructive and interesting historical talk […] given by Mr. W.T. McIntire B.A., who had kindly come over from his home at Haversham near Kendal for the purpose.

The project to reach unemployed youth in the mid-1930s was at the initiative of the national WEA. In the first year, existing youth groups such as the YMCA, YHA, Scouts and Guides, Toc H, Churches, Labour Party League of Youth and the Co-operative League of Youth were contacted to identify and, as it is put, 'create demand'. In all, sixty-eight organisations were contacted. A mixture of study groups, linked lectures, and day schools were offered by a panel of voluntary tutors, with one paid organiser, Mr. J. Irving. Corbett (2003) records that from 1936 to 1940, the scheme was financed by the Carnegie Trust. The panel of tutors offered two hundred and thirty-one study group subjects and 1,285 single lectures. The most popular subjects were of a 'sociological character' such as social and economic history, politics and psychology, with minority interests in international relations, and in the second year, literature and science. The District Secretary reflects perhaps somewhat hopefully that this 'indicates a tendency towards a widening of the interests of the groups making use of the Scheme'. The intention to broaden out to include 'unattached youth' did not apparently take place, choosing rather to build on the contacts made the previous year with a group of people it was no doubt challenging to work with. The scheme reached over three hundred young people from fifty-five different groups: a considerable achievement when relying on voluntary tutors and only one paid co-ordinator, with little support from the branch network. Indeed, the branch network was patchy in some places and not always coterminous with the demand from youth groups. Reports from this scheme suggest that it was very similar in its challenges to the targeted project work the WEA undertakes today.

In the second half of the 1930s there was growing concern at developments in Europe, and in 1937 the District Secretary, Bertie Abrahart, and Chairman, Frank Blackwell, expressed their views forcefully:

> With authoritarianism of one brand on one side battling remorselessly with authoritarianism of a different brand, but similar essence, on the other, it is difficult for the purveyors of thought to make their voices heard. It seems it is only necessary to shout loud enough to win support for anything and thought is at a discount amid the noisy dictatorships which have discovered this. Educationists can only continue their efforts hopefully […]

On a lighter note, it is almost amusing to record how major national events are seen almost as an irritant to the smooth running of the Northern District's programme. In 1932, when the controversial National Government was sealing its position in a second election, the *Annual Report* notes that:

> the work of organising classes at the beginning of the session was impeded to some extent by the election in October […] many of our classes did not meet for one or two weeks […]

> In 1938, class work in spite of a bad start caused by the international crisis at a vital time in the session, has shewn a steady advance.

Further on in the report a more measured response to the crisis and the possibility of war was made, including the National Circular exhorting the Districts to continue their work at all costs. The branches were 'to regard their voluntary work as of supreme national importance'. In 1947, unsurprisingly, the first item of note was the extremely bad winter weather:

> which had affected both attendance at classes and the reporting and recording of statistics […] and led to […] the virtual stoppage of much non-grant earning work.

Passing reference has been made to the subjects of study chosen by students. There is continuing debate about what is 'useful' and whether students will choose more 'applied' or 'relevant' subjects in time of crisis. It is clear that new subjects came to the fore. Charles Hocking in the 1959-60 *Annual Report* recalls that already in 1912 there were nine tutorial classes and of these eight were in Economics, the ninth (at West Stanley) being in Literature. R. H. Tawney promoted the study of international relations during both the First and the Second World Wars with a view to being prepared to create a more just and lasting peace afterwards. It is easy to forget that subjects such as economics, sociology and psychology were new and exciting in the 1930s. J. R. Till, a tutor from 1950, recalls in Chapter 16 that any course containing the word 'social' in its title was considered trendy and perhaps a little daring. He also suggests that working people were drawn in by such practical subjects as economics or politics and then moved on to the more academic ones. Yet perusal of both branch and summer school programmes suggests that the two streams always existed side by side.

There were also practical considerations. John Carmichael was the Honorary Secretary and part-time organiser for the Sub-District of Cumberland and Westmorland. He was paid an honorarium of £10 per year 'whilst holding down his real job as a carpenter' (Corbett 2003:25). He described the problem of responding to requests for 'new subjects of study, such as Psychology' in 1932 to 1933:

> Our difficulty is that of co-ordinating the demand on the student side with that of supply on the teaching side. Sometimes our offers of subjects for which there are available tutors do not meet with the popular fancy. In other cases we are defeated by such factors as space and time in association with transport and finance.

Writing in the WEA's national newsletter *The Highway* in 1939, W.E. Williams puts in a word for what he calls more 'escapist' subjects:

> Even if it is impossible to persuade our politically minded members that there is no such thing as an escapist subject, it should not be impossible to get them to regard poetry, painting and music as permissible 'anaesthetics' for war-time living.

Even R. H. Tawney, in the same 1939 issue, admitted that 'what matters is that knowledge and inspiration which a man gets from his study, which necessarily varies with individual tastes'. And there we have it. Wisdom may be gained from study of 'practical' subjects but insights and understanding may just as easily come from liberal studies. After all, the Pitmen Painters, suffering poverty and unemployment in Ashington in the 1930s, chose what the 1936 *Annual Report* confusingly calls 'Theory of Applied Art'.

William Feaver, in his book *Pitmen Painters: The Ashington Group 1934-1984*, quotes their tutor Robert Lyon: 'I was invited to join in with a number of men in Ashington who had met to discuss the possibility of forming an art appreciation group in that district' (Feaver 2008:14). Two points arise: the WEA under grant regulation could run classes in 'Appreciation of Art', but not in practical painting. Interestingly, Lyon's thesis, written in the 1930 and perhaps influenced by his experience in Ashington, was 'The Appreciation of Art through the Visual and Practical Approach'. Lee Hall's play, *The Pitman Painters*, has shown us the way this class transformed itself into a vibrant and creative art course through the tutor's recognition of the wishes of his students actually to put paint to paper and express themselves. This was obviously a topic which provoked discussion elsewhere at the time. In Darlington in the mid-thirties, a sub-committee on branch re-organisation suggested as a possible topic for a speaker meeting: 'Should the WEA do Craft Work?'

After the Second World War, and following the implementation of the Butler Education Act, the WEA had to find a new role for itself in the developing culture of the time. More diverse topics were taken on as a more liberal and wide-ranging approach to education evolved. With increased political stability, and improved communications and transport, students could not only study international relations and our growing links with Europe but actually visit places, either in association with language classes or trade union activities. These topics are dealt with in other chapters of this book. The breaking of the link with the universities and the demise of the three-year tutorial class has led to the predominance of shorter courses, perhaps better suited to the pace of modern life and the needs and expectations of our learners. The widening of topics permitted in our curriculum range has led to classes such as 'Craft Work' and 'Health and Wellbeing' which our predecessors would never have dreamt of. In the world around us climate change and environmental issues may well have replaced 'War and the Rise of Dictators', but they are still topics which our students wish to study, alongside the more enduring subjects such as history and literature. All these changes serve to illustrate how the WEA has managed not only to survive for over one hundred years, but to renew and refresh continually its outlook and its offer to learners.

SOURCES CITED

Corbett, Ivan, 2003. '"So noble an institution": A History of the Workers' Educational Association Northern District 1910-80'. In: Standen (2003a:5-81). [Originally published 1980.]

Feaver, William, 2009. *The Pitmen Painters: The Ashington Group 1934 -1984*. Ashington: Ashington Group Trustees. [First published in 1988.]

Hadow, William Henry, 1926. *The Education of the Adolescent; Report of the Consultative Committee*, London: HMSO.

Standen, Michael (ed.), 2003a. *A hunger to be more serious …: The Story of the WEA Northern District*. Newcastle-upon-Tyne: WEA Northern District.

Stocks, M., 1953. *The Workers Educational Association: The First Fifty Years*. London: George Allen and Unwin.

Tawney, R. H., 1939. 'The W. E. A. in Wartime'. In: *The Highway*, 32, 4-6.

Williams, W. E., 1939. 'Notes and Comments'. In: *The Highway*, 32, 1-2.

WEA, 1953. *The Workers Educational Association Northern District (1903-1953) Jubilee Brochure*. Newcastle: WEA.

The Northern District and the Men from the Ministry — Aspects of the District's Relationship with Whitehall, 1924 to 1968

Ian Roberts

Even before the opening of the Northern District Office of the WEA in 1910, the Association had already begun to influence prominent supporters of the organisation to engage the government in taking notice of its activities. Several leading figures in the Association who were Members of Parliament had begun to involve themselves in the extension of the movement's work as, for example, when C. W. Bowerman and D. J. Shackleton joined Albert Mansbridge and others on a committee set up between representatives of Oxford University and the Association in 1907. This was the committee which produced the report entitled *Oxford and Working Class Education* which appeared in 1908 and which became a major force in promoting the reform of Oxford and Cambridge through the post-war Royal Commission and the amendment of statutes in 1926. The earnest and responsible attitude of the WEA members during this committee's deliberations, together with the strength of their arguments, had a positive effect on Prime Minister Asquith and the Liberal government and from 1908 arrangements was made with the Board of Education to grant financial assistance to the WEA.

Perhaps at a less exalted level, members of the WEA from all regions became involved in seeking to raise the school leaving age and bring in secondary education for all, both in the period before and at the time of the passing of the 1918 Education Act. Additionally, there was some disappointment in WEA circles that there was no reference to adult education in that Act, either as an end in itself or as a mechanism for providing education at a later stage in life for those children who had been unable to enjoy the benefits of secondary education. This sense of disappointment turned to one of apprehension in 1917 when draft regulations from the Board of Education suggested that in future payments for non-vocational adult education would be switched to Local Education Authorities (LEAs). As Mel Doyle (2003:30) succinctly explains:

> However, this potential threat to the WEA's funding base was removed in 1919 with the publication of the Final Report of the Adult Education Committee of the Ministry of Reconstruction (chaired by A L Smith, Master of Balliol College). The Report recommended (in guarded language) that voluntary organisations, including the WEA, should receive direct grant for one-year courses, and a commitment was given that there would be no grant changes for the next five years.

Thus assured, all regions of the WEA began to make steady progress in rebuilding in the wake of the war. Again, as Doyle (2003) points out, there were potential pitfalls in receiving such a grant as it placed the WEA at the mercy of changes in government policy and changes in the economic circumstances on which such finance depended. No more was this so than in 1924, when the five-year moratorium on grant changes came to an end. Doyle goes on to explain that new arrangements were made whereby government grants could be paid to approved associations. For the WEA this meant support for one-year and shorter course provision in non-vocational adult education, or liberal adult education in WEA terms. In addition, WEA Districts in England and Wales became Responsible Bodies 'able to receive grants and make provision in their own right'. One such body was the Northern District of the WEA.

Ann Morton (1997) has explained in her guide to educational records in the National Archives that unfortunately all of the papers dealing with bodies providing adult education up to 1924 have been destroyed and thus we have no knowledge as to the mechanism that the WEA put in place to deal with the new financial arrangements, either centrally or in the Districts. For the period after 1924, all papers in the National Archives subsequently dealing with the WEA and its relationship with the Board of Education and later the Ministry of Education have been collected together under File Reference ED73. There are four files relating to the Northern District in this section which are ED73/33:1927-35, ED73/82:1936-39. ED73/121:1947-55, and ED73/174:1956-68. The first three of these files were closed for access until 1986 while the last one was closed until 1999. This suggests that the next file in the series runs to a date after 1980 and is still closed under the thirty-year rule. However, the files, when read against the WEA District *Annual Reports* provide us with a picture of many aspects of the way in which the Districts and the government department interacted.

As a Responsible Body approved by the Board of Education, the WEA was able to make claims for grants during each year for courses of a type that were permitted under Chapter III of the Regulations drawn up in 1924. The year ran from 1 June to 31 May and a statement of the grants received had to be sent to the Board of Education by 31 October in the same year. Thus, the first document in ED73/33 is a 'Statement of Receipts and Payments' for the year ending 31 May 1927. The Receipts page shows that in 1927 there were four headings under which income for these particular courses was paid to the Northern District — Board grants, LEA grants, fees paid by students and money transferred from the General Account of the Responsible Body. In 1927 the total sum was £1128 8*s*. 10*d*., of which the Board of Education grant amounted to £488 3*s*. 2*d*., while the LEAs of Northumberland, Cumberland, Sunderland, Darlington and Middlesbrough contributed £215. The money was used to pay for items listed on the Payments page, including some money for office expenses, books and room hire, but the bulk of the money, £900 10*s*. 0*d*., was spent on the salaries of the teaching and non-teaching officers of the WEA Northern District. In addition to this information, the form also had attached to it the General Accounts for the Northern District of the WEA as a whole, so that Board officials had a picture of the remainder of the Association's activities in this District.

The files for 1928, 1929 and 1930 show the details of Payments and Receipts set out as in 1927, except that the receipts from both the Board and the LEAs fell in these years — in the Board's case to £326 12*s*. 9*d*. in 1928, £283 7*s*. 6*d*. in 1929 and £231 0*s*. 5*d*. in 1930. No reason is given for this fall in revenue and the District's *Annual Report* for 1930 does not provide any information either. There was no mention of the economic problems facing the country and the problems that these created for financing by government and voluntary associations. Perhaps their presence was so widely known and accepted that it was felt that further reiteration was unnecessary.

The *Annual Report* for 1930 begins with a statement of WEA policy which is clearly national in its scope, stating very strongly that it is non-sectarian and also non-political and that it co-operates and works with the Board of Education and LEAs as it does with trades unions, co-operative societies and working men's clubs. In the main body of the report, the Secretary suggests that there had been some apprehension about the Northern District not having sufficient funds during the year to meet all the activities planned but this proved to be without foundation. Donations from members and also from the affiliated organisations had more than fulfilled the requirements, giving the impression that, although the aid from the Board and LEAs was welcomed and assisted in broadening the work of the District in this period of economic adversity, it was not a crucial factor for its success.

The year 1931 saw a marked change in this situation. In the words of Ivan Corbett (2003):

> 1931, [Alderman W N] Smith's last year in office, [as District Secretary] was also the "coming of age" of the District. Income was £1877 with a healthy surplus of £127; grants totalled £1122. Completed classes were 171 with 3457 students with a disappointingly low proportion of members at 776 in 26 active branches, paying 5/- for the privilege

Among these riches, the grant from the Board of Education was a massive £732 0*s*. 7*d*., and accounted for almost all of the increase in grant income between 1930 and 1931.

At the same time that he was adding these figures together, Alderman Smith was able to report that there was hope for even more riches from the Board during the succeeding year. The regulations regarding payments for adult education courses were to be amended and Smith reported that one of the main features would be that provision would be made for short courses of not less than six weeks duration while there would be additional payments for university extension classes and some other advanced courses. John Carmichael, in his report on the Sub-District of Cumberland and Westmorland, also drew attention to these new regulations, pointing out that they gave an additional opportunity for the extension of WEA work to some of the remoter rural areas where it was only possible to deliver short courses.

If we exclude the remarkably high payment of Board grant in 1931, Smith's and Carmichael's predictions appear to have been fulfilled. The grant from the Board in 1932 was £372 1*s*. 9*d*. — a larger grant than any before this date as far as we are aware. However, the 1932 *Annual Report* sounded a word of caution about the future of grants. The Chairman, Frank Blackwell and James B. Hall, the new District Secretary, explained that the change of government in August 1931 from a Labour administration to a National Government had led to the issue of a circular which indicated that, as a result of the continuing economic depression, 'cuts' would in future be made in grants towards the fees of WEA tutors. This news was unwelcome in the North-East and at the District Council in October there was reference to the 'savage blow' that had fallen on education in general, followed by a resolution of protest against the 'economy proposals'. The same feelings were reported in the Sub-District of Cumberland and Westmorland, where Carmichael's report contained several instances of additional classes, some in areas where the WEA had not operated before, but all of which were as a result of the enlarged grants. Such developments would be jeopardised in the future by the new government measures.

The imposition of the cuts duly came in the following year. The *Annual Report* for 1933 set out the problems very clearly:

> Under the (Adult Education) Amending Regulations of the Board of Education, we have succeeded in introducing new types of classes which are specially provided for sparsely populated areas, and we are hopeful of being able to develop along these lines, particularly in Cumberland and Westmorland, but restrictions imposed upon the Board of Education by the Treasury made such developments very difficult, as the number of classes held during the 1932-33 session almost used up the whole of the money available to this District. With a continuance of these financial restrictions it may be very difficult to break new ground in future, and as this report is being prepared we already know that we shall only be allowed a stabilised programme for 1933-34. In this connection it is only fair to state that our relationship with the Board of Education is very cordial, as when their officials met the representatives of the Responsible Bodies in June and July, 1932, there was a sincere desire on the part of all concerned that the usual percentage increase in the number of classes should be continued, but in common with other Departments of State the Board of Education has been compelled to restrict the activities of the Responsible Bodies owing to a limitation of grants from the Treasury. (*Annual Report* 1932-33, p. 5)

The return of Receipts and Payments for 1933 shows no entry for a grant from the Board of Education and this resulted in stronger feelings about the measures being introduced by government. The file in the National Archives contains a newspaper article taken from the *Northern Echo*, dated 11 December 1933, which reports that at a meeting of the WEA District Council in early December, the Chairman had reported the problems being faced as a result of government policy and had moved a resolution 'placing on record the regret of the delegates [to a meeting with the Board] at the attitude of the Board of Education to the restrictions under which the work of the WEA is carried on'. The Secretary explained some of the difficulties arising from the policy of stabilisation of tutors' fees and said that they hoped to hold a future meeting with the Board about the matter. The article was 'noted' by the civil servants at the Board and then placed on file.

No further material is to be found in the file, but in the *Annual Report* for 1934 the Secretary makes it clear that the WEA was still operating under financial restrictions as a result of the Treasury cuts. He made an earnest plea to the LEAs to continue their valuable support work as it was crucial for the maintenance of the Association's work. However, there were some rays of hope. Carmichael included the following statement in his report from Cumberland and Westmorland (p. 29):

> It may here be stated for the information of our responsible local officers that the Board has recently intimated that there is to be some relaxation in the severity of the economic policy imposed in 1931. Some expansion in grant-aided classes is to be permitted, at any rate to the extent of seven and a half per cent increase on the figures for 1933-34.

There was also a grant to the Northern District for this year of £641 8s. 9d. which strongly suggests that the Board officials and the WEA had come to a compromise over the figures for 1932-33 and 1933-34, and that a figure to cover payment of grants for both years had been agreed. In the District accounts for 1934 it is shown as £363 10s. 6d. for 1933 and £277 18s. 3d. for 1934.

After a long illness, James B. Hall, the Secretary of the Northern District, died in September 1935. The disruption caused by his illness and death prevented the compilation of an *Annual Report* for that year and it is not possible to gauge the impact of the Board of Education grants for that year. The Receipts and Payments form in ED73/33 shows that the size of the grant was £370 5s. 6d., and as this is larger than the grant in either of the previous two years it makes a powerful case that the Board (and probably the Treasury!) had begun to relax some of their earlier strictures. Further evidence is also provided in the form of a general letter from the Board dated 26 August 1935, a copy of which had been sent to Mr Hall. The Board had begun to consider grants under the Adult Education Regulations for the following year (1935-36) and had discovered that there had been an under-spend of about £5,000 in the current year. The Board proposed to make much the same sum as in the current year available for the following year and to carry forward the

£5,000 so that there might be an increase in classes to absorb this money, and on which there would be no restriction save 'the usual scrutiny on educational grounds will be imposed on the programme submitted by individual Responsible Bodies for the session 1935-36'.

But what was 'the usual scrutiny'? None of the reports refer to scrutiny procedures for the courses or the tutors who worked for the WEA at this time. Lists are given in each of the reports of courses taking place at a variety of levels and the names of tutors and successful students appear regularly, however, there is no mention of inspection or scrutiny or approval procedures. In the National Archives file ED73/33 there is a clutch of documents which throws some intriguing light on this question although a complete answer is not provided.

The first course referred to in these documents took place in Newcastle and was concerned with elocution and dramatic art. A local HMI, Mr Dann, had decided that this course did not meet the requirements for a grant because it was too concerned with elocution, and the tutor had also been guilty of some registration errors. These matters had been drawn to the attention of Mr Hall, the District Secretary, but he had died before any changes could be brought about. The matter was passed by Mr Dann to the Board which decided that, in view of Mr Hall's death and the possibility that he had been unable to deal with the complaint, the course could continue to its end provided that a revised syllabus was submitted and adhered to until the course ended. Mr Clear, the Assistant Secretary temporarily in charge after Mr Hall's demise, put the matter to the tutor who refused to revise the syllabus. This was communicated to the Board and the decision taken to withdraw all support for the class so that no grant would be paid.

The second case contained in the file involves the work of a tutor, Mr John (Jack) Hemingway, in Darlington. Mr Hemingway was to become an important and influential figure in the Northern District, both as a tutor and as a member of the District Committee on which he ultimately served as Vice-Chairman.[1] Mr Hemingway had been teaching a one-year English literature course at two working men's clubs in Darlington and then, in late 1935, began to teach the first year of a full three-year tutorial course in English at one of these clubs. The matter was drawn to HMI Dann's attention, probably by the Darlington LEA which employed Mr Hemingway as a full-time teacher at Darlington Grammar School. HMI Jack was sent to look into the matter.

Mr Jack visited the class and watched the tuition and then had a discussion with the tutor and the students. He made some comments on the work and then summed up his experience, 'I have seen many worse literature courses in their first year without feeling called upon to criticise the tutor to the R[esponsible] B[ody]'. He then reported back to the Director of Education for Darlington. The Director was interested in four matters: first, was the class of 'University Honours Standard'; second, ought a secondary school teacher teach a class that purports to be of university standard; third, should the tutor be receiving additional pay for this work when the salary given was meant to be part of a staff tutor's salary, especially when the teacher/tutor already had a full-time post; and, finally, should a full time teacher devote more than one night a week to such work?

Mr Jack commented that the Director had raised all these points with him on previous occasions and then explained in reply that he would not interpret regulations but that although the class was not faultless, it was better than many he had seen and that secondary school teachers were taking many such courses in many places around the country, including a considerable number in County Durham. He also said that the fees were paid equally to whoever took the course and that Responsible Bodies did not differentiate between tutors who were doing the same work. The last point made by the Director was discussed at length although Mr Jack reiterated that he had heard many of the Director's comments before, including the Director's view that 'a secondary school job, if properly done, was literally a "full-time" job, and that he had, or ought to have, no time for extra classes'. He also made it clear that the LEA normally limited teachers to one additional evening's work. This appears to have been the only point that Mr Jack felt worth considering, as he advised the Board that the Durham Committee and the Northern District of the WEA should be written to in order that at Christmas Mr Hemingway should relinquish one of the two evening posts he held.

These two incidents are the only examples that seem to have survived of HMI involvement with the work of the Responsible Bodies. A search of HMI records at the National Archives has failed to uncover any further correspondence in the period before the Second World War. What is apparent, however, is that HMI was instrumental in making checks on the work carried out by the Responsible Bodies and in ensuring that

---

[1] For further information on Jack Hemingway see Chapter 5 below.

the correct work was being carried out in grant-aided classes. The records described above relate to incidents in 1935 but the familiarity of the official with adult education would strongly suggest a continuous HMI involvement that may have been less formally recorded but nonetheless ensured that the appropriate standard of the work was maintained.

The nature of the incidents does not appear to have affected the relationship of the Northern District with the Board of Education in any way. Indeed, no mention of either incident occurred in the *Annual Report* of the District for 1936, which further strengthens the argument that such visits were commonplace and rarely reported other than when some problem was experienced with the course. Indeed, the Northern District received a grant of £284 6s. 1d. for 1936 and there were words of appreciation in the report for favourable policy changes at the Board. The new District Secretary, B. W. Abrahart, concluded his report with the following statement:

> A welcome contribution to the expansion of our work was made by the final withdrawal of the restrictions imposed by the Board of Education in 1932. Excepting the limits imposed by our own resources and those of the Durham and Armstrong Extra-Mural Boards, there is now no restriction on development of Grant Earning Class-work. Moreover as a happy augury of future progress, the issue of Circular 1,444 to Local Education Authorities by the Board of Education reveals a strong desire on the part of the Board for an expansion of adult educational activity. We venture to hope that the LEAs within the North Eastern District will respond to the Board's gesture and will extend wherever possible the support they already give us (*Annual Report* 1936, p. 13).

Abrahart's confidence appears to have been well founded. The remaining three years before the outbreak of war in September 1939 were very productive for the Northern District. In the three years up to the war, 1936-37, 1937-38 and 1938-39, the Board of Education supplied the following grants: £492 12s. 10d.; £614 7s. 6d.; and £824 6s. 11d. — all significantly greater than any single grant since 1927. No mention is made of this in any of the three *Annual Reports*, while on the Board's part the information about its activities as represented in ED73/82 is totally different from the previous file. Only two forms of letter exist in the file. One is a cover letter supplying the names of the places where courses for which approval for grant might be given and the distinguishing number of that institution which had to be used on any correspondence with the Board. The second is a letter stating that there is an attached list of the courses which have recognised for grants. Both types of letter were issued all the year round for the whole of the Northern District and sent to the office in Newcastle, as the Sub-District of Cumberland and Westmorland had now been fully integrated with the North–Eastern area. In the case of the second type which provided details of grants, most of these arrived in the two months at the end of the year but they do not give details of the amount earned for the particular courses listed. The file ends abruptly in March 1939, the last document being a copy of the Northern District *Annual Report* for 1938-39.

As we have no *Annual Reports* for the war years and the files at the National Archives do not resume until 1947, an account of the relationship of the Northern District with the Board of Education has to be sought elsewhere. Corbett (2003:42-54) provides a brief overview of what transpired but the most thorough account of the WEA during the war has been provided by John Field (2003). Based on much original research in the National Archives, Field provides the most detailed account of the Association in this period to date and redresses the slight treatments given to the topic in earlier studies. He also provides an admirable backdrop to the relationship between the new Ministry of Education and the WEA as described in the post-war District *Annual Reports* and the surviving papers in the files at the National Archives.

ED73/121 is catalogued as covering the years 1947 to 1955 and contains material dealing with the official documents concerning the relationship between the Northern District of the WEA and the new Ministry of Education. The file has three original documents, as well as a copy of the District reports for 1954-55. Two of the original documents are concerned with the work of the Tutor Organisers employed in the District while the third is the report of a survey of courses in Public Affairs in Newcastle and Gateshead. In comparison with the two pre-war files, much less can be learned about the official view of WEA work in the Northern District in this period. Even when read with the District reports from 1949 to 1955, the picture is not as clear as before the war. In part, the war may well be responsible for this. The dislocation of the war years had resulted in the government dealing with the headquarters of the WEA rather than with the individual Districts. At the end of the war, the 1944 Education Act created the Ministry of Education, charging it with many new tasks and it was often seen by government officials as more efficient to deal with a central authority rather than a group of scattered Districts. At the same time, changes had also taken place in the regulations governing the delivery of adult education. The 1944 Act made it mandatory rather than voluntary for LEAs to provide adequate further education facilities for adults in their areas. Corbett (2003:54-55) shows that the number of evening institutes doubled between 1947 and 1950 and that although many LEA courses were vocational and recreational, the legislation also created a rival provider of some of the same types of course as those offered by the WEA. In 1945, the regulations regarding government grant-aid were relaxed so that, in future, grants would be related to the size of the District's programme of classes. Encouraging though this was, in 1946 the grant regulations were altered so that the distinction between the work which was considered appropriate for Universities and that delivered by the other Responsible Bodies, including the WEA, was to be abolished. This had the effect of opening doors for the universities and making the relationship between them and the WEA competitive rather than collaborative.

In the Northern District, there was no immediate conflict. Relations were cordial and work shared for some years to come but, as Corbett (2003) has pointed out, there was an expansion in the number of extra-mural tutors appointed to the Durham and King's College northern staffs, to the disadvantage of the District. The great strength of the WEA at this point was the strong Tutor Organiser operation that District Secretary Abrahart had set up prior to his leaving the WEA in 1946. It was the importance of these officers and the manner in which they were deployed that attracted the attention of the Ministry of Education. Only concern for these matters, and their capacity to earn grants, can explain the presence of two documents containing reports compiled by the District Secretary which give details of the work of these officers in file ED73/121.

The reports are dated February and December 1948 and contain details of the work of the three Tutor Organisers in Northumberland, Tyneside, Durham, Cumberland and Westmorland. The information is comprehensive and covers the work done in all three terms of the year. Teaching work is found under headings such as terminal courses, lecture courses, single lectures and day schools, while organisational work embraces lectures arranged, One-day courses arranged and visits to centres. Mostly, each Tutor Organiser's work covered two foolscap sheets and occasionally three. The attached letters from Charles Hocking, Abrahart's replacement as District Secretary, are stamped with the Ministry's date of receipt and also 'DW' for 'dealt with'. They are also marked 'No action taken' with a reference to a file coding, thus indicating that the documents had entirely fulfilled the purpose for which they were collected. It would seem most likely that this was a method of ensuring that appropriate work was being undertaken by the Responsible Body and that the grants paid were merited. At the same time that this was taking place, entries in the *Annual Reports* for 1949 to 1955 state that the District staff were grateful to the Ministry for help and also to the HMIs who regularly visited the classes offered, giving valuable suggestions and advice to the tutors and students. The only other references in the reports to involvement with the Ministry are occasional comments on current policy, usually voiced in terms of the whole Association rather than, as before the war, with particular reference to the District.

The third document in the file is the 'Survey of Courses in Public Affairs in the County Boroughs of Gateshead and Newcastle-upon-Tyne' which was held between September 1948 and May 1949. This was a long-term study of a wide range of courses offered by the Extra-Mural Department of King's College and the Northern District of the WEA as well as evening institutes, youth clubs and some other groups. The purpose of the study was an 'attempt to inquire into the provision of classes and other types of instruction aimed at furthering a knowledge of or stimulating an interest in "Public Affairs" at all stages'. The survey was not intended to test the efficacy of course delivery but rather to understand the type of people attending the courses and their interests, as well as finding out how to encourage more people to participate in and learn about public affairs. There was obviously a deep concern about the amount of knowledge people had about public affairs and some of the report contains sentiments reminiscent of discussions about courses on 'citizenship' in the twenty-first century. The relationship between the extra-mural tutors and the WEA was found to be very friendly and their courses appear to have been judged to be very satisfactory. One problem clearly demonstrated was that participation was stronger from those in the professional sphere than those engaged in manual work. Another area of concern was the participation of women, the ratio of men to women being twenty-two to nineteen. Here the WEA did very well as large audiences of housewives attended many of their public lectures. Another concern was the low participation of younger people. It was felt that Tyneside youth was articulate about problems and the work of government but unwilling to take part in discussion or learning about the topics on offer.

The reports concluded that valuable work was being done by the Responsible Bodies and that the pioneering work of the courses surveyed had promise for the future. Specially mentioned was the need for greater co-operation with the LEAs and the provision of more evening institute courses. It was also felt that integrated publicity might help and raise awareness for the future. All of which, if applied to the WEA would have led the Ministry to see that the 1950 grant of £2825 7*s*. 9*d*. was money well spent.

The type of documentation found in the National Archives file ED73/174 covering the period 1956 to 1968 is very similar to that of the previous file. ED73/174 contains four sets of papers relating to the work of the Tutor Organisers from 1956 to 1960, two copies of a special report on weekend courses for students drawn from the trades unions and a 1963 special report on the work done by the Northern District of the WEA in County Durham. In addition, there are also three sets of papers covering work done on the Special Science Project between 1963 and 1968.[2]

The first papers in the file deal with the survey of weekend courses conducted by the Northern District of the WEA and the report of a conference held between the HMIs responsible for the survey and members of the Northern District's Executive Committee. The relationship between HMI and the WEA was portrayed in all the District Reports as very cordial. HMIs visited classes on a regular basis and 'inspected' the work taking place. These visits were not inspections in the strict sense but visits in which the inspectors offered advice and guidance on teaching matters and help for those who were having difficulties in coping with the workload. As they saw a large number of classes, they were able to bring comparative knowledge to the tutors and often helped them devise new work approaches that created a greater interest and higher standard among the students. The survey of the weekend courses carried out in the 1958-59 session was a similar exercise to the review of Public Affairs carried out in the 1940s. HMIs attended and observed a large number of courses and drew together the information gathered to provide a broad view of the enterprise in hand.

The weekend courses at the centre of the survey were based on a WEA initiative concerning the trades union members. As the authors of the survey report explained:

> In 1954 the WEA realising the special needs of the Trade Unions, decided to conduct an experimental drive to provide classes for their members. Three areas, namely Tyneside, Tees-side, and the Port Talbot District of South Wales were selected for this major effort, which became known as the Trade Union Pilot Scheme.

In the Northern District a special report (WEA 1957) had been issued which covered the scheme between 1955 and 1957. It described the scheme in detail and drew conclusions about the problems encountered, their possible solutions and made suggestions about how the work might continue in the future. Because some of the problems faced by students working in industry were related to business hours, shift work and the tiredness of many after a day at work, it was considered that some of the best teaching and learning had taken place during the weekend courses. As a result of this and because the Ministry of Education had assisted the project financially, HMIs undertook to survey these particular courses, to discover what could be learned from them and judge the extent of their success. HMIs investigated all aspects of this work from the location and facilities of the courses through to administration and finance, the tutors, students, conditions of teaching and conduct of classes. Their conclusions contained some criticisms and suggestions for improvement, but the final paragraph was optimistic:

> In spite of these criticisms some very good work has been done in the weekend schools, and the linked series, with their more favourable teaching conditions and a more protracted period of study, deserve special commendation. The steady recruitment from weekend schools to the more formal classes proves their value as a training ground. For some classes there are more applicants than can be accepted. Improvements in teaching conditions and the satisfying of the demands for education which have been stimulated may well hinge on more generous financial support.

Here then was a hint to both WEA and the government to provide more aid for a successful experiment. This was an important role of the HMI — the ability to investigate an activity from an informed and experienced point of view and subsequently make clear recommendations for improvement. The supportive role of this governmental body was much appreciated by the WEA and led to constant expressions of gratitude in successive *Annual Reports*.

The four programmes of work of the full-time tutors (or Tutor Organisers) revealed that the tutors spent rather less time on organising and more on teaching. HMIs and civil servants examined the proposals and were happy to comment and suggest changes. They were also keen to see that workloads were evenly distributed and money fairly earned. Interestingly, when the 1957 to 1958 programmes came up for review, it was suggested that some changes be made to the work of one of the tutors who had been unsuccessful in retaining full classes the previous year. A letter from the Ministry was suggested, but one of the senior officials considered this to be unethical and a much too heavy-handed approach. He felt, and this was agreed,

[3] This project was considered at the time to be an important one for the WEA and has been explored in greater detail in Chapter 14 below.

that the matter should be informally handled through one of the HMIs. The matter could be raised at an appropriate point in conversation and the changes made in a more subtle manner.

All of which is consistent with the regular approach of HMIs and the way in which the Inspectorate and Ministry attempted to work in partnership with the Responsible Body. As in the case of District Secretary Hocking, they were attempting to build up a team of tutors working consistently in their delivery of successful courses throughout the north of England. It is interesting to note in this context that the trade union tutor was expected to deliver the same types of courses to trade unionists as were taught in the branch-organised meetings. The strength of the WEA lay in the collegial way in which education was delivered, so that on some occasions it was reported in the *Annual Reports* that the trade union classes could be taught through the branch structure. Again HMIs seem to have supported this on behalf of the Ministry. Such support was important as the Ministry was financing the project through the grant to the Association and any detailed criticism of the way the courses were being delivered might well have put this grant, which was such an essential part of Northern District finances, in jeopardy. By 1960, the grant had risen to £6,800 and accounted for over half the education budget for the District.

The report on the activities of the WEA in the Administrative County of Durham for the year ending 31 July 1963, which is the final document to be examined in ED73/174, confirms much of what had been expected both from the work of the Tutor Organisers and the Trades Union Project. This report was drawn up by District Secretary Hocking and, as one might expect, began with references to the harsh winter conditions which had prevailed during the first few months of the year during which the Association had continued to deliver its services in an exemplary manner. Hocking then went on to point out the successes of the year in terms of courses and enrolments — he showed that there had been an increase in class meetings from 355 class meetings in 1959-60, to 530 meetings in 1962-63. He explained this success by referring to the programme of single lectures delivered by the Tutor Organisers and the uptake of courses by trade unionists. One of the most successful places was Consett where there had been a considerable measure of co-operation from the authorities at the Iron Works. It is important to note that these courses were being delivered as part of the WEA programme, and the Trades Union Project developments were being gradually and seamlessly drawn into the network of provisions made by the Northern District as a whole, as HMIs had hoped. Corbett (2003) has been critical of the lack of follow-up for what he regarded as a very successful Trades Union Project and considered that the failure to appoint a specialist tutor for some years was detrimental to its legacy. However, a perusal of the list of courses delivered in Durham shows that a significant number had their origins in the Project and this must be judged as an example of successful integration from which emanated the engagement of a wider audience.

In addition to the authorities at the Consett Iron Works, Hocking also drew attention to the work of the University's Extra-Mural Department. He praised the close co-operation between the WEA and the university staff in organising this work and stated that this had resulted in 147 courses being put on by both bodies with a total student enrolment of 2,440. Hocking also paid warm tribute to the Director and Deputy Director of Education for the county and also to the Library Service, all of whom had helped to make the year a very successful one in terms of the adult education service provided.

In conclusion, there is almost a Whiggish sense of continuous progress in the relationship between the Northern District and the government between 1924 and 1968, by which time the ministerial authority had become the Department of Education and Science (DES). In part, this is supported by the almost continual rise in the size of the grant from the Department which had inexorably climbed to £17,330 by July 1968. However, as Corbett (2003:73-76) points out, there were underlying problems in the financial structure of the organisation of the Northern District which were to lead to a crisis in the 1970s in which government help in 1974 was not taken as the warning signal for action that it undoubtedly was. Responsible Body status had been a marvellous status to gain, but it appears to have led to over-dependence on state funding and an assumption that the aim of providing university-type education for the working person was universal and everlasting. In the files of government, with their record of approbation and carefully constructive criticism, there may be factors in need of fresh examination to see what evidence they provide for institutional complacency and an inability by the Northern District, if not the WEA as a whole, to adapt more speedily than they did to the changing educational and social scene. The next release of government files will present an interesting opportunity for further research activity into this area.

SOURCES CITED

Corbett, Ivan, 2003. '"So noble an institution": A History of the Workers' Educational Association Northern District 1910-80'. In: Standen (2003a:5-81). [Originally published 1980.]

Doyle, Mel, 2003. *A Very Special Adventure — The Illustrated History of the Workers' Educational Association.* London: Workers' Educational Association.

Field, John, 2003. 'Survival, Growth and Retreat: The WEA in Wartime, 1939-45'. In: Roberts 2003:131-52.

Roberts, Stephen K. (ed.), 2003. *A Ministry of Enthusiasm: Centenary Essays on the Workers' Educational Association.* London: Pluto Press

Morton Ann, 1997. *Education and the State from 1833*. Richmond: PRO Publications (Public Record Office Readers' Guide No. 18).

Simon, Brian, 1974. *Education and the Labour Movement, 1870-1920,* London: Lawrence and Wishart. [First published 1965.]

Standen, Michael (ed.), 2003a. *A hunger to be more serious …: The Story of the WEA Northern District.* Newcastle upon Tyne: WEA Northern District.

WEA, 1957. *Trade Union Education 1955-56-57: Work on Tyneside.* Newcastle: WEA Northern District.

'Over the hills and a long way off...'
— the Development of the Bellingham Branch of the WEA in Rural Northumberland

Ian Roberts

It is true to state that in most towns and villages of any note in the country there is to be found a WEA class or group of students, who are quietly and steadily at work endeavouring to equip not only their own minds, but also trying to create in their fellows the desire to search into these subjects which have a vital bearing on life's questions and problems, and thus help to create a society based upon a recognition of the value of the things of the mind. (*Annual Report* 1932-33)

Thus, in the concluding paragraph of the Adult Education section of the Statement of Policy in the Northern District's *Annual Report* for 1932-33, its authors reflected on the progress of WEA classes in the North East of England in the preceding thirty-three years. From the contents of the remainder of that report, there seems little doubt that the above remarks were justified in terms of the progress of the Association on Tyneside and Durham. There were encouraging reports of large numbers of well attended classes covering a wide range of subjects, supported by weekend courses, a summer school in Durham and many other activities. However, with respect to rural Northumberland, no sign is found of branches or classes among the 'villages of any note' in places such as North Tynedale, Redesdale or Coquetdale.

This is not to denigrate the efforts made to bring WEA classes to these rural areas prior to the Second World War. A university extension course on 'Immortality' took place at Wark-on-Tyne (hereafter Wark) in 1934, while some WEA services were offered at Kielder in 1936, probably in association with the industrial training camp that the government had set up near the recently established forestry enterprise in the same area. Both WEA activities were supported not only from the District office in Newcastle but also later by the Hexham Branch, which was established in 1937 and had become a flourishing centre by the end of the 1930s, offering several courses each year. The success of the Hexham Branch, no doubt arising from the hard work of District Secretary Abrahart and his assistant, Mr Clear, could have paved the way for further developments. However, as Ivan Corbett (2003) makes clear, the outbreak of war in 1939 created conditions such as blackout, limited transport and loss of accommodation, all of which made the growth of the organisation difficult to sustain.

In spite of these wartime privations, the first genuinely rural WEA branch to be established in North Tynedale took place at Barrasford in 1941 with a total of eighteen members. Little is known about those early days at Barrasford but the village was a likely centre for such activity because of its special circumstances. As might be expected, there was a well established farming community, but the villages of Barrasford and Gunnerton were also the site of a number of quarries exploiting the whinstone prominent in the area, as well as a couple of small coalmines employing up to twenty men. However, the most significant employment centre was the local sanatorium which had been opened in 1907 for the treatment of tuberculosis cases. Originally with room for fifty patients, by 1921 it had doubled in size and the number of staff had also increased commensurately. A railway station for the Border Counties line to Hexham situated conveniently close to the village, serviced all of these activities. As a consequence, the parish of Chollerton, in which the village of Barrasford was located, had a population of over 1,200 people.

The size of the community, as well as the large number of workers from non-agricultural enterprises, made this a fertile environment in which the WEA flourished so that the branch continued to operate throughout the years of conflict and for a significant number of years after the war had ended. The Barrasford Branch had the same secretary, Mr J. Campbell of Gunnerton, during its lifetime but did not have a large membership. However, it ran at least one course each year containing more students than just those who had elected to take WEA membership.

Unfortunately, this success was localised. Barrasford did not immediately become a model for other villages, so that for a number of years it was the only WEA branch in the valleys of north-west Northumberland. Tutor Organisers made visits in the period just after the war. In 1947, Mrs McNair made organisational visits to Barrasford, Falstone and West Woodburn, while in 1948 Mr Quigley visited Barrasford and Kielder (The National Archives, ED73/121). Later, occasional lecture courses were held, such as one in Local History at Elsdon in 1952 and two weekend courses at Otterburn in 1954, but there was no sustained activity until 1957 when a class in International Affairs was held at Bellingham for sixteen students and which met twenty-two times. This was succeeded over the following two years by classes in Economics. Classes continued into the 1960s, until in 1963-64 a class in Foundations of Christianity was offered and conducted by the local vicar, the Rev. B. W. Garman. There are no records of any class after this until 1969, when the *Annual Report* for the Northern District lists Bellingham as having a branch of the WEA whose Secretary, Martin Sumner, lived at Wark and was also the local school attendance officer. Given the success of the Barrasford Branch, why did it take so long for another branch to be opened in the North Tyne valley?

Corbett (2003) reports the success of the new Tutor Organisers from the early 1940s onwards in widening the work of the WEA in the North-East and in particular in Northumberland. However, there were limitations to the scope of this work. Finances were always restricted but there were other factors to be considered as well. One was clearly the size and composition of the communities in the more remote rural areas. Bellingham had always larger than Barrasford by about two hundred people but its population was more scattered. There were fewer full-time agricultural workers than in Barrasford where more arable farming was undertaken. Bellingham was principally concerned with pastoral agriculture and many of the farm workers were hill shepherds with homes situated far from those of their fellow workers. Although other forms of employment existed, such business concerns were small and there was also very little trade union activity. Moreover, there was limited transport around the villages. The railway lines to both Morpeth and Hexham were closed in 1952 and 1956 respectively. Thus, public transport was left in the hands of bus drivers while railway work, another type of employment that might have attracted the attention of the WEA, now ceased to exist. Visits from WEA tutors or members of the District Office staff could only be made with difficulty or by the use of a motor car. All these factors meant that when the WEA classes began in Bellingham, they were usually restricted to people who lived in or around Bellingham village and attracted those who were interested in one-year classes rather than courses linked to a university-type education.

One potential source of employment in the area had failed to materialise as had once been hoped. This was the development of the forestry around Kielder in the far north of the valley. A shortage of timber after the First World War had led to the founding of the Forestry Commission and sustained efforts on the part of government to create a British forestry industry. Kielder had become the centre of what was to be the largest man-made forest in Britain. Plans were made after the Second World War to increase its size and to establish a group of eight new forest villages that were to be the homes of approximately 2,000 workers in the timber production industry. However, changing methodology and increasing use of mechanisation meant that just three villages were built and hundreds rather than thousands of employees came to live in the North Tyne and Rede valleys. Although some forestry workers lived in other villages such as Falstone, these were quite small and none of the settlements, forestry or otherwise, was large enough, nor was the demand great enough for the WEA to be requested to offer classes, let alone open a branch.

This, then, was the nature of the Bellingham area when the branch began in 1968 and explains why Bellingham Branch was to be the only one opened in the area beyond Barrasford. The new forestry villages were too small and too remote, with only one type of employer in a single industry. The populations of the older villages continued to decline, except for Bellingham, where WEA classes were held in a wide variety of subjects throughout the 1970s. The variety on offer was considerable, not only from year to year but also within the annual programmes. In 1972, for example, there were classes on 'Man in Society', Astronomy and Criminology and the closing one on Roman History was delivered by no less an eminent academic than Professor Eric Birley of Durham University, an internationally renowned authority on Hadrian's Wall. Although Bellingham's example did not produce other branches in the area, classes were organised in some of the other villages such as those at Kielder between 1970 and 1973, and a class for lovers of music which met in East Woodburn for several years.

Unlike Barrasford, where Mr Campbell of Gunnerton continued as the Secretary and where classes were held increasingly at Wark, the Secretary's post at Bellingham changed hands a number of times. Martin Sumner was succeeded by Mrs P. Gaskin and then by Mrs Ruth Everatt. Ruth Everatt recalled that the classes were always popular but members were sometimes only drawn from the village. She has also recalled that although the use of a school room or the staff room in Bellingham's Middle School was sometimes the venue, classes were often held informally in people's homes and books and papers stored in someone's sideboard between classes.

The 1980s saw a number of changes in the WEA's provision of classes in Northumberland. In 1982 the long-time Tutor Organiser, Skeff Vaughan, was replaced by Freda Tallantyre who has written her own recollections of the period in this post during the years 1982 to 1986 in Chapter 11 below. Bellingham would probably have been one of her more conservative branches, pursuing its own interests rather than attempting to be part of the new movements taking place elsewhere which embraced feminism and new ways of political thinking. One of Freda's successes was the formation of the federal Tynedale Branch based on Hexham, which introduced many new ideas into the area. However, this period saw the demise of the Barrasford Branch in 1984 and left Bellingham as the sole branch in the North Tyne valley. Although the branch was successful and a new student group had been established at Otterburn, Ruth Everett recalled that the Bellingham Branch members sometimes felt they were a little on the periphery compared to the vibrancy that seemed to be elsewhere in places such as Hexham and Ashington.[1] Freda Tallantyre herself recalled that resources were often a little thin and some of the rural areas had to survive on less than they really deserved, but given the demands of her job which included a significant amount of teaching as well as administrative duties and her work in the Women's Education Programme, it is remarkable how much she achieved in four years.

Freda left WEA service in 1986, initially on secondment, and was replaced by Peter Bennet who held the post of Tutor Organiser temporarily until 1987, and then permanently for the next fifteen years. In 1984-85, new regulations about the payment of grants to WEA classes had been issued by the Department of Education and Science (DES). The new regulations stipulated more strictly the number of students that had to be enrolled to ensure class viability and grant aid. As a result, one of the courses in Bellingham had to be cancelled. This undermined the Bellingham Branch's structure, which was further weakened the following year when the same rules caused the cancellation of the Otterburn class. Thus, when Peter took over in 1986, Bellingham Branch was no longer in existence and only two WEA classes were being held in Bellingham and East Woodburn.

Freda Tallantyre had only taken leave of absence for one year to work at the then Newcastle Polytechnic but her appointment was made permanent in 1987 and Peter Bennet was then confirmed as the permanent replacement Tutor Organiser in Northumberland. In the previous year, despite being new to the post, he had managed to revive the Alnwick Branch. In 1987, he succeeded in reviving the Bellingham Branch with the help of Ruth Everatt and Marian Young. Three factors helped bring this restoration about. First, Peter lived only a few miles from Bellingham and was concerned to restore a branch that he knew had the potential to succeed. After all, he was the only Tutor Organiser who had actually tutored in Bellingham. Second, there was a group of people including Ruth Everatt and Philip Liddell from East Woodburn who were keen to restore Bellingham's fortunes and maintain classes in their villages. Finally, Peter knew Marian Young, who had recently come to live in Bellingham, and believed that she was the ideal candidate for Branch Secretary who would work very well with Ruth Everatt and the other local WEA supporters.[2]

It was remarkable how prescient this choice proved to be. Marian Young has frequently admitted that her knowledge of the WEA was very sketchy when she joined the WEA and the Bellingham Branch. However, her formidable abilities as an organiser and as a teacher of English Literature, honed by a successful career in teaching, latterly as deputy head of a large Newcastle comprehensive, meant that she soon had the branch back on its feet. From this grew Marian's abiding affection for the WEA and its ideals, her membership of the Regional Committee and, ultimately, her holding of national office.

In Bellingham village and its surroundings, the branch revived and maintained its strength. Despite a heavy teaching load and an ever-increasing number of administrative duties, Peter lent much support to the branch. One of Marian's innovations was to develop two one-day courses — one in the autumn and the other at the start of spring. These were open to all interested local people, as well as regular WEA students, and they fitted in admirably with Peter's advertising slogans: 'Friendly Courses for Thinking Adults' and 'WEA — the College in your Village'. Peter has taken part in a number of the day courses, both before and after retirement, and contributed greatly to their success. He is, therefore, the embodiment of a model Tutor Organiser, both administering his area and supporting the branches and classes with his own teaching. As Peter acknowledges in his oral history interview with me, the role of the Tutor Organiser has been relentlessly transformed into

---

[1] Personal communication - Ruth Everatt to Ian Roberts, 29 March 2010.
[2] Oral History interview - Peter Bennet talking to Ian Roberts, 10 March 2010.

full-time administrator by the never-ending changes in regulations and funding structures applied by successive governments to the adult education sector. Peter quite clearly believes that the original Tutor Organiser model had great strengths, particularly when applied to WEA branches in rural communities. It is easy for these branches and their classes to feel isolated and disregarded if they are not nurtured by contact with the Regional Office. Happily, Peter's successors have been very supportive and even though they may not teach the classes, their visits and constant attention to the welfare of branch officers and the tutors has been a source of strength to branches such as Bellingham.

Over the last decade, the demands of twenty-first century Adult Education have generally been fulfilled in Bellingham Branch through the strategy of offering one longer course supported by two day schools. Within this scenario, one of the most significant difficulties faced has been financial. Many of the students are elderly and the rising costs of tuition fees and room hire could have proved a disincentive to participation. However, more economical but equally up-to-date facilities such as those at the New Horizons Centre, or in the Methodist / United Reformed Church Hall have replaced the use of classrooms in local schools and have also helped to defray costs. Surpluses from some of the most popular day courses have also helped to maintain the branch's solvency, as has the success of the longer course ventures.[3]

In 2005-06, a study of local educational history coupled with a continuation of oral history work begun in a previous course created a desire among the students of Bellingham Branch to chart the history of elementary education in North Tynedale and Redesdale. Much hard work, both in research and writing, produced an original and very worthwhile book: *Telling Tales Out Of School — A History of Education and School Life in North Tynedale and Redesdale from 1870 to 1944*, published in 2008. Launched in the House of Lords in London and also in Bellingham, this book was not only an enormous event in the life of Bellingham Branch and a tangible achievement for the members of the class, but has also produced some much needed income and publicity for the branch as well as raising the profile of the WEA in the region.

The class has now switched its focus to studying the lives of people in the two valleys in twentieth century wartime. An exhibition of the class's findings has been held this year in the Heritage Centre in Bellingham and in several local schools, and a book is now planned. Readers interested in investigating the vibrant life of a rural branch in the second century of the WEA in North East England should begin here!

SOURCES CITED

Corbett, Ivan, 2003. '"So noble an institution": A History of the Workers' Educational Association Northern District 1910-80'. In: Standen (2003a:5-81). [Originally published 1980.]

Roberts, Ian David, 2009. 'The hill farms are dying and the folk all but gone: rural employment 1950-2000'. In: *North East History* 40.31-57.

Roberts, Ian David and Bellingham WEA Group, 2008. *Telling Tales Out of School: A History of Education and School Life in North Tynedale and Redesdale from 1870 to 1944.* Seaton Burn: Northern Heritage.

Standen, Michael (ed.), 2003a. *A hunger to be more serious ...: The Story of the WEA Northern District.* Newcastle upon Tyne: WEA Northern District.

---

[3] Oral History interview - Marian Young talking to Ian Roberts, 10 February 2010.

Bound to Flourish: the Story of a Successful Urban Branch[1]

Ruth Tanner

> The more lively the branch, the greater the breadth and depth of participation in its affairs, and the better its activities are locally known and appreciated, the more effective the WEA as a whole will be. Democracy starts in the class and continues through the organisation.

These are the words of Asa Briggs, National President of the WEA, quoted in the 1967-69 Northern District *Annual Report*. If these were, and are, the conditions for a successful branch, then Darlington was bound to flourish. In 1969-70, according to the Northern District's *Annual Report:*

> the branch presented a very large programme ranging from tutorials to day conferences. This included a number of morning and afternoon classes with crèche facilities. This branch makes a very substantial contribution to the activities of the town and the surrounding district.

In the following year, HMIs carried out an inspection of adult education work in Darlington, including that of the WEA, and recorded that:

> the outstanding success of this branch in recent years is largely due to the enthusiasm of the branch officers and members, not least the professional attitude towards the work of the Branch Secretary, Mrs. Joan Hutson, her assistant Mrs P. Garrod, and their loyal immediate supporters.

This had always been the case in Darlington Branch, from the time of Jack Hemingway and his colleagues in the early and mid-years of the twentieth century to the tireless and dedicated work of the late Val Portass with Kate Singlehurst, and George and Brenda Flynn more recently. Continuity, links with the community and consistent enthusiasm are certainly the hallmarks of this branch.

There seems to be some uncertainty as to the start date of the branch. The national WEA *Annual Report* for 1907 (p. 33) lists a Darlington Branch starting in September 1906 with fifty individual members and as 'a federation of the Trades Council, the Co-operative Society, the Mechanics' Institute, seven trade unions, and four various societies'. The secretary was R. Murray, 10 Fern Street, Darlington, who also acted as a voluntary District Secretary for a few years. Apparently, the branch made use of university extension lectures and had twenty students enrolled on a lecture course in Astronomy, in which 'some useful practical work had been done with a telescope' (National WEA *Annual Report*, 1908, p. 37). Astronomy was hugely popular in working-class communities in the late nineteenth and early twentieth centuries. Darlington was still listed as a branch in the 1909 *Annual Report* but not in 1910. There is also mention of a Darlington Branch in 1909-10 in later Northern District publications (for example, in the *Annual Report*, 1981-82). However, a document exists in the branch archive putting the start date for the Darlington Branch as 1913. This document is a report in the *Northern Echo* for Tuesday 16 January 1913 of a meeting in the Technical College 'to consider the advisability of forming a branch of the Association in Darlington'. Mr Lee, District Secretary at the time, recalled at that meeting that 'some six years ago an attempt was made to form a branch of the Association and since then matters had moved very rapidly'. Possibly there had been a false start in 1907-10, and the branch had fallen into abeyance for a while. Discussion followed, and it was felt that 'this was a ripe constituency' for the work of such an association as the WEA. 'It was decided to form a branch … and a provisional committee was appointed'. The Darlington Branch never looked back.

By 1921, a young Jack Hemingway was lecturing to members of the Harrowgate Workingmen's Club, and soon became Branch Secretary and then Chairman. By 1929, the branch held three three-year tutorial classes, in Economic Organisation and Theory, Appreciation of Music and Psychology.

There was one university extension course, in dramatic literature, two one-year classes, in aspects of English literature and two terminal classes, as they were called, both in elocution and dramatic art, apparently a popular subject at the time. They also held three public lectures, one by William Temple, then Archbishop of York, and were already conducting educational visits. The *Annual Report* records that 'the Branch Committee is very active and desirous of further developments'. The following year it states that the branch helped to influence the LEA to provide University Adult Education Scholarships. It had twenty

[1] Material for this chapter has been drawn from WEA Northern District *Annual Reports,* 1929-90; Minute books of Darlington WEA Branch for the years 1939-60 and personal conversations with Brenda Flynn and Kate Singlehurst.

individual members and the CIU and LEA were affiliated.

Darlington was never a branch to let the grass grow under its feet. In the mid-thirties, among the beautifully hand-written notes of the branch Minute Book, a typed sheet records the 'Recommendations of a Sub-Committee on Branch Re-organisation'. It was suggested as regards meetings that 'in addition to one Day School and two social evenings we organise a big meeting in October or November and another in February, each to be addresses by a well-known speaker'. Suggested speakers were (again) Dr. Temple, plus Hugh Dalton, an economist and Labour MP for Bishop Auckland who later became Chancellor of the Exchequer in the post-war Labour Government, and Arthur Greenwood, who had been Minister of Health from 1929-31. The branch believed in aiming high!

It was also recommended that they set up a Research Sub-Committee and a Propaganda Sub-Committee, and that there should be:

> more advertising than in the past by means of pamphlets and by the printing of programmes drawing attention to our Day School, classes, etc., plus direct appeals at the big meetings from the Chair and by printed forms asking for names and addresses of members desirous of joining.

Each class was to have a Chairman and Secretary to 'look after class matters' and these two class officials should be the representatives to the Branch Executive. These plans obviously bore fruit. By 1938-39, the Archbishop had indeed visited again and the number of branch outings had increased to five with a total of two hundred members taking part. Membership was also up to seventy, with four affiliates, including the Union of Postal Workers (indoor), and Darlington Rolling Mills Athletic and Welfare Club.

By this time, Jack Hemingway, Branch Secretary since 1932, was also the branch's representative on the District Committee and no doubt contributed hugely to the outward-looking aspect of the branch's activities. He gave classes and lectures, initially in English Literature, but later on added Modern European History, World Affairs and other political topics. Frank Robson, a recent Mayor of Darlington and now 86 years old, recalls Jack Hemingway, his schoolteacher, as 'a wonderful man!' The following tribute appeared in the Northern District *Annual Report* for 1962-63, when he retired from branch activities:

Jack Hemingway: a stalwart member of Darlington Branch

Some forty years ago a young schoolmaster at Albert Road Boys' School, Darlington, Jack Hemingway was invited to lecture to members of the Harrowgate Workingmen's Club and so began a long and active association with the WEA. Hundreds of students have attended classes and weekend schools taken by him and scores of them have expressed their appreciation and debt of gratitude to the world of ideas and the new horizons opened up by the teaching of Jack Hemingway. His influence extended far beyond the class room: as secretary and later chairman of the Darlington WEA Branch he enthused local activities with his dynamic qualities. For thirty years he was a member of the District Executive Committee serving for a time as Vice-Chairman. And his interests extend far beyond the educational work of the WEA. He is now Chairman of the Darlington Borough Magistrates and a visiting JP to Durham Prison.

He moved [...] from Albert Road [...] to the Queen Elizabeth Grammar School and in 1950 joined the staff of the Extra-Mural Department of the University of Newcastle upon Tyne as staff tutor in Services Education. For many years he has been on the panel of tutors of the Extra-Mural Department, University of Durham.

The Association is deeply grateful to him for all the services he has given to the WEA ... and although he has decided to give up his active connection with Darlington branch we are very pleased that he has agreed to continue taking some class work.

When he died in 1978 he was remembered as 'a forceful supporter of the WEA ideal as tutor, District officer, but above all as a prop and inspiration to Darlington branch'. A fund was set up, the Hemingway Prize, to be awarded each year for an outstanding piece of work by a student.

In a newspaper article reporting the branch Annual General Meeting for 1934-35, Mr Hemingway used a phrase which is redolent of its time: 'We expect the members to be the cream of the working classes, those people who are thinking for themselves'. He also said that it was very much a part of the work of the Association to 'get women-folk interested', and that they (the branch) were already attempting some co-operation with the local Townswomen's Guild. Little might he have known what floodgates he was opening!

Women were obviously expressing the wish to be included in class visits. We read that in 1938 'a visit to Darlington Rolling Mills could be arranged for our lady members, and that we could all visit the Darlington

Wire Mills if we desired'. A letter was also read from the Darlington Forge Ltd stating that 'they had been pleased to allow the visit and would advise us if it was ever possible to allow lady members to tour the works'. At the 1945 Annual General Meeting, 'much discussion took place about women not being allowed to attend the Working Men's Club classes, and they were demanding a class on International Relations'. In 1946 there was still a reference to the 'possibility of women being allowed to attend the Harrowgate Hill class'.

Through the 1950s we have records at Northern District of the numbers of men and women attending classes and proof that women attending were gradually catching up and then overtaking men in numbers, though it is noticeable that women tended to predominate in classes tutored by women. In 1955-56, the District records 'informal lecture courses' for women in the Co-operative Women's Guild and the Townswomen's Guilds, which were to be regarded 'as a means to more sustained study'. This comment presumably refers to the traditionalists' loyalty to the old tutorial class formula. In 1962-63 it notes that after several years of providing such classes 'the most striking development has been in Darlington, where the branch provided ten classes, with an enrolment of 142 women'. These were experimental day courses for women in Literature, tutored by Mrs. Benson, and the 'Scenery of the Tees Valley', by Vera Chapman. Well into the 1960s, afternoon classes were being provided specifically 'for housewives and retired people'. The shorter daytime class was here to stay.

In 1960 Jack Hemingway gave up the secretaryship to Miss Sybil Mais, who had been his assistant for some years, and she also remained active in the branch for many years to come, becoming, like Hemingway, President of the Darlington Branch until her retirement in 2000. Joan Hutson took over from her as Branch Secretary in 1966, and not only worked tirelessly for the branch but also had her own achievements as a student recognised. In 1961-62, the District *Annual Report* paid tribute to the:

> much good work done by Mrs. Joan Hutson, who has conducted an intensive publicity drive amongst women's organisations and a door-to-door distribution of leaflets [...] Our branches in other large centres might well usefully use the experience of Darlington branch in the development of similar work.

In 1965, Mrs. Hutson won a Travelling Scholarship from the Durham Extra-Mural Department for her essay on the novels of Iris Murdoch.

Another factor contributing to the success of the branch was its social activities, which in time became, or perhaps always were, also fund-raising. Here again it gained the admiration of the District Committee. In the 1951-52 session, Darlington and Barnard Castle branches together organised a weekend school at Sharrow Bay, Ullswater, and the link continued through until 1969-70, when 'with Barnard Castle Branch, dinner was held at the Black Horse Hotel on 13 May.' By 1971-72, the branch was offering over thirty courses, and in 1977 fifty-one classes were offered with over eight hundred students.

Times were not always easy, however. The minutes of the branch during the Second World War show that it had to work hard to follow the exhortations of both the District and national Association to keep classes going during the emergency. At first, even the social life of the branch was maintained. In 1940 it was decided to hold the annual summer outing in Keswick instead of Durham 'to give it more of a holiday aspect'. In 1941, the Annual General Meeting reported a difficult year, with many students unable to attend classes because of the need to work longer hours or because they were on Civil Defence duties. Tutors had to hold extra classes to compensate for those disrupted by air-raid warnings, and over fifty lectures were given to HM Forces. The Secretary of the branch, Jack Hemingway, was acting as temporary Tutor Organiser for Leeds regional division, and assisting the District Secretary. A musical evening was planned at the home of Lady Starmer, second wife of the proprietor of the *Northern Echo*. She was Vice-President of the branch and elected President in 1948. An unusual and sad event was the death of the then President and ex-Chairman, Councillor Abraham Hildreth, presumably during a branch meeting, as it was recorded that it was 'perhaps unique in the history of the WEA that the Secretary should have performed the last rites for him'. The 1942 Annual General Meeting recorded 'another difficult year' with eight classes, two tutorial, one sessional and five one-year. The number of classes did not fall below ten all through the war years, and membership rose slightly, from seventy to over one hundred. Against this the Chair's call in 1944 to 'banish apathy and complacency and recruit more members — 700 members would only represent 1% of the population' seems a little ambitious! An interesting development in 1942 had been a series of lectures for bus drivers, probably those transporting the 'Aycliffe Angels', as they were called, to the munitions factories, which later formed the basis of the post-war industrial estate and new town:

Lady Starmer had written some time ago asking if we could do anything for bus drivers who had to spend several hours waiting at Aycliffe between shift periods. The result was that for ten weeks lectures and talks had been held in a bus up there, but recently other arrangements had been made for the drivers.

In 1943 the branch had taken on three Civil Defence classes, and in 1944 'Messrs Thomas Summerson had requested a series of discussions on Russia to be held in its canteen for the workforce'. Support from the National Union of Teachers, the Co-operative movement, the Trades Council and Civil Defence workers was acknowledged and the Chairman expressed the hope that, with the passing of the Butler Education Act, the 'WEA's voice would now be heard on educational matters'.

There was no immediate improvement in branch affairs after the war, however. 1947 was recorded as a 'year of hard work with great difficulties due to lack of accommodation and bad transport'. By 1948 links with the LEA were being built upon, and the branch was working hard to counter the feeling that 'some people now thought that there was no longer any need for voluntary bodies within adult education'. The year 1950, however, was recorded in the Annual General Meeting minutes as:

one of the busiest in the branch's history. The autumn University course had attracted as many as 130 students and 100 had attended the full course. It had been the most successful course in the Northern area.

Joint meetings and outings with Barnard Castle Branch became regular events from this time, as were lecture-discussion meetings at Lady Starmer's home, Danby Lodge. Summer outings were also re-established, although in 1956, the 'outing to Masham and Bedale had been cancelled through lack of interest', and in 1957, perhaps due to the rise in fees, the membership was down again from over one hundred to just thirty. By 1963, however, when a new fee system was introduced whereby students automatically became members of the WEA, membership rose to a total of one hundred and thirty-eight.

The branch was continually working to find the subjects which interested its students. A lessening of interest in Economics and Biology had been noted, with an increase in take up of archaeology and astronomy classes. Single lectures were always popular with the branch and topics ranged from the controversial 'A Leisured Class is essential to Real Progress' in 1951, to Sir James Duff's 'Education — a life sentence' in 1956, Mr J. Summerson on 'British Railways' in 1957, and the ubiquitous Jack Hemingway on 'A Changed and Changing World' in 1959. In 1964 a series of monthly meetings held at Crombie's Hotel had proved popular, with almost seventy people turning up for a talk by Vera Chapman. The meetings at Crombie's only lasted until 1966 when they were discontinued due to poor numbers. However, Vera Chapman proved a highly successful tutor for the branch for many years, with her courses on the Flora and Fauna, Geology and History of Teesdale and South Durham. A four-week course in 1965 had record attendances.

Talks were initiated in 1964 with the District Secretary, Charles Hocking, regarding the acquisition of a permanent building for the branch. This bore fruit eleven years later when the branch moved into Bennet House and is considered in more detail below.

The branch also continued to support the WEA's District and national work. In 1973, they hosted a Branch Officers' Conference at which the main speaker was Bernard Jennings from the University of Leeds on the subject of the Russell Report. The contents of the report, which laid the basis for the 'Three Strands' approach to adult education which we still use today, was received with some misgivings by some branch members, but Darlington seized the opportunity with its usual enthusiasm and by the following year was putting on five day-release courses in Industrial Studies. New subject topics were noted such as 'The Jazz Session', and in more traditional vein: 'Before a large audience at the Darlington WEA Branch Open Meeting an address was delivered by the Lord Bishop of Durham, his title being "Learning and Un-learning".'

In 1973, Val Portass, who had been Branch Secretary since 1971-72, attended the National Conference at Harrogate as one of the District's representatives. Val had come north from the Hatfield Branch of the WEA and threw herself into the life of Darlington Branch from the start. It was she who, with Kate Singlehurst (then Kate Anderson), became involved both in setting up and running crèche facilities, a development which arose almost naturally from the provision of afternoon classes for women, and in acquiring Bennet House as a base for the branch in the mid-1970s. This eighteenth-century townhouse in the centre of the town was owned by Darlington Borough Council which, since the 1950s, had been generous in finding accommodation for branch classes in local schools. The Council had refurbished the building in connection with the hundred and fiftieth anniversary of the Stockton and Darlington Railway in 1975 and had then made it available for adult education. The branch, the Open University (OU) and the Department of Adult and Continuing Education of Durham University (DUDACE) not only co-existed in the building, but also worked closely together, along with the local Council for Voluntary Service (CVS) and the Citizens' Advice Bureau. Val was employed by DUDACE as Administrator, and the 1976-77 session was 'the first wholly based in Bennet House'. Enrolments were greatly increased and there was a whole range of informal activity. The Northern District *Annual Report* 1981-82 contains an account by Val Portass of a year in the life of the Darlington Branch, which is reproduced below:

At Bennet House: a year in the life of the Darlington Branch

A large part of July and August was spent in preparing and distributing advertising material for September, which began with our Open Day on the 7th of the month. Many people came in on that day […] to choose courses from what is provided in other establishments as well as our own, but there are also many passers-by who look in out of mild curiosity and find (almost to their surprise!) interesting courses to attend.

The Northern District Committee was invited to hold one of its regular meetings at Bennet House, to give members the opportunity to see the building and meet members of Darlington Branch Committee. The meeting took place on 12th September and a buffet lunch provided by the branch committee members added a somewhat social atmosphere to what was the last committee meeting with Mrs. Lee Fairlie as Chairman.

14th September saw the Branch Open Evening, which is the traditional beginning to the winter programme. The lounge was filled with people wanting to hear about the history and the re-fit at Hartlepool of HMS Warrior, the only remaining Victorian battleship, a talk ably given by Mr. Brownley, a Master Mariner closely involved with the vessel. Classes began the following week, the clocks were put back and Winter had arrived!

Two fundraising events came in November. It was pleasing to see donations from many of our students for our cake stall at the CVS Fair in St. Cuthbert's Church Hall. Books arrived in even greater quantities than cakes, and the following week our Saturday Book Sale was an even greater success than it had been the previous year. Very many thanks to all who contributed to both these events

The Christmas party brought the autumn session to a close, before the snow began. That snow created some problems, and several courses had a delayed start in January. Rail strikes weren't any help! Two tutors […] were ill and had to cancel their courses — we send them our best wishes […]

The DUDACE Librarian visited Bennet House in January and congratulated the branch members on acquiring such a good selection of back-up reading for the courses. Soon we shall have to consider what space may be found to house more books as they arrive.

The District Committee again asked to hold a meeting at Bennet House on the 23rd January, bringing three groups of four officers from our own District, Yorkshire North and Yorkshire South. Again we provided a buffet lunch. Brenda (Flynn) and Kate are becoming quite famous for quiche and salad, not to mention Kate's expert boiling of vast quantities of rice.

Staff from the Open University joined us for one of our regular Saturday coffee mornings on 30th January, when they gave advice and help to people interested in working at home for a degree. Many enquiries are received at the basement office all the year round for advice on courses available.

This year we have had our usual quota of day release courses, eight sessions of ten days each, organised by Tom Ellison, the District Organiser for industrial courses, and I am pleased to report that our connection with the Regional probation service continues with their programme of in-service training days.

Friday Forum continues to flourish. On one evening the Darlington recorded Music Society were our guests, when the Gaelic Society visited us, and sang songs in Gaelic and English. Another evening was shared with the Darlington Astronomical Society, when their speaker, Dr.Harding, gave a lecture, 'The Scale of the Universe'. Arising out of Dr. Gibby's Ancestry course, another forum became a social evening for genealogists who offered each other tips to help in their researches. Yet another local connection arising from the Friday Forum is that with the local branch of the Embroiderers' Guild, who mounted a display of some of their work for an open day.

The Wednesday morning crèche continues, occasionally visited by 'old' boys and girls — the granddaddy of them all being now 13! Kate soldiers on, assisted again this year by Jill Morgan […]

Income from coffee in the evenings and especially from Saturday mornings this year, continues to warm the cockles of the Treasurer's heart. The work and commitment put into providing an unflagging service still comes from too small a band of coffee makers, notably Miss Shaw, who is soon to take an extended holiday: how shall we manage?

No doubt they did manage, and very well indeed! This description shows how the hard work put in, in addition to the regular programme of classes, provided social contact and a service to the community, additional learning and a great deal of enjoyment. Sometimes classes themselves provided fund-raising opportunities, as when Mrs Ibbotson, long-standing tutor of an antiques class 'surpassed herself in a fund-raising venture with the branch'.

The face of women's education in the eighties was provided by Darlington's own variation on New Opportunities for Women,[2] which it called 'Take Tuesday Afternoon for Yourself'. This course drew a mixed group of students learning study skills with Janet Atkinson, supported by specialists from DUDACE in ecology, economics, literature and history — 'a truly joint course'. Janet Atkinson recalls how she had been attracted to 'the other side of the desk' by her own tutor on a NOW course, Mary Cooper. Many of the students needed to brush up their study skills before re-applying for work, or for moving into new areas. Janet recalls one student who had been a laboratory assistant and had gained enough confidence to re-train as a science teacher after encouragement from her tutor. Val Portass recalled only hearing peals of laughter coming from the basement on a Tuesday afternoon.

The year 1985 saw the tenth anniversary of the move to Bennet House. The branch marked this with a multi-lecture programme and a new venture, 'Script to Stage' — a course of creative writing leading to a production at the local theatre. The use of Bennet House undoubtedly contributed enormously to the continued success of the branch, its central position in the market place making it a hub of community life, as well as providing a high profile for adult education in the town. In addition to a thriving and varied branch programme, a Trade Union Studies Group had also developed from a Shop Stewards' course and a twenty-week course in 'Photography and Publicity Production' was held in 1985-86.

The late eighties also saw a crop of publications by branch members growing out of local history courses. *Bygone Cockerton* (Curran and Singlehurst 1989), *Cockerton Collection* (Curran and Singlehurst 1994), and *Darlington in 1850-1851* (Singlehurst 1999) were published by the Darlington Branch. George Flynn, at that time an active tutor and Chairman of the branch, produced *Darlington and its Telephones* (Flynn 1985) and *The Book of Darlington* (Flynn 1987).

In 1992, Val Portass retired on the grounds of ill-health. On her retirement she was described in the *Annual Report:* 'for fifteen years the heart and soul of adult education in Darlington'. She was succeeded by Kate Singlehurst who had been her assistant, and who worked on until 2000, when all was to change. In that year the Durham University Adult Education Department closed. Once the university had pulled out, the WEA was 'on borrowed time', to quote Brenda Flynn, current Chair of the branch (2009-10), as the contract for Bennet House had been between Darlington Borough Council and the University, the WEA only being present as partners of DUDACE. Kate was made redundant and then employed, first on a casual basis and then part-time, by the WEA. Paul McGee, Tutor Organiser in Tees Valley attempted to keep the centre open by moving some of his own staff in, but soon the WEA began gradually to give up its basement rooms to the Citizens' Advice Bureau and retreated to the second floor. In 2007 the WEA was asked to move out, but since they had already planned their autumn programme, they negotiated for another year's grace while they looked for alternative accommodation and financial support. The Council agreed to help with this, and after several attempts to find appropriate accommodation, it agreed to lease a room in e-VOLution (the new name of the CVS) across the Market Place. The move took place from April to June 2008. The move out of Bennet House was a sad one but was, says Brenda:

> very much a team effort on the part of the branch committee, plus two "pressed husbands". Several committee members stayed on an extra year to see the move through, enduring frequent committee meetings in very cramped surroundings. The bulk of the furniture (signed over to the branch by the university) and our other possessions were transported manually with the aid of a sack barrow. For the heavy items we hired a "man with a van" the whole move costing only £50.

The Darlington Branch now functions from one room in e-VOLution, with its courses spread around the branch area, determined to continue but missing the luxury of 'its own' building, and finding it less easy to organise social functions. The key to why Darlington branch has retained the loyalty of its members over the years is summed up by Kate Singlehurst, still working for the branch on a voluntary basis, as Enrolment Secretary:

> I first came to the WEA as a student in a Local History class. At the end of term, the then Chairman of the Branch, who was in the same class, invited me to an Open Meeting to discuss the following September's programme. Towards the end of the meeting, a desperate plea was put out for someone to run the crèche and I somehow found

---

[2] See Chapter 9 for further information about this.

myself volunteering. I thought it would be good for my 3-year-old to mix with others. My 3-year-old is now 38. Apart from the interest and knowledge gained in classes over the years, for me the WEA has meant, above everything else, friendship, of fellow students, of tutors and of committee members at both branch and regional level. In so many ways, the WEA has enriched my life.

Sometimes though, the value goes yet deeper. Brenda Flynn recalls how a WEA distance learning class organised by Peter Bennet, Northumberland Tutor Organiser, helped her son to recover from a serious road accident sustained while he was undergoing his police training. From being unable to speak, read or write, Colin recovered and was able to go on to take a university degree.

Brenda and George Flynn, along with Kate and Val, have been stalwarts of the Darlington Branch for over 30 years and have continued to build on the foundations laid by those early pioneers, Messrs Hemingway, Hildreth and Pickering, Miss Mais, Mrs Hutson and all the others, who gave so many hours to ensure the continuation of just one of the cogs so indispensable to the great wheel of locally planned and student organised adult education, the WEA branch.[3]

SOURCES CITED

Curran, Sylvia, and Kate Singlehurst, 1989. *Bygone Cockerton.* Darlington: WEA Darlington Branch.

Curran, Sylvia, and Kate Singlehurst, 1994. *Cockerton Collection.* Darlington: WEA Darlington Branch.

Singlehurst, Kate, 1999. *Aspects of Darlington 1850-1851.* Darlington: WEA Darlington Branch.

Flynn, G., 1985. *Darlington and its Telephones.* Darlington: WEA Darlington Branch.

Flynn, G., 1987. *The Book of Darlington: Saxon Settlement and Railway Town,* Buckingham: Barracuda Books.

---

[3] Just as we went to press, we were very saddened to hear of the death of George Flynn, a long time supporter of the WEA and a local history tutor.

WEA Northern District in Crisis, 1973 to 1976

Jonathan Brown

The office staff [...] were aware from 1973 that the District was being run incompetently. (No committee meetings were held in the District offices after 1972). A combination of loyalty and efficiency helped to disguise the facts for some time [...] By the summer of 1975 the problems of the District were common knowledge and at the AGM elections were contested and a new Committee appointed. With the help of the Administrative Assistant it was possible for the Committee to appreciate the state of the District which was 'that it was on the point of collapse'. The District Secretary avoided a confrontation with the Committee which [...] came to the conclusion that it was impossible to justify the continued employment of Mr Evans [...] Mr Evans pre-empted this by resigning. (Corbett 2003:74-75)

As Ivan Corbett shows, the crisis of 1973-76 came to a head at the sixty-fifth Annual General Meeting of the Northern District. Held on 11 October at Burt Hall in Newcastle, the packed meeting elected a new District Committee. The AGM also refused to accept the financial accounts for the year 1974-75. Of the elected officers, only the Chair and Treasurer remained in post. Professor Peter Kaim-Caudle came in as Vice-Chairman with Liz Armstrong, Lee Fairlie, G. Smith and Professor Teddy Allen joining the Committee. Looking back, both Lee Fairlie and Liz Armstrong recall that they were asked to stand for election as part of a list of 'new' (or 'renewal') candidates. If contested elections were uncommon at WEA District AGMs, the refusal to accept the accounts which followed that election was quite unprecedented. The resignation of the District Secretary, Tudor Evans, at the July 1976 District Council meeting was an inevitable consequence of the 1975 AGM.

This is but an outline of what happened to the Northern District between October 1975 and July 1976. The account raises questions about why the District was in such a dire position, how the crisis was brought to a head and how it recovered from these events. Each of these three questions will be answered in turn.

Why was the Northern District in crisis?

In the 1960s and 1970s, the WEA Districts faced a series of challenges. Some of these challenges relate to being a small voluntary organisation, others related specifically to the educational role of the WEA itself. Against this background any of the several WEA Districts could have encountered a crisis of the kind which arose in the Northern District in 1973-1976. But what were the challenges encountered? At least four kinds of issue can be identified: structure and government of the WEA; management; finance; uncertainty and change.

Structure and government of the WEA

Like many voluntary organisations in the late sixties, the Northern District had a complex and quite confusing constitution which was based on that of the national Association rather than the effective governance of the District. Although two bodies (District Council and District Committee) were identified, their purposes were not entirely clear and they operated from the late 1960s somewhat spasmodically. The constitution had not been revised to meet newer circumstances and there was no system for succession of lay office holders: indeed, once first elected, officers seemed to serve on until illness or even death intervened. For example, Thomas Nelson Kerr was Treasurer from 1965 until just before his death in 1972. Victor Bell was Chairman or Vice-Chairman from the early 1960s until 1976. Such practices may give continuity but do not give refreshment to the organisation. From the late 1960s, Committee meetings became spasmodic and the officers led by the District Secretary ran the District with little oversight from either the District Committee or Council. There was no transparency. To work effectively, a small voluntary organisation needs to engage with its membership and its operations need to be visible.

Management

From the mid-1960s through to 1976, the District had a small headquarters in Newcastle with its professional staff dispersed over a wide geographical area. Usually in this period the chief officer (District Secretary) was supported by no more than four (often only three) administrative staff with seven (later eight) Tutor

Organisers. Such a small organisation requires effective routines and high morale. In leadership terms the District Secretary was the key person. Responsibility for the administration, educational direction and financial planning were in the hands of this one individual. Much depended on the innate skills and flexibility of the office holder.

Finance

From its inception, the WEA was always short of money. Year after year *Annual Reports* comment on this shortage. The position was a persistent one. In the eleven years after 1966 there were only two years where there was a surplus (and these two positive outcomes were quite small ones) on the end of year accounts: the other nine years showed a deficit. Just before his retirement in 1969, District Secretary Charles Hocking spoke of his term of office as 'twenty year's hard labour' (Corbett 2003:63). Hocking had instituted several cost saving measures including printing *Annual Reports* every other year. Whilst this might have been a wise temporary measure, in the longer term it was not good practice. Moreover, then as later, there was little or no reserve for the District to fall back on. So his successor, Tudor Evans, who was appointed in 1969, inherited an organisation with in-built financial stresses. Mr Evans knew the District well having served as Tutor Organiser in North Cumbria for eight years before moving to Bootle Borough as Adult Education Officer in 1965. That the District remained afloat was largely due to supplementary grants from the DES and emergency donations from branches.

The income the District was heavily reliant on throughout the period from the mid-1960s to the mid-1970s was external funding, which included the DES grant, contributions from LEAs, corporate members and branches. The fee income from core class activity remained quite small. As shown in the table below, student fee income contributed between 10% and 12.6% of Northern District income.

Student Fees as a Proportion of Northern District Income

	District Income	Student Fees	Proportion
1965-66	£ 27,240	£ 3,433	12.6%
1974-75	£ 84,764	£ 8,476	10.0%

Increases in Inflation and Northern District Expenditure

	District Expenditure (actual)	Staff costs	Proportion
1965-66	£ 27,240	£ 21,966	80.6%
1974-75	£ 84,764	£ 76,532	90.2%

Using the Measuring Worth Calculator of relative values of the UK £sterling over time, the 1965-66 figure (£27,240) is calculated to be worth £60,400 in 1975 based on the Retail Price Index. But as so much of the WEA's expenditure was on salaries (and on-costs) a more realistic figure would be that based on based on average earnings which gives a 1975 equivalent of £78,100 (**www.measuring worth.com** accessed on 21 June 2010).

The other challenge was inflation which during this period was rampant. In the 1974-75 Northern District *Annual Report*, it is noted that for the previous two years 'Salaries and National Insurance have risen by 23% in terms of District Office and by 29% in respect of full-time staff" (*Annual Report*, p. 6). In times of inflation it is difficult to see what is really happening. How do expenditure figures of £27,240 (1965-66) and £84,764 (1974-75) actually equate?

As the WEA's expenditure is substantially on salaries it can be argued that the apparent increase over the period is illusory and, at best, the expenditure had risen quite slowly in terms of purchasing power. However, inflation on this scale presents very real budgetary challenges from one year to the next.

Uncertainty and change

The 1960s and 1970s were a period of quite rapid change in terms of adult education. Excitement had been created by the establishment by the Wilson Government of the Open University. The first students of the OU started out in January 1971 in the middle of a protracted postal strike. The visibility of the new institution was there for all to see with prime time course-specific broadcasts on BBC2. Traditional universities were expanding their continuing education programmes and new offerings for part-time studies were being offered by the polytechnics. Local Education Authorities were also expanding community and adult provision in both schools and colleges. In the Northern District, both Cumberland and Northumberland had exciting schemes for community provision.[1] There were also demands from the field for specific educational programmes including those from the Pre-School Playgroup Association described in Chapter 7, the Women's Education Programme described in Chapter 9 and trade unions described in Chapter 12. Demand for courses was well in advance of the necessary income to mount them. 'There seems to be no limit on the opportunities available for [...] special project work on Tyneside: the only very real limits are time and money' (WEA Northern District, *Annual Report* 1974-75, p. 8).

At the same time the uncertainty about the role and purpose of the WEA was magnified by the work of the Russell Inquiry which had been set up in February 1969 to 'assess the need for and to review the provision of non-vocational adult education in England and Wales' (Russell 1973:iv). Russell had been set up under the Labour Government but reporting to the Conservative Government in 1973. Most providers, including the WEA were 'waiting for Russell' between 1969 and 1973. For the WEA this created real uncertainty and doubts. In fact, the Russell Report when issued endorsed the WEA position:

> The needs perceived in the WEA's original purpose still persist: it is as necessary as ever (if not more so) that the educationally and culturally underprivileged should have a chance to share in and contribute to the intellectual and cultural heritage enjoyed by others. Moreover, the voluntary nature of the WEA, with its active student participation in planning and organisation serves as a model and training ground for those who may wish to apply the lessons in social, political and trade union activity. And continuing access to the knowledge on which an informed critique of society can be based is an essential element in the preservation of a free society (Russell 1973:§22,7).

However, having accepted the Russell assessment, the government then challenged the WEA to live up to its claims by incorporating social targets into the grant settlements (the so-called 'Russell categories'). This gave rise to another form of uncertainty as much of the traditional branch activity did not fall into the Russell categories.

How the crisis in the Northern District was brought to a head.

So the background to the WEA Northern District crisis of 1973-76 can be seen in the challenges of its structure and government, its management style, deep-seated financial stresses in an era of uncertainty and change. Finance was at the heart of the District's problems. This was not helped by a secretive management and a decay of good practice in the voluntary structure (especially long periods in office by key District Officers).

The crisis in the Northern District was brought to a head after the democratic changes in the District Committee membership following the 1975 AGM. The new Committee soon found that its relationship with the District Secretary was breaking down. This led to the resignation of Tudor Evans in July 1976. The *Annual Report* of the District 1975-76, presented to the 1976 AGM, explains the position of the new Committee. This explanation is in a statement by Professor Teddy Allen who had joined the District Committee as a result of the 1975 elections and who chaired the District's Finance and General Purposes Committee. Allen writes that events during the year 'have shaken the Northern District to its very foundations and brought into the brink of collapse'. There were for Allen three key issues:

> First, relations between [the District Secretary] and his staff, both tutor-organisers and office had been driven to a point of deplorable strain [...]. Second, financial control had become slack: losses were incurred which should have been avoided: there was a failure to ensure receipt of payments which keener and sharper watchfulness would have safeguarded. Third, there was an increasing tendency on the part of the District Secretary to be uncooperative in providing the committee with the necessary explanations of financial statements; and this phase of relationship ended with his absence from three successive meetings of the Finance and General Purposes Committee, at the last of which he had promised to furnish an explanation which had been urgently requested. (WEA Northern District *Annual Report* 1975-1976, pp. 7-8)

Throughout the crisis the National WEA had backed the existing status quo and seen the new Committee as maverick. After the resignation of Tudor Evans, the General Secretary and the National Executive of the WEA treated the new 'regime' with suspicion and hostility. This ruptured relationship was an added difficulty of the recovery phase.

How the Northern District recovered from these events.

The Northern District Committee, put in place a number of measures to restore normality. These included identifying temporary cover for the departed District Secretary; introducing a budgetary plan; commencing careful scrutiny of cash flow; and striving for greater transparency both with the voluntary movement and

---

[1] For more details about the Northumberland scheme, see Brown and Galleymore, 1976.

with the staff in the conduct of its affairs.

Much of this was anathema to the National WEA. They had concerns about the departure of Tudor Evans. They objected to the designation of the temporary Chief Officer as 'Acting District Secretary', especially when the temporary officer was a Tutor Organiser (Michael Standen). The National WEA was 'very strongly against the designation of a tutor organiser as Acting District Secretary' (letter of 27 September 1976 from Reg Jeffries, General Secretary of the WEA, to Teddy Allen). The National WEA also wanted a full investigation of the Northern District by a Committee of Reconstruction.

However the District Committee felt that it was essential to move forward speedily to rebuild confidence in the organisation. Their response to the National WEA was robust. The District Committee agreed at its 22 October 1976 meeting that:

(1) At all times the Committee had acted within the District Constitution. A delegate from the National Committee is welcome to attend its meetings though the District would not meet the expenses of such a delegate. The District Committee would be very pleased to benefit from closer co-operation with a National representative.

(2) It sees no purpose in setting up a 'Committee of Reconstruction'.

(3) It will not appoint an Honorary District Secretary and will continue to support the Acting District Secretary.

(4) It will review the District Secretary appointment after six months.

Eventually the position returned to something like normal. This was helped by an understanding local HMI, Laurie Speak, who arranged for the DES to pay a supplementary grant to meet the 1974-75 deficit of £9,293 in full. However, the renewal of the Northern District was achieved by returning to conventional voluntary governance, professional procedures within the office and by skilled leadership from Michael Standen, who was later after national advertisement and interview appointed as District Secretary. Michael's own account (Standen 2003) of what was to become nineteen years 'in the driving seat' is republished in this book in Chapter 13. He may have been in the driving seat but came to that role:

[…] with a wholehearted belief in the voluntary movement if actively and sensitively encouraged and a genuine respect for staff colleagues in whom one had to trust and to whom delegate as freely as possible. The District's recent history also suggested a working principle, to make all information widely available to all. (Standen 2003:83)

It was from such belief at the collegial helm that the District recovered to take up the challenges of the Russell 'targets', so that the Northern District in Standen's words 'led the WEA in delivering priority categories for many years' (Standen 2003.85). Testimony to the strength of this recovery is given in several other chapters of this book. For example, Eileen Aird in Chapter 9 recalls her time with the Women's Education Programme in the 1970s and 1980s as being the 'richest experience of my working life'. Tom Nesbit, then working for the TGWU talks of his 'memories of the WEA Northern District recognise and celebrate its general collegiality and good humour […] the District was one of most vital of the WEA's regions' in Chapter 12. Speaking of her experience at much the same time, Lee Fairlie recollects in Chapter 7:

'the delight in discovering that the WEA could offer the opportunity for adults to expand their horizons and use their talents in ways which would not have been possible in the prevailing rigid pass/fail exam system'.

The Northern District emerged from the 1973-76 crisis as a stronger and wiser organisation. It was able to do so through internal democracy. Change started at the 1975 AGM with contested election and the rejection of the accounts.

SOURCES CITED

Brown, J. and D. C. Galleymore, 1976. 'Adult Education and Local Government Reorganisation; the Effects of Change in Three Local Education Authorities 1973-5'. In: *Studies in Adult Education* 8,1:29-42.

Corbett, Ivan, 2003. '"So noble an institution": A History of the Workers' Educational Association Northern District 1910-80'. In: Standen (2003a:5-81). [Originally published 1980.]

Russell, Edward Lionel, 1973. *Adult education: a plan for development. Report by a Committee of Inquiry appointed by the Secretary of State for Education and Science under the Chairmanship of Sir Lionel Russell C.B.E.* London: HMSO.

Standen, Michael (ed.), 2003a. *A hunger to be more serious …: The Story of the WEA Northern District.* Newcastle-upon-Tyne: WEA Northern District.

Standen, Michael, 2003b. 'An Uphill Drive: The Northern District, 1976-1995' In: Standen (2003a:82-93).

The Arrival of a New Member Organisation: PPA joins the WEA

Jonathan Brown

They were exciting times. I met the most stimulating, thoughtful people who believed in sharing ideas and skills, supporting one another and thus supporting families and communities. (Jill Gladstone)

Introduction

In the mid 1970s the Pre-School Playgroups Association (PPA) and the WEA were at different stages of development. The WEA, begun in 1903, was some seventy years old, had a rich past in adult education, strong links with the trade union movement and a burgeoning mythology, but, at least in the Northern District, was also running into structural problems largely associated with ageing. These structural problems were magnified by financial strain and leadership problems. A full account of this crisis of 1973-76 is described in Chapter 6. After this crisis, restructuring of the WEA Northern District was required. It was in this process that the PPA played a significant part as a new member organisation .

If the WEA was an ageing organisation facing a mid-life crisis, the PPA, on the other hand,was a vigorous child of the 1960s. The Playgroup Movement and the PPA grew rapidly after being set up following a 1961 letter to the Guardian Women's page by Belle Tutaev (Liebman 1996). The PPA quickly developed group, branch and regional structures. During this expansion, the PPA quickly discovered that it had specific training and educational needs to enable its members to undertake key roles within playgroups themselves and within the expanding organisation. So it approached many providers of adult education for help to meet its need for courses at a range of levels. Those approached included LEAs, Local Adult Centres, Further Education Centres, FE Colleges, Teacher Training Colleges, Universities and the WEA. A variety of responses to such approaches for access to courses was inevitable. How this worked out in the North of England is traced by written thoughts collected in 2009-10 from people active in the PPA in the 1970s. Testimony on responses from educational providers is given in the section below headed 'Access to courses'. Other sections drawn from the submitted recollections are: 'The students', 'The tutors', 'Timetabling issues', 'Curriculum', 'PPA and constitutional and structural issues for the WEA', and 'People'.

It should be noted that the testimony is given from the perspective of members of the PPA who were involved in their organisation joining with the Northern District of the WEA for specific purposes.[1]

Access to courses

As Lee Fairlie recalls, 'Our major difficulty in the North was finding courses to fit the needs and build upon the strengths of parent run playgroups'. But approaches to educational providers were quite difficult. PPA was a new and relatively unknown organisation, did not really comprehend educational structures or the language of education and training, had needs that as an organisation were not fully thought through, and wanted to do things 'their way', which did not fit well with others in what might appear to be the same arena, such as Nursery Nursing, Teaching and Childcare.

Jill Faux remembers well the issues she faced as the newly-appointed Training and Development Officer in Cumbria:

> We were feeling increasingly hamstrung: not by lack of funds but by the expectations, rules and intransigence of the further education establishment. Our needs could not be met within their framework and we needed to either change or subvert the system. Our students were young mothers. Schools opened themselves for evening classes between the unrealistic time (for mothers of young children) of 7.00 pm and 9.00 pm. The FE tutor's expectation was that we would ask for a course, he (and it nearly always was a man) would find a tutor and a classroom — often with no access to water and sometimes with strict instructions not to move the furniture and that the course would last about 10 weeks. Also, unless there were around a dozen students, the class would not run. Most FE tutors, with some honourable exceptions, were frankly astonished when we had gently to tell them that our students didn't need a primary teacher to 'tell' them how to do it. The local 'tech' was even worse, they assumed we needed a woodwork teacher to run the session on woodwork in the playgroup and an art teacher to tell us how to organize art for the children, despite the fact that these tutors knew nothing of the needs of young children and were frankly

[1] The following people assisted in the drafting of this Chapter: Maureen Marsden, Jill Faux, Lee Fairlie, Jill Gladstone, Joanna Matthews, Ruth Tanner and Pat Wilcock. All are thanked for their help.

uninterested in what they were being asked to do, and were astounded when we asked that the course tutor should be present at every session.

As Jill Faux found out there were entrenched positions and empires to defend especially in some FE Colleges, where the nearest professional context in terms of lecturing staff were tutors on NNEB courses. As Joanna Matthews recalls at her local FE College in Cumbria:

> The NNEB Tutor was also doing courses for Playgroup personnel, which we considered totally ineffective. They seemed […] fixed on […] certain very dictatorial forms of supervision in the playgroups: e.g. a painting session in which children were only allowed one colour at a time, and at a given order from the supervisor had to exchange that colour for another with their neighbour.

It was against such attitudes that PPA officers looked for help from elsewhere.

Even though PPA was 'a new kid on the block' the requirements of PPA were relatively clear, as Jill Faux reported:

> Our need was to run a class in the daytime, locally, often in the hall that was used as a playgroup for two or three sessions a week, using one of our members (who knew the situation) as a tutor and to have the facility to pay another tutor occasionally.

In looking elsewhere a Welsh colleague suggested to Lee Fairlie that responses from the WEA were much more helpful as it:

> […] had the structure to organise local courses and employ tutors. PPA could identify suitable tutors and recruit class members. We started there, with small courses run locally based upon pre-school playgroup organisations.

Lee Fairlie can still recall:

> […] the delight in discovering that the WEA could offer the opportunity for adults to expand their horizons and use their talents in ways which would not have been possible in the prevailing rigid pass / fail exam system. We had fun meeting together in cold church halls, sharing the ups and downs of life with young children and making an impact upon our communities. Having grown up in a different culture, I felt included by the support and friendship of like minds working together for a common goal.

In Cumbria, Jill Faux followed the lead from Newcastle:

> We cast around looking for solutions and luckily for us, my colleague Lee Fairlie saw opportunities in collaboration with the WEA. She, Mike Standen and Jonathan Brown set up a scheme to suit our particular situation and arranged for the funding to be made available to us to run the courses.

Jill goes on to remember progress from:

> […] the moment we joined forces with the WEA, things improved. We were able to proliferate courses when needed, often at short notice to serve the demands of a growing movement.

The contact, once established between the WEA and the PPA, proved to be worthwhile for both organisations. Pat Wilcock writes:

> When I think about WEA in those early days my thoughts are of tremendous respect and gratitude that PPA was recognised and supported as it was. The characters involved and the way that life was witnessed and shared set a standard that hasn't really been equalled anywhere else.

The partnership between the two organisations flourished from the early 1970s until 1991 when reorganisation of the PPA and its transformation into the Pre-School Learning Alliance led to closure of the Northern Region of the PPA after some twenty years of joint work (Standen 2003b:91).

The students

The focus of the courses was pre-school children and their development in the family, the community and playgroups. However, from the start there was almost inevitably a 'hidden curriculum' in terms of the personal development of the students themselves.

> Courses themselves are neutral, just a journey from one point to another. What is of interest is that the students want to start and do not always know where and how fast they are going (Henderson 1978:62, my italics).

As a result students not only undertook roles within playgroups and PPA, but moved on to other learning:

> As both the WEA and PPA were indeed voluntary adult education organisations, our parents and leaders developed through playgroup courses into related and unrelated adult, further and higher education […] It was the playgroup

courses which opened horizons to adults who had begun by meeting together in a hall to organise play for their pre-school children and 'went on' to do more both within and without the playgroup movement. (Lee Fairlie)

The courses were held at an increasingly wide range of levels and durations, but their specific focus was on the pre-school child. This attracted the students from diverse prior educational and vocational experience.

Their education spans the whole range — from those who thankfully left school at the earliest possible moment to PhDs. Their jobs before marriage were anything from interesting and responsible careers and professions through to the dullest of dead-end jobs. (Fazackerley 1975:239)

The process was that:

our parents and leaders developed through playgroup courses into related and unrelated adult, further and higher education. This was the time when a very small percentage of the UK population had had the opportunity of degree education (perhaps 6%?) and new institutions were developing — the Open University and polytechnics becoming universities: a general university expansion in both numbers and diversity. (Lee Fairlie)

In terms of personal development the process was most marked in that:

[...] many intelligent undereducated women discovered a new capacity and interest in learning and went on to undertake further academic or vocational courses, sometimes changing their lives forever. (Jill Faux)

Jill Gladstone observes:

Women found strengths, skills and abilities which they had and which had hitherto lain dormant. With this new awakening at grassroots level they were empowered to go on to higher training, e.g. teacher training, JPs, school assistants, playgroup leaders and also WEA tutors.

Some of this personal development would have and did occur in courses sponsored by other providers, but the WEA philosophy was particularly favourable as:

The WEA always recognized and celebrated the fact that we were about adult education almost more than child education which was an enormous relief. (Jill Faux)

Some gave testimony based on their own experience as WEA students, so that for Pat Wilcock:

On a personal level as a WEA student I was encouraged to discover and appreciate ideas and experiences that were often different from my own, so it followed that when I was asked to tutor I remembered to make enough time for everyone and value each person's contribution.

Jill Gladstone remembers so well:

looking forward to Tuesdays when I was on the Fieldwork Course tutored by Lee Fairlie. Each session was always interesting and eating lunch together was sociable.

Many PPA students approached their first course with some trepidation. Maureen Marsden recalls:

I was feeling a little anxious as this was the first serious course I had attended since leaving school. I do remember a relaxed atmosphere, a structured course that was relevant to the work I was doing in the playgroup and it certainly reinforced my belief that I could do this work. Building confidence was a major outcome.

The tutors

From first contact with possible educational providers, the PPA envisaged the appointment of tutors who had little or no formal training for such a role with adult students. Moreover, although more than one tutor might be needed for any course, there had to be a lead tutor:

It was always important to have a host tutor who took several of the sessions and who knew about playgroups. It was the host tutor's job to help them to recognize what they already knew about children, the way they play, their physical and mental milestones of development and how to provide appropriately for them. The tutor also had to know the pitfalls and joys of organizing a group and be someone who would start with them on a journey of exploration and be content to be diverted from time to time into sometimes quite abstruse discussions about the running of a business, or the horrors of cot death. As a tutor it was demanding work, recognizing the relevance of diversions but always pulling it back to the main task — of building a team out of a group of mothers to run a playgroup. It was important to be able to find out the answers even if you didn't know them yourself and to build up a network of useful and helpful people who would contribute if asked. We were always conscious of what Lee called 'the good model principle' — the need to demonstrate in the way we did things, the way in which they could do things. I well remember one tutor running successive courses — one in a middle class village in the local church hall and the next in an old mining village in the pigeon fanciers' hut and telling me of the hugely different approaches and responses she had had to adapt to. (Jill Faux)

As already noted, most education providers were concerned about the qualifications of potential tutors:

> Many who would be appropriate tutors in terms of playgroup experience may be unacceptable to educational organisations which have defined qualifications for part-time teachers in a formal way. (Brown 1975:242-3)

In many cases the WEA had less rigid regulations and were much more flexible over tutor appointments.

In 1981 Jonathan Brown recorded his visits to five playgroup courses at a variety of levels in preparation for a talk at the PPA National Conference. All five courses had experienced PPA tutors (Brown 1981:12). By that time the 'battle' over tutor appointments had been won by the PPA. Ruth Tanner recalls her experience of being tutor:

> After my degree I did teacher training, but soon realised I had neither wish nor aptitude to teach in schools. I found child development in the under-5s fascinating, and enjoyed working with 'the mums' — as they largely were then — in playgroups. Tutoring the Playgroup Foundation Course was a gift, but it worked on several levels. The Foundation Course syllabus had already "sussed" this ('The Child and the Playgroup', 'The Child and the Family', etc.). It gave mums like me who were full time carers and had come to playgroup for their children's sake, some time and space to think about themselves and their own needs (a NOW Course in disguise?). I recall one student on a Foundation Course in Durham who went on to study right through to degree level and became a lecturer in the Durham University Business School.

> For me as a tutor it operated at a third level also, giving me the opportunity to dip a toe into adult education work, develop the self confidence I so lacked, gain experience as a team worker, and respond to a number of unexpected challenges, not the least being to run a course on 'Play with your Children' for women on remand in Durham's Franklands prison, this itself having the hidden agenda of allowing them to 'play' and be children and be appreciated, sometimes for the first time in their lives.

Timetabling issues

The requirements of the PPA were to run classes in the daytime, locally, with a PPA member as the tutor, with the ability occasionally to pay a visiting speaker. Such requirements often meant that the best location was the hall in which a playgroup was often held two or three times a week. This approach raised timetabling issues of a kind which the WEA seldom encountered in its traditional provision. Prior to the link up with the PPA, most WEA courses were single sessions of between ninety minutes and two hours. There was little experience of running a crèche or playgroup alongside the class meeting. But most PPA course students were young women with pre-school children. So the playgroup alongside the course was a prerequisite for student enrolment. Also the courses had to be in school term time and have breaks for half-term holidays. The longer courses, particularly foundation and fieldwork, required more than one session during the day. So, as well as demands for access to appropriate courses, the PPA came along with requirements in terms of suitable locations for holding both the PPA course and an accompanying playgroup for the students' pre-school children. Often this required timetabling over a 10.00 a.m. to 3.00 p.m. day, with up to three conventional sessions. However, the WEA had always coped with issues over finding suitable locations for its work and had built-in flexibility over timings.

Curriculum

During the 1970s the curriculum was being developed not only by feedback from experiences of courses, but also by the development of guidelines by the national PPA. The PPA was adept at being what would now be called 'a learning organisation'. At the beginning of her tutorials, Jill Faux writes:

> I started tutoring short courses in Cumbria, working with parents of small children, starting from where they were and helping them to set up and organize activities for their children. In the first instance, they were very practically based and concentrated on the 'how' rather than the 'why'. But it soon became very clear that an understanding of human development and relationships were the key to a successful group. We discussed different forms of control ranging from the anarchic to highly controlled. We looked at 'free play' versus 'structured play'. We began to realize that the control and management lay as much in the way a group was set out and the expectations of the adults as it did in the premises and equipment available.

Lee Fairlie comments on the development over time on a curriculum:

> based upon child development, child-centred activities, business management and the involvement of adults in a voluntary organisation. Over time the courses diversified, sometimes becoming more formal, other times they were very practical activities, playing with dough, finger painting and making puppets, but always the core of the session was based upon discussion of practicalities and drawing out the underlying issues.

In 1975, the national PPA published the *Guidelines for a Playgroup Foundation Course* (PPA 1975). Although these were national guidelines, there was a strong Northern District input as the final version was drafted by Lee Fairlie and Margaret Bell working in Newcastle. The Guidelines were a way of bringing together good practice from around the country. As Joan Fazackerley (1975:239) wrote:

> Courses have developed in an 'ad hoc' way over the country to meet local need. PPA now feels sufficiently confident of having identified the essential elements required in such a course to launch the guidelines.

The publication itself called this 'the evolving pattern'. Although specifically aimed at creating coherence for the Foundation Course, the guidelines saw this as part of pattern of courses from the informal short introductory sessions through to a foundation course and complementary specialist courses. In curriculum terms the Foundation Course would have three sections: 1. The family and the child; 2. The child and the playgroup including the why and how of playgroups and play activities; 3. The playgroup and the community, (PPA 1975). So from the mid-1970s onwards there was a clearer understanding of the content and style of playgroup courses.

By 1981, Jonathan Brown was recording the impact of the guidelines in producing clearly written syllabuses, writing that:

> there is a clear emphasis on the child in the family, playgroup and community settings. There is practical work in dough / clay / water. Also there is consideration of organisational issues such as finance / mother and toddler groups and the acquisition of observation and reporting skills (Brown 1981:12).

PPA and constitutional and structural issues for the WEA

> WEA was going through a rough time in the early 1970s but the link forged between WEA and PPA held fast as Lee Fairlie and Jonathan Brown wrestled with the [WEA] constitution. (Jill Gladstone)

In constitutional terms, the PPA in the North Region became a corporate member of the WEA Northern District. In this sense the PPA joined many trade unions, co-operative societies and other organisations as members of the District. But, as indicated at the start of this chapter, the District in the 1970s had internal problems, both in terms of personnel, management and constitution. On the constitutional side the PPA assisted in the small constitutional review group established in 1976. As a result a simpler, reformed constitution was adopted by the WEA Northern District.

Like other work with affiliated organisations, attempts were made by the PPA members and branch to integrate with WEA branches. This was not altogether successful as Maureen Marsden comments: '[…] regional collaboration was more evident than local coming together'. Also, as Pat Wilcock found out, WEA branches had their own agendas:

> I was involved with the Durham Branch committee for a while but didn't feel that I could contribute anything here or at regional meetings. I was, at best, an observer with much to learn about WEA as an organisation and as a spring-board for some people and a life-line for others. I hope that I remembered to report back.

However, the joining of the WEA by the PPA allowed several joint projects to take place. In 1978, the Northern District joined forces to obtain funding from the Manpower Services Commission (MSC) through the Special Temporary Employment Programme (STEP). The two organisations steered the project which was known at the time as The Women's Education Project.[2] Two project workers were appointed, Margaret Barnes to work in Cleveland and Maureen Marsden on Tyneside / Wearside. An edited version of the report by Barnes and Marsden (1979) follows:

- The Sponsors had expected that the workers would use existing links between PPA and WEA in the first instance, and this proved the case. Margaret Barnes worked closely with Cleveland PPA during the year and was instrumental in revitalising the Stockton WEA Branch. Maureen Marsden in her first approaches for courses utilised the interest of parents in local playgroups.

- In addition to providing more courses for women about the needs of their children, the sponsors expected wider interests to emerge as the women came to realise that Education and Learning are not things which came to an end on leaving school. Maureen Marsden's first course venture 'Now We Are Six' centred on studying the development and needs of school children. The courses that followed, 'Aspects of Play' and 'A Woman's Place' reflect the widening scope of the first group's outlook.

- The third expectation was that groups of women would begin to look at their own educational needs and ways of meeting them. (This led to conferences on Women's Education in Newcastle, Durham and Cleveland.)

---

[2] This project was separate from the wider Women's Education Programme which is described by Eileen Aird in Chapter 9.

1. Bennet House: home to Darlington WEA Branch 1975-2008. *(Darlington WEA Branch)*

2. **The WEA at work:** Janette Hilton, Oral History tutor, with two students, mounting a local history exhibition in Sunderland City Library. *(WEA North-East Region)*

3. Celebrating the Right to Learn: Adult Learners' Week was created in 1993 to recognise adult learner achievements. On the first selection panel were Nigel Todd, Professor Bill Williamson (DUDACE), Sheila Brown (Tyne Tees TV) and Jonathan Brown. *(WEA North-East Region)*

4. A branch stalwart: Jack Hemingway of Darlington, sometime Vice–Chair of Northern District.
(Darlington WEA Branch)

5. A District Secretary in Time of War:
Jack Trevena was District Secretary,
1914-1920 and subsequently served in a
similar role in South–West District.
(Tyne and Wear Archives - WEA collection)

6. A WEA residential school in The Great War, January 1916. *(Tyne & Wear Archives - WEA collection)*

7. Programme planning: Liz Armstrong of
Newcastle Branch with two Tutor Organisers,
Skeff Vaughan and Victor Cadaxa.
(WEA North–East Region)

8. A WEA administrator at work: Judy Champion In the District Office c.1985 *(WEA North–East Region)*

9. Michael Standen: a poet and novelist who was District Secretary 1976-1995
(WEA North–East Region)

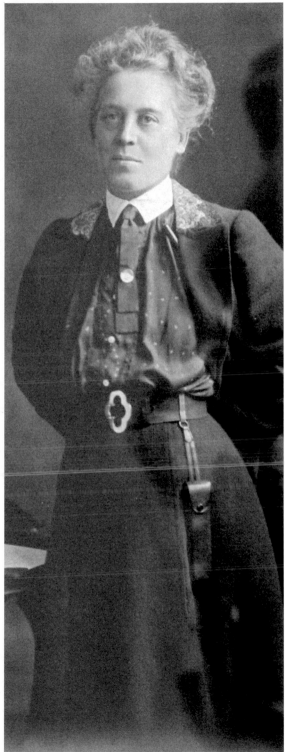

10. A WEA tutor and womens' suffrage activist:
Dr. Ethel Williams.
(Dr Gillian Rye)

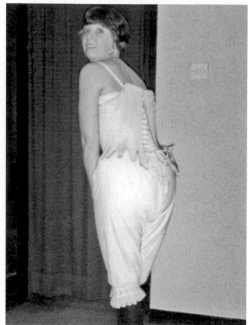

11. From Branch to district to National Office: Marian Young of Bellingham Branch who became Chair of the District (1992-1998) and later National Vice–President. *(WEA North-East Region)*

12. The Antiques Day School: Kate Singlehurst of Darlington rediscovering Victorian undergarments. *(Darlington Branch Archive)*

13. A tutor looking forward: J.R. (Roger) Till with daughter and granddaughter 1991. *(Roger Till)*

- Help was also given to investigate openings for women with other educational providers. So that individual students could find their interests already met within the existing framework of education. It had been implicit in the work to counsel such people towards existing provision.

- All courses [...] have been planned with the student's needs in mind, i.e. during school hours, with childminding facilities, and as close to the students' home as possible.

- If nothing else, the project convinced us that the present provision does not meet the educational needs of women, particularly ordinary women. Both sponsors would have liked to continue beyond the first year [...] However the MSC were unable to continue their support and applications for aid to other organisations [...] were unsuccessful.

- Although we are clear that [...] (the project has contributed to the thinking of both WEA and PPA) if we are to make progress a much longer term exercise is necessary.

People

> Mike Standen's name and image appear in my mind before anything else as the main link between WEA and PPA. (Pat Wilcock)

There is general agreement that in personal terms and from the start the WEA co-operation with PPA was facilitated by Michael Standen. This started when he was Tutor Organiser in Durham (1967-76) and was continued when he became District Secretary in 1976, as he himself describes in Chapter 13. But from the PPA side of the partnership came a succession of District Officers. Details are given in the table below.

PPA Officers who became WEA Officers

	PPA Office(s)	WEA Office(s)
Lee Fairlie	Regional Training & Development Officer (TDO)	Vice-Chair of District Chair 1977-81
Ruth Tanner	Regional TDO	District Chair 1998-2002
Minna Ireland	National Treasurer	Treasurer

Michael Standen recognised the contribution of Lee Fairlie 'who had gained much experience with the PPA and had an American 'can-do approach' (Standen 2003b:87).

Conclusions

The recollections gathered here show the coming together for mutual benefit of two organisation which had similar principles and values. Both were committed to the right of adults to learn and to progress, individually and collectively. Both believed in democratic voluntary effort. Both the older WEA and the much younger PPA sustained each other through joint the provision of courses, the sharing of officers and the pioneering of new forms of learning. Writing in 2003, Michael Standen (2003a:3) says of the WEA:

> It has existed long enough to seem a desperately old fashioned idea: education for its own sake, 'the fellowship of learning'. Weirdly, it can still be found in good shape [...].

On the other hand, those coming in via the PPA in the 1970s and 1980s found, as Jill Gladstone says at the head of this chapter, 'stimulating, thoughtful people who believed in sharing ideas and skills, supporting one another'. This chapter is a tribute to the enduring relevance of the WEA ethos and its ability to adapt to changing circumstances.

SOURCES CITED

Barnes, M. and M. Marsden, 1979. *The Women's Education Project 1978-1979.* Newcastle: WEA Northern District.

Brown, J., 1975. 'Pre-school playgroup courses 1973-4'. *Adult Education* 48(4):241-43.

Brown, J., 1981. 'Never a Dull Moment: The Challenge of Education for Playgroup People'. Script of talk given at 20th Annual Meeting of PPA in Newcastle 3-5 April 1981 (mimeo by PPA Northern Region).

Corbett, Ivan, 2003. '"So noble an institution": A History of the Workers' Educational Association Northern District 1910-80'. In: Standen (2003a:5-81).

Fazackerley, Joan, 1975. 'Preparation for playgroup work'. *Adult Education* 48(4):238-41.

Henderson, Maude, 1978. *Cogs and Spindles: some impressions of the playgroup movement.* London: Pre-School Playgroups Association.

Liebman, George W., 1996. 'Mum's the word in British day care'. *Policy Review* May 01:11-21.

PPA, 1975. *Guidelines for a Playgroup Foundation Course.* London: PPA.

Standen, Michael (ed.), 2003a. *A hunger to be more serious ...: The Story of the WEA Northern District.* Newcastle-upon-Tyne: WEA Northern District.

Standen, M., 2003b. 'An Uphill Drive: The Northern District, 1976-95' In: Standen (2003a:82-93).

An Approach to Art: the Birth of the Pitmen Painters[1]

Robert Lyon

Mr Lyon, who is Master of Painting at Armstrong College, Newcastle, describes a new development in WEA Classes. The Ashington Group have decided to go further with the experiment this year, and a second group has been started at Bensham Grove Settlement, Gateshead.

A year ago a group of men associated with the colliery town of Ashington, Northumberland, met to discuss the possibility of the formation of an Art Appreciation class in their district. It was perfectly obvious that these men had decided views on what they did not want the class to be, and also that they had no illusions as to their own technical ability.

A course of study of the history and theory of art for its own sake was quite impracticable, whilst the most obvious alternative, that of a technical training, undesirable. Yet a desire persisted to make some contact with art other than that which could be provided either by an art school or a study of the philosophy of art. It was not sufficient to rely purely on one's instinct, and without experience — or perhaps with experience of the wrong sort — development was almost impossible. The class, however, could be formed or brought together provided some common experience could be discussed, and it was on this basis that the class commenced its activities. The 'common experience' was to consist of lectures on art history, discussion of some particular aspect of art, technical demonstrations from time to time by the lecturer, and a series of practical exercises in various media by members of the class. The progress of the class with its unusual course was one of particular interest for it was possible to attempt experiments which did not rely for success on a high standard of technical ability, but rather on a creative experience similar to that of a practising artist. The choice of a technique employed by the artist being one in which he can best express himself, so, 'expression' can be better appreciated when some personal experience has been enjoyed in the possibilities of a medium.

With this idea in mind the course was developed, after a number of practical difficulties had been overcome, on the following basis. Some particular aspect of art was chosen, for example, decorative painting, and a series of evenings were devoted to this subject. The first consisted of a lecture during which examples of decorative painting of different periods and different techniques were examined and discussed. Primitive paintings on plaster, pure fresco and *tempera* could be considered in relation to period and purpose. The development of these media might be traced to later and richer periods, but the interest was rather more centred on the elementary form of the medium and of its simple function. Examples of early Christian and pagan symbolic painting could be considered conventional in comparison with the freedom exercised by painters of later periods. This freedom permitted developments in technique and experiments tended toward the discovery of a more plastic medium, one which would permit of a greater variety of expression. It was readily appreciated by the class that it was inevitable in some hands that these technical discoveries led to uncontrolled licence, exhibitionism and decadence. Recognition of the advantages in varying circumstances of one medium over another is of the greatest importance. An artist could not be expected to produce his best if he was obliged to work in some medium which he felt was not best suited for the purpose.

From the discussion arising out of the lecture many interesting questions promoted lively debate. For instance, it was asked why some artists preferred *tempera*, as a medium, to oil paint, why some preferred water-colour to the engraved and etched line. It is a matter of selection, the response of the mind and hand of the artist to the sympathetic qualities of a particular medium. So in an attempt to appreciate the imaginative qualities in a decorative composition some contact with the creative ability of the artist was established by the class through an insight into the selection of a medium.

The second stage in the series was devoted to some demonstration in a particular medium as in the case of "Decorative Painting". Some small design was prepared, that is, the idea had been translated into terms of a sketch design or composition. A suitable medium for the execution of the design was then considered and prepared beforehand. One demonstration, in *tempera*, may be cited as an example of the procedure: the design having been decided upon, the panel on which it was to be painted was then prepared. The panel consisted of a piece of strong ply-wood, butter muslin being glued on both sides to provide a "keyed" surface.

[1] This article originally appeared in the December 1935 edition of the WEA house magazine *The Highway*, pages 42-43. The WEA is grateful to Robert's grandson Jasper Lyon for permission to republish it here.

When this had hardened, a mixture of whitening and parchment size was applied until, by polishing with fine glass paper, a smooth surface was obtained. The painting of the design itself was done as a demonstration, and the procedure explained to the class. The paint used was made from powdered earth colours mixed with the yolk of an egg. This medium, as demonstrated, is too elaborate in the sense that, for a class of this nature, practical exercises in the medium would make too heavy a demand on the time allotted to that particular phase of the course. It is necessary, however, to bear in mind that it was from this early method of painting that experiments produced other and simpler methods of painting. So, for the purposes of comparison, if not actual practical experience, some knowledge of this method of *tempera* painting is desirable if only to appreciate it as the source of our more familiar and contemporary methods of painting.

The exercises by members of the class, which followed the demonstration, were carried through on similar lines, that is, the technique employed being of the same order as that used in the demonstration itself. It was not possible or even desirable to make any elaborate preparations for these exercises and, provided that the class appreciated the discipline and limits of the technique concerned, some simpler methods were used. These varied according to the whim of the student. Instead of the pure *tempera* painting, some elected to use pieces of cardboard, packing or brown paper. They were prepared and painted with decorators' water-paint tinters, poster-paint or water-colour and ink. This was important in the sense that it provided the actual creative experience of 'doing' as apart from the 'critical' experience. There were, of course, many difficulties to overcome before a definite working arrangement was possible, but, by a process of trial and error, it was ultimately established that no student was expected to develop any high standard of technical ability and that 'picture-making' for its own sake was not to be considered within the scope of the class. As the programme developed and the confidence of the class in the experiment matured, discussion and appreciation developed in an atmosphere of greater freedom than would have been possible if technical ability, in the academic sense of the word, had been allowed to become important in itself.

The selection of subject matter for these elementary practical exercises was left to the individual student, and if (at first) there was a tendency toward over-elaboration and the superficial, it was because ideas tended to be self-conscious and derivative rather than the natural statement of a familiar experience. After a few false starts literary and romantic illustration were abandoned. The 'trying-to-think-of-an-idea' state of mind is hopeless and usually ends in the production of something so dull and depressing that it is never worth the doing. Once the class realised that their own experience would provide sufficient in the way of incident for self-expression, and that nothing is commonplace unless we make it so, there was an end to the difficulty of making a start in the practical experiments. The technical difficulties acted as a strong deterrent to any reckless extravagance in some of the early attempts; they also developed in the class an awareness, or 'put them on their guard' when meeting with examples of this type of work. A medium which demands the simplest and most orderly treatment may not be used in any other manner, and this would naturally be the medium to select if we felt our 'subject' that way. On the other hand one would not for the same 'subject' use a medium which by its composition is capable of permitting almost unlimited freedom, though this is a fault which may be observed in many pretentious examples of painting and sculpture.

Other branches of art dealt with during the course included engraving, water-colour painting and portraiture, these affording sufficient range for an introduction to the subject of art appreciation. In each of these series the technique was considered in relation to the imaginative structure of examples selected from some particular phase of art and, in turn, was followed by a class exercise.

In addition to the routine of the course it became the practice for each member of the class to bring each evening some small design based on a subject set the previous week, and a portion of the evening was devoted to a general criticism of these compositions. In this way the class began to feel more intimate with the actual making of a design and to share with each other the creative impulse.

Further developments are taking place this autumn in Ashington, and I hope to let HIGHWAY readers know how the experiment progresses in its more advanced phases.

SOURCE CITED

Feaver, W., 2009. *The Pitmen Painters: The Ashington Group 1934-1984.* Ashington: Ashington Group Trustees [First published in 1988].

Opening the Door to a Whole New World:
Reflections on the Women's Education Programme[1]

Eileen Aird

The New Opportunities for Women (NOW) courses, which were at the heart of the Women's Education Programme, gave women a voice, encouraging them to read, write and discuss, to explore the factors shaping their lives, to desire change for themselves and others and to plan for their futures. Writing now, in 2010, I want to provide memories of the courses and reflections on their meaning through several voices. Many memories are common, some are particular. Pathways into and out of the work, over the lifetimes of tutors and students, but also reflecting the influences from previous generations, have an intricate pattern of repetition and difference. The work itself was concerned with both similarity and difference. It drew together women from very different educational and social backgrounds, women with and without children, women who were employed and women who worked in the home, women with radical views about change and women who saw change as a slower, more incremental process.

Several factors coalesced in the creation of this work. Debates about adult education's function and focus flourished (Russell 1973). The concept of the negotiated curriculum and an emphasis on the partnership between student and tutor reshaped the idea of the tutor as expert and the student as learner. We began to see that learning took place in many contexts, and that the lives of adults in the home, in the work place, in political, cultural and social activity, influenced their choice of study. These ideas belong to the tradition of the WEA but they were being re-evaluated for the 1970s. This was not always a comfortable process. Some established WEA branches and stalwart voluntary members welcomed innovative work bringing in new students and potential WEA activists. There was suspicion too: a feeling that successful women's classes, overflowing with new learners and tutors with a deeply felt commitment to their work, might pose a threat to the existing structures. The idea of 'women only' classes was difficult: it cut across a universalising principle that education was open to all. Trade union education and later programmes for the unemployed did not raise the same anxieties.

Tutors on the NOW courses were often first generation university graduates. They knew from their own lives about the not always comfortable power of education to effect individual and social change. They were born into the evolving welfare state. They benefited from the struggles of their parents' and grandparents' generations and took for granted free schooling and at least the possibility of further or higher education, even if in practice it remained closed to many. Our students were often women for whom educational opportunities had been curtailed:

> I came to the NOW courses an educationally deprived 40 year-old. Born a miner's daughter in a small County Durham pit village during the Second World War, chances for girls were not a high priority. I wanted to study French, Literature, Art and History but the Education authority decreed that all girls should study office skills. So for two years, four hours a day, five days a week, I was taught Shorthand, Typing and Book-keeping. I hated every minute. (Shirley Rodham)

> I was attracted to the NOW programme in the mid 1980s as a means of thinking where to go next in career terms. At the time I had just had my third child and had given up work to concentrate on family issues and was feeling a bit 'lost'. I had been a nurse for 15 years with a strong sense that this was not what I wanted to be doing for the rest of my life. I had always had a strong interest in politics but with no idea how I might pursue this in terms of further study. Going to university had not been an option for me in leaving school at 16. (Rosie Cunningham)

While the funding of adult education has never been anything other than marginal, it was much more readily available in the seventies than in our current utilitarian times. It was possible to establish the NOW courses with even the full fee at a level which would not deter too many students. For those for whom the fee was a barrier to attendance concessionary fees were available. Inspectors of adult education were often enthusiasts themselves, ready to encourage innovation, unhampered by the need to achieve nationally set targets or to tick simplistically captioned boxes to provide widespread data. Having said that, we had some challenging encounters with HMIs who were more conventional.

[1] I am very grateful to the following tutors and students who generously agreed to write about their memories and then trusted me to select from their accounts: Jean Barr, Joan Briggs, Jonathan Brown, Sheila Cross, Rosie Cunningham, Cynthia Fuller, Jan Hewitt, Judy Lown, Barbara McKay, Chi Onwurah, Shirley Rodham, Freda Tallantyre.

I well recall the visit of an HMI to my Washington class when we were studying the representation of women in women's magazines. Coming up to me after class, he asked if I did not think the subject matter had been rather one-sided. Inwardly seething, I asked him if he did not think the treatment of women had been rather one-sided for centuries and challenged him to find me an article at that time in a woman's magazine which did not treat women as pretty little sideshows for men. Probably not a wise challenge to an HMI, but he did not have the nerve to fail my class. (Freda Tallantyre)

Evaluation, both spoken and written, of the NOW courses was taken very seriously from the start, was ongoing in the course and was firmly focused on student response as well as tutor analysis. We considered the content and process of the courses, what facilitated learning and what impeded it. As far as possible we tried to involve students in the development of their learning. This climate nurtured experiment, development and locally created initiatives and networks (WEA 1989).

The most influential factor in the provision of women only education was the Women's Movement. Feminism was not a single activity: women were drawn to it for varying reasons. Analyses of the need for women's liberation were wide-ranging and sometimes at odds with each other. There was sisterhood in abundance but also, as in any revolutionary movement, competitiveness and hostility. The NOW courses, because of their educational objectives and settings and their limited contact of one day a week for twenty weeks, were mainly able to draw on commonality and support, despite differences of class, race, sexuality and age, which interwove in a complex way with the shared experience of what it was to be a woman. A widespread hopefulness infused the courses and women's lives generally.

These are the words of one of my colleagues looking back on her work:

Recently seeing 'The Pitman Painters' at the National Theatre was a moving experience for me, as it reminded me of how many people of my grandparents' and parents' generations had no access to formal education, yet of how many venerated and craved it. For some, the WEA gave them their first vibrant and relevant educational experience, and it should have carried a government health warning: this experience changes lives!

It should perhaps have been surprising that the same thing could be said of many of my contemporaries who were women, since they had been in the main part of the post-war generation who had benefited from compulsory schooling up to the age of 15 at least. However, the attitude to schooling for women then still questioned its value, since the expectation was that women might work for a year or two, but would leave to have children, and stay at home for decades to bring them up. As a consequence, most of my female friends left school as soon as legally possible, and never dreamt of a university education.

When the feminist movement of the 1970s began to challenge why women's life expectations should be any more limited than men's it found a ready uptake amongst women of all classes who were hungry for greater self realisation. Some Women's Education programmes referred to 'women returners' but for most of our students, this was no return, but an entirely new start. Our title, New Opportunities for Women, was as much a sociological as a personal reference.

My first personal engagement with the programme was in itself revealing as I came to teach English Literature to a group of 20 women for my own first venture back into the adult world after the birth of my first child. Leaving the six-week-old baby with a child minder for the first time was a harrowing experience, but greatly relieved by the reassuring words of my more experienced maternal students. Who was the tutor, and who the student, I wondered, as we supported each other through our individual crises, in a peer approach that characterised the whole programme. To have this intellectual challenge in our weeks, alongside more mundane chores, was a liberation for us all. (Freda Tallantyre)

NOW in Newcastle with an October starting date was launched in the summer of 1974 by a feature article in the *Newcastle Journal.* Before talking to the journalist two parallel sets of discussions had taken place. The first discussions were between Eileen Aird and Jonathan Brown who became the joint tutors of the first two courses. After drafting the outline of the course informal consultation took place with a range of statutory and voluntary organisations.

The main features of the course were as follows.

- A full-day session was offered once a week from 09.45 till 15.00 for twenty weeks.
- A three-session day was also offered, the first and third sessions being academic.
- The middle session was a mixture of information and counselling in which ideas for progression were introduced often by outside speakers with individual tutorials with the course tutors.

- The two academic sessions provided a contrast in terms of discipline, usually being Social Science and Humanities.

- Tutors placed high value on discussion, reading and writing, the values of liberal adult education.

- Whilst the course aim and rhetoric were about opportunities, individual progression and plans for the future NOW did not prescribe outcomes. For example, although for many students progression to degree courses was a foreseeable outcome, it was not a prescribed progression. In this sense NOW was not a standard Access Course, or what came to be known as an 'Access Course' in the later 1970s and 1980s.

- NOW required pre-enrolment which was not the norm in the Department of Adult Education in 1974.

- At the point of enrolment all students had a pre-course interview with one of the course tutors. This was not a selection interview: NOW was open to all women irrespective of previous education or employment. The interview was a start to the process of self-assessment, choice and progression.

- We aimed to have a maximum of twenty students on any one course.

- In 1974, although the course day reflected or implied childcare issues, we did not have an accompanying playgroup or crèche. Later courses did have associated childcare provision. My memory is that the issue was discussed in the consultation process but that advice at that stage was that the length of the day raised significant issues for pre-school age children.

As Jonathan Brown remarked, response to the *Newcastle Journal* article was immediate and reassuring. In October 1974 two courses were run rather than the planned single course. Within eighteen months seven courses had been run enrolling eighteen students.

Although the NOW courses were the first to be offered in a university department or WEA District, Ruth Michaels had run the first ever NOW course at Hatfield Polytechnic in 1973. Shorter than the Newcastle course and more vocationally orientated, it was similarly influenced by feminist principles. Other courses were starting up in different areas of the country and within different educational contexts. The term 'Women's Education' was used to indicate a curriculum which was wider than the academic and so was separate from Women's Studies, which was seen more as the province of higher education internal departments and sometimes forming a component of the wider Women's Education course. In practice on a national basis the terms were used interchangeably, but the distinction was an important one for the Northern District. Descriptions of programmes run by two colleagues in other settings follow:

> To begin with there was no conscious plan. Adult Education in the Essex garrison town where I lived in the early 1970s attracted a lot of women from a variety of class and ethnic backgrounds. There were women with pre-school age children who could make use of the playgroup, older women whose children were at school or had left home, "army wives" who found themselves billeted in yet another new place with few friends and connections, retired women, unemployed women, women seeking a new direction in life. The curriculum in the LEA Adult Education Centre, in which I worked, had been expanding around this time beyond a range of creative arts and crafts and associated subjects to provide a growing number of O and A level courses. Many of the women enrolling for these courses had missed out somewhere along the line in gaining academic qualifications. Some had accrued them in the past but found the subjects they had studied no longer inspiring or suited to their current interests and concerns. Some wanted companionship and stimulation. One or two arrived because "there was no room in the Life Drawing class. Classes in such subjects as Sociology, Social History, English Literature and Politics were bursting at the seams. Many were filled solely with women. Within the content of these courses women found themes that related deeply to their own lives. In Sociology they could speak from their experience of growing up in and raising their own families, of having been participants, and parents of children, in the education system, of having been involved in youth culture, political groups or work environments of various kinds. (Judy Lown)

> My work on women's issues in the North East started in September 1973. It was a short daytime course in Stockton-on-Tees for the Extra Mural Department of Durham University. I called it 'A Woman's Place?' although the organiser, Mary Cooper, had wanted me to call it 'The Case for Women's Lib'. I never liked the term 'women's lib', to my mind it trivialised important issues although from a marketing point of view it might have worked well. However, the course did attract media interest as it attracted the attention of the women's editor of the local paper, *The Evening Gazette*, resulting in a long feature, the first of many articles on my courses and the two campaigns in Cleveland that the courses eventually inspired. (Sheila Cross)

As we had gained exemption under the Equal Opportunities Act, enrolment to the Newcastle NOW courses was restricted to women only. Occasionally a man would enquire in either a rueful or an angry tone why the course was not open to him, but in the main it was accepted that this was single sex provision. The curriculum created was focused on the specificity of women's experience while taking into account structural differences between women. New resources were becoming available all the time. Virago, The Women's Press and other smaller women's publishing houses were publishing novels, poetry, short stories and essays by women which had been previously published, particularly at the end of the nineteenth and the first half of the twentieth century, and then gone out of print. Feminist scholars and activists were researching and analysing aspects of women's experience such as housework, childcare, pregnancy, birth, and workplace roles, which had so far received scant attention, even in the tradition of working-class or trade union literature. Enticing collections of Virago books, with their distinctive green spines and covers showing images of women taken from portraits, paintings or photographs, lined up in bookshops, alongside the more sober black and white of The Women's Press publications, with their small spine icon of a domestic iron. Literary analysis of women's writing delved into the conditions under which novels and poetry had been written, the history of publishing in rejecting women's work and the perspectives adopted by reviewers and critics of women's writing. Explorations of texts, their language and imagery from a gendered perspective began to emerge. We saw our work as tutors and organisers as part of a widespread and lively development, as the following statements show:

> One of the key aspects of the Women's Movement for me was the recognition that women's roles, experience and achievements were undervalued and the need to work towards changing that. My work in women's education centred on building confidence and a belief in creativity through encouraging students to find their own voices, and through exploring neglected and forgotten women writers and artists. Courses with such titles as 'Breaking the Silences', 'Women's Words', 'Finding a Voice' put at the centre women's lives and experience and created the opportunity to put into words their stories and their imaginings. Literature classes gave students the chance to study novels and poetry then left out of the traditional syllabus.

> My most vivid memory is of my first experience teaching a women's autobiographical writing workshop. For the first exercise I asked the group to choose a 'small incident' to write about. I stressed 'small' but the group heard only 'incident'. There were 22 students of varying ages and the next week nearly everyone read out a piece about the worst thing that had ever happened to her. It was an emotional session, though ultimately, I think it bonded the group in a very positive way. It left me aware that skills in teaching creative writing were not going to be enough. It left me more aware than ever of the importance of getting experience into words and the drive to do that. It gave a disturbing snapshot of women's experience and showed how readily the group were prepared to share their stories.

> Teaching literature meant introducing students to writers who were often new to them and seeing the excitement when they discovered a novelist or poet who seemed to reflect back to them their own thoughts and feelings. Strange as it seems now, the idea of writing about washing and ironing, giving birth, caring for an elderly relative, seemed to many to be inappropriate, so introducing students to women writers like Marge Piercy, Adrienne Rich, Audre Lorde changed the sense of what poetry could be. Then thanks to the work of Virago, novels by such writers as Willa Cather, Winifred Holtby, Mary Webb, became available and a whole new sense of history and development became apparent. It was a very exciting time to be studying women's writing both for tutors and students. (Cynthia Fuller)

> The NOW courses on the whole appealed to women who had been submerged in domesticity for a period and had lost confidence, if indeed they had ever been confident. Typically they felt 'now it's time for me'. It was incredibly rewarding teaching a NOW course, although emotionally draining, as you watched the women grow before your eyes, week after week. The women found the sociology I taught interesting as we focused on family and gender in a way that related to their lives. (Sheila Cross)

> There was a conscious expansion of the curriculum to include non-examined courses specifically designed by and for women. Tutors consulted with students about their interests and offered such courses as 'Women's History', 'Women Writers', 'Lives of Women' and 'Women and Education'. Uncovering the lives of women hidden from history was strongly linked to the reclaiming and assertion of women's lives in the present. Women grew in confidence and opened to new ways of seeing themselves and their possibilities. This found expression in initiatives such as magazines of women's writing, and fund-raising, together with similar ventures associated with local women's projects. (Judy Lown)

Students were engaged and excited by curricula which enabled them to reflect on their lived experience:

> That it took women's perspectives and their experiences as central was important in raising my confidence. It started a process of 'remaking' myself, of thinking through my ideas, instead of vaguely assuming that I had to be part of some kind of consensus. (Jan Hewitt)

> Listening to the stories of other women in the group was also inspiring in terms of the difficulties they had overcome and their aspirations for the future. I can honestly say that the NOW programme changed my life in ways

I could not have imagined. (Rosie Cunningham)

Written work was an important part of the NOW courses. Students were encouraged to write, even if their first piece was only a paragraph long. Work was read and commented on fully, both in writing and in a general way in class, and each student was supported in her own academic development. In classes which included a wide range of previous educational experience and attainment, written work varied hugely in length, content and perspective. The development in written skills for many students over the twenty weeks of the course was remarkable.

> Though they were really daunting, I also enjoyed writing the essays, the first I had ever written at such length. I relished the thoughtful and supportive feedback from tutors who took my work and, importantly, my feelings about it and my responses so seriously. Although I enjoyed the work I still carried with me multiple humiliations collected from schooldays and was sure that I would be 'found out' in front of others. But one-to-one feedback — as well as classes and discussion groups — gave time to talk through things, to think about them in relation to me, and to build a relationship with my tutors that centred around being accepted for who I was. (Jan Hewitt)

Sandwiched between the two academic sessions of the NOW course was a session called Opportunities, although the whole course was the real opportunity. This session included study skills, presentations by outside speakers, sometimes about particular employment fields or about voluntary work, or on occasions local writers would come in to read some of their work and discuss it with the group. The first term was pre-planned by the tutors, the second term negotiated with the students according to their specific interests.

Counselling, both individual and group, played a central part. I had worked as a volunteer counsellor in Off the Record, a youth counselling service, and had become very interested in the way in which counselling is not just a way of exploring problems but can provide a context for looking at change and choice. It was clear that major educational or employment change in adult life brings with it dilemmas, as well as prospects, and especially so for women who may be revising their sense of what it means to be a woman. The only prerequisite for enrolling on a NOW course was to attend an advisory interview with one of the course tutors and this is where an approach influenced by counselling as well as good educational practice began. We rang students ourselves to make an appointment and made a point of going to meet them in the waiting area when they arrived. The interview was not for selection: we did ask various things about previous experience and reasons for choosing the course but we also explained the structure and process of the course and answered any questions which came up.

> When I did eventually meet you. I told you how I had been a failure at grammar school and how I was not good at articulating myself to others; my first real NOW memory is being rather taken aback to have you assure me I was articulating myself perfectly well to you! (Jan Hewitt)

After this meeting women were asked to get in touch and let us know if they wanted to enrol. The majority of women coming to an advisory interview did enrol and the drop out rate was very low. Choosing not to enrol was a positive outcome for some women. The advisory interview ensured that each woman coming to the first morning course knew at least one of the tutors:

> One sunny autumn morning a small group of nervous women met in a beautiful old building in Newcastle. You joined us with another tutor. You introduced us to women's literature and encouraged us to talk about women's lives. We laughed, we cried and we bonded as a group. Friendships were formed. We took each other at face value without the baggage of our private lives. (Shirley Rodham)

Each student was also offered an interview with one of the tutors towards the end of the first term. This could be used as the student chose: to discuss course work, future progression or more personal issues. Three group counselling sessions were programmed in. These were non-directive, facilitated by both course tutors and allowed a space in which the group could explore anything which seemed relevant and important. This was not an easy process. Very painful issues came up and were almost always explored with great sensitivity. Domestic roles and responsibilities were often the focus. I remember with pleasure the tide of appreciative laughter which met one student's proud statement that she was no longer going to spend at least an hour a week sorting and rolling together the many pairs of washed socks of her otherwise all male household! This was a choice more easily made than choices struggled with by women enduring domestic or sexual abuse or social or economic privations.

> I do not think that we manufactured discontent, but rather unearthed it and allowed it to be articulated and legitimised. In the early days, the subject matter was more traditional liberal arts than women's studies, but the personal stories came flowing out in opportunities sessions in a way that was at first shocking to a young naïve well-educated tutor like me. I had not knowingly encountered before the middle class woman who was

nevertheless beaten up by her husband on a regular basis, the women who were given scarcely a penny by their husbands to bring up their children, while the men drank the money away at the club, the women who had cultivated active and social lives of their own despite bringing up children and caring for elderly relatives only to be required to care once again when demanding husbands retired. (Freda Tallantyre)

Initially we didn't offer childcare provision but with the agreement of the supportive Head of an LEA Adult Education Centre and advice and practical help from the PPA, we were later able to offer a crèche alongside a course. This gave opportunities to a further group of women:

When my youngest child was three years old I discovered the WEA. I did a few short taster courses and loved using my brain again. I then heard about the NOW course, I was ready to study again but didn't know what I wanted to do. The course appeared just at the right time and very importantly it provided a crèche and fitted around the school day for my two eldest children, vital in those days with no parents or relatives around to help out. (Barbara McKay)

The building had to be appropriate for childcare though. We later tried to run a crèche alongside classes in the WEA offices at the top of an old building in Newcastle's Grainger Street. The District Secretary, Michael Standen, and I had to go down and eat humble pie with the solicitors on the floor below who didn't appreciate the slow seepage through their ceiling from water play on the floor above!

Work on the Women's Education Programme was both exciting and challenging for tutors and staff development and tutorial support was integral to the programme. The issues which came up for our students were also part of our lives and perhaps because the work was lively, successful and expanded widely throughout the Northern District, we encountered negative as well as positive and supportive responses. The work challenged both educational and social structures: some saw this process as well within the traditions of radical adult education, others felt that it was a deflection from those traditions.

Working as a member of a group of Women's Education tutors was also very important. Sharing experiences and concerns, trying out ideas on each other, debating issues of feminism made the work a personal journey for each tutor but with the active support of colleagues. We were often in the position of having to justify what we were doing to those who found it disruptive or challenging and being part of a group was extremely rewarding. (Cynthia Fuller)

Students also established support structures beyond the course, drawing on the traditions of connection and communication already rooted in their lives and further encouraged by the counselling component of the NOW course:

Eventually I left school aged 15 and trained to be a ladies hairdresser. I was the first person in my family to have an apprenticeship or trade. Meeting women every day, talking to them and listening to what they had to say was a kind of education. I learnt a lot about people and different lives. Each woman had a tale to tell, a viewpoint to put forward. Women relax while having their hair done, often having no one to listen to their feelings at home, so talking to a sympathetic listener at a time when they are relaxed is very therapeutic. (Shirley Rodham)

I enjoyed the course simply for what it gave me, and I didn't immediately focus on doing anything further with it. By the time it ended I had a real sense of myself as one in a community of women who relished their learning and who had been stimulated into thinking about themselves and their lives in the light of the ideas we discussed both in and outside the classes. Groups of us met for coffee afterwards, we did things together, and we talked so much about ourselves and what was important to us that I just wanted to carry on with it. (Jan Hewitt)

Outcomes of the course varied from student to student. Many went on to higher education and we were able to build relationships with university departments which enabled students without matriculation requirements to have their applications considered and to gain entry to degree courses. This was before concepts of non-traditional entry were well established. Vocational training, especially in social work or teaching, was also a frequent choice, as was work with voluntary organisations either in a paid or voluntary capacity.

With my newly found confidence, gained from the tutors and other students, I applied for and was accepted as a trainee social worker at the local college. That was 23 years ago. Since then I have worked for a large children's charity as a qualified social worker. Alongside this, I also furthered my studies: I became a practice teacher encouraging and teaching students, many from a similar background to me i.e. women with young families who had a zest for learning and wanted to contribute something. I gained counselling / therapeutic qualifications and eventually a BA(Hons) in Social Work. I also became a visiting lecturer to a number of universities, both in the UK and abroad (Italy and Denmark). I eventually managed a large busy team of twelve practitioners and for the last eight years I have been a social care inspector appraising and developing practice across the UK. (Barbara McKay)

In 1985 I discovered the WEA. I had not been in full time education, or taken exams since leaving school in 1959, after which I worked in a bank, married and had two children. The course I attended was NOW at the end of which my tutors encouraged me to apply to university. At first I resisted saying 'people like me don't go to university' but after much persuasion and an interview for a four-year BEd (Hons) I was unconditionally accepted. I was then 44 years old and most of my fellow students were 18-19 years old. How exciting! I attended full time. […] In 1990 I graduated with a 2.1 degree. Success! Our income was doubled when I got my first teaching post. My first year as a teacher coincided with my daughter commencing her degree in pharmacy at Sunderland and the following year my son went to Leeds to become a computer scientist. […] later he realised he had made a wrong choice of career and wished to train as a doctor […] it was decided that my salary would pay for his five-year course. My son is now a consultant radiologist at a large teaching hospital in Leeds thus combining his computer training with his skill as doctor. My daughter serves the people of Sunderland as a pharmacist. None of this would have been possible without that push into higher education by the WEA. I have discovered a lifelong love of learning helping hundreds of children to read and write […] and made many good friends. (Joan Briggs)

Where am I now? What am I doing? I'm a registered Reiki Healer and Psychic Medium. Another door opened to another dimension and untold wonders. (Shirley Rodham)

There were implications for families as well as individuals. Chi Onwurah, now Member of Parliament for Newcastle Central, remembers the impact of her mother's study:

In the mid-seventies we were living on a council estate in North Kenton, Newcastle. My Mum had been frustrated in her desire to continue her own education and then seen her marriage torn apart by war in Nigeria, so she was left to bring up three children on her own in poverty. In retrospect, then, I can imagine the NOW course was a light in the darkness. I didn't know this at the time, I was about nine, and all I knew was that suddenly my Mum's reading, interests and friends became even more diverse than before. Some of the books I remember still: *Round About a Pound a Week*, where I learnt the grinding detail of real poverty; *How to Lie with Statistics* which fuelled my admiration, if not my respect, for mathematics.

My Mum went onto the Open University and eventually to study Social and Political Sciences at Newcastle Poly, as it then was. She was almost 60 when she graduated, her degree did not enable her to go on to a better job or higher wage. Yet it made such a difference to all our lives, and not only because her mature student's grant was higher than benefits we had lived on. As she said herself, her degree enabled her to look anyone, including her children, in the eye and know what she should have known anyway, that she was their equal. (Chi Onwurah)

I have very positive memories about the NOW programme, the tutors and the women in the group. The whole experience was uplifting and empowering and provided a major impetus for me to change career. At the end of the programme I was supported in my application to do a degree at Northumbria University in Politics and I followed this with a Masters in Politics at Durham University. The initial support was invaluable as, when I was growing up, no one in my family had been to university or had aspirations to do so and I would have lacked the confidence to take such a step by myself […] I had a fantastic time as a mature student, made a whole new circle of friends and subsequently taught Politics part-time at Durham and the OU before coming back to Northumbria University […] More recently I was successful in my application for a personal chair (teaching and learning) and I delivered my inaugural lecture last November on Women, Power and Politics in the 21st century. In summary, the opportunity to pursue a personal career in academia stemmed originally from the NOW course for which I will always be grateful. It has enriched my life immensely. (Rosie Cunningham)

For some students there was disappointment that we were less able to open up employment opportunities, although a well-written application supported by a reference and the production of written work could sometimes open previously closed doors. Many students wanted to continue their learning in the WEA and, as we developed a policy of only being able to do a NOW course once, an inevitable outcome was the development of a range of further courses. These included day and evening provision and weekend intensive courses, sometimes held residentially. Amongst the courses which sprang directly from NOW was Study Link, offering modular study of a range of subjects including at various times Economics, Politics, Sociology, Literature, History, Psychology, alongside a study skills component. Study Link was open to men as well as women but in practice was almost entirely taken up by women. Other courses were: 'Day Out' with an interdisciplinary curriculum, 'The Other Woman', an interdisciplinary women's studies course and Creative Writing and Health courses.

The WEA educated me in a way that suited my lifestyle. When my husband came home on leave I wanted to spend my time with him. Other educational establishments had fixed timetables and goals. WEA was flexible and understood that people need different things out of life. What is a priority for one person isn't important to another. In the last twenty odd years I have studied various subjects: creative writing, holistic health, history, art, literature and philosophy. All for pure pleasure and I have liked every minute. (Shirley Rodham)

I enrolled myself on to other Women's Education courses, and it was after one of these ('The Other Woman?') that one particular tutor really pushed me into thinking about studying for a degree. My immediate (and predictable) response was 'Oh no, that's not for someone like me', but in truth the idea had taken hold during the NOW course itself, when a sociologist from the university invited us to one of his seminars. That was my very first view of the inside of a university and I cannot tell you just how strong an impression it had on me. Partly it felt an impossibly alien environment — this small room with its rough-textured brick walls, white paintwork, slim vertical windows and a large table with a group of students — and the three or four of us sitting together feeling scrutinised, a bit like specimens. But as we were drawn into discussion, giving our ideas and our perceptions about families and home, I actually felt rather comfortable. It was very similar to what we'd been doing each week at NOW. Knowing that I could do that gave me a further push towards putting in my application. (Jan Hewitt)

The first NOW course began in Newcastle in 1974. Ten years later with funding from the Equal Opportunities Commission and other trust funds the Women's Education Advisory Group of the WEA Northern District organised a national conference in Durham, the proceedings of which were published as *Women's Education: Making Our Future: Change in Women's Education* (WEA 1984), a misleadingly optimistic title, perhaps, given the general political climate. All of the voices of this chapter so far have been those of 2010 looking back on work which began in 1974. In 1984 Jean Barr, then WEA District Secretary of the West of Scotland, gave a closing speech at the conference critiquing both the strengths and weaknesses of Women's Studies. Very importantly she emphasised the structural context: bodies of work like the Newcastle Women's Education Programme, however successful, could not be divorced from wider social, cultural and political power:

> In looking forward we have to be realistic and canny as well as imaginative and ambitious. And in trying to devise a future strategy for women's education we have to acknowledge that our views on this will depend not only on the values we hold but on our views on how society as a whole works and how social change as well as personal change can be brought about.

> My own belief is that if we are to safeguard existing gains for women in education and seek further change we must work towards alternative policies not only for education but for the whole of society and its economy. This means organising on a broader political front. If women don't adopt such strategies then they will bear more than their share of the burdens imposed by present political, social, economic conditions. For we have to recognise that bias against women is much more subtle than blatant, clear sexism and frequently takes the form of the exclusion of women rather than overt bias against them. (Jean Barr)

Twenty-six years later it is worth wondering how much has changed. The feminist movement is in one of its periodic quieter moments. Individualism rather than collectivism reigns. There is little optimism about education as a force for political, social or personal change: functional objectives are paramount.

> Looking back it is clear that grassroots development of this kind would be extraordinarily difficult today. If that is so (and I believe it is) then how many opportunities to develop appropriate, stimulating, life-enhancing educational provision for adults are being missed today? (Jonathan Brown)

There are changes in women's lives, hard fought for but lived out by our daughters:

> We have all paid a price for it, as I feel every time I discuss with my daughter how on earth she will balance her personal ambition, her blossoming research career, and her desire to raise a family. These are not easy choices that our young women make, and they are often painfully unaware of what it took to win them the right to them, but I could never regret that we fought for them and won. (Freda Tallantyre)

The content of the mainstream educational curriculum has changed and widened:

> Courses teaching women's literature highlighted the narrowness of conventional syllabuses and other groups have followed in challenging the exclusion of black and Asian writers, working class writers and gay writers from literature syllabuses. Today literature syllabuses and options look very different from those of the 1970s. (Cynthia Fuller)

The work was important in insisting on the value of affective as well as cognitive learning. We saw no dilemma in studying, discussing and writing about texts alongside an exploration of inner worlds. Change came about because students were introduced to bodies of knowledge which excited and stimulated them. At the same time they began to believe in their own right and capacity to reach out for opportunities not previously available to them. It was understood that this was not just an individual matter: women had been systematically excluded:

> Many educationists and politicians simply don't see women as part of the social world. To be asked to make a conscious decision to include women is therefore something of a problem for individuals who have previously

refused to recognise the issue exists. (Jean Barr)

Students from NOW courses were often influenced by the way in which their learning had taken place, building similar approaches into their own lifelong work, as seen in the following statement:

I also brought from NOW a nascent feminist perspective that I found I could build on right across my studies. I did this in a number of ways, and certainly with my third-year theory studies after I had been blandly told that feminist theory was not included on the course because it was 'just bits and pieces of other theories'. I'd probably argue now that that's what any theory is, but then it simply provoked me enough to dig my heels in and take off on my own tack, determined to bring into my wider curricular work the ideas from the feminist critics and historians that I sought out. It did me no harm and, to my mind, certainly helped towards finding the voice that eventually got me a first class honours degree, a prize for work on W.B. Yeats and a British Academy award from research into women's poetry.

Twenty-four years later (!) I am now a senior lecturer in English Studies at another post-1992 university. I teach large numbers of what are still routinely referred to as 'non-traditional students' — students who I used to think were similar to myself. In terms of background and so many other ways of course, they are — and I was always very open in telling them that I too had been a 'mature student', rather complacent in the assumption, I now suspect, that if they could see that just as I had succeeded so could they. But could I have done my degree as a single parent, as many of mine are, and holding down one, possibly more, jobs as well as doing a supposedly full-time degree? I rather doubt it. In a political, economic and educational environment that is so drastically changed from when I did my own studying, I feel enormously privileged to have been able to do my NOW course so much on my own terms.

I find that as a tutor I am still committed to the values that underpinned my perceptions of what worked for me from the NOW courses. They are fundamental to how I teach: I take time for groups to know each other to make discussions easier. It almost always entails furniture-moving and 'parlour games' to establish names and personalities before settling into the academic business of my modules, but for me it is worth it. Increasingly it means stretching impossible deadlines and workloads to incorporate time for one-to-one feedback, but these I know clarify things for students personally and more directly than any amount of computer-generated feedback. It often means thinking through students' learning experiences to find new and different ways to make ideas meaningful, on their terms as well as those of the syllabus. It means stressing social interactions as part of the ways of building continuity and process for students who can so easily feel alienated by the various dictates of HE structures, existing jobs and future career prospects that are inevitably emphasised in and by the current economic climate.

In my own mind there is a clear correlation between such practices and my experiences from the NOW course. It was being an integrated and forward-thinking collaboration fostered by a socially-committed group of intellectuals, which made it the turning-point for my own achievement in both academic and personal terms. It has fostered my belief ever since that learning always needs time and a supportive social environment and that we need each other to find ourselves and our individual voices. (Ian Hewitt)

I want to end with a voice from 1912. In the archives of the WEA Northern District there exists a pamphlet, *Women in the WEA*, written by Ida Hony, then Secretary, Women's Department of the National WEA. In it she argues in the language of her time, but with an uncanny similarity to the arguments of the seventies, for specialist women's provision appropriately funded and designed:

Life seems nothing but cleaning up dirt, a working mother once said to us — and there was a world of pathos behind the words. We must labour unceasingly to give her and her sisters the chance of seeing how much more than this it both may and must mean […]

Afternoon or evening meetings of an informal and friendly nature might be arranged fortnightly or monthly in different parts of the district (if it be a large one), and it would not be a bad plan to tackle one street at a time by distribution of invitations from door to door. After a short simple address on some attractive subject had been given, refreshments might be given, or sold at cost price, and perhaps a little good music provided; but, in any case, plenty of time should be left for talk. Every member should feel herself a hostess, and make it her business to see that the new-comers become interested, and that no-one is left out in the cold. […]

Careful consideration, too, needs to be given to the question of expenses, so that poverty should bar no one from attending. It is suggested that a fund should be raised to which everyone should subscribe something — no matter how little — and from this the fares of those unable to afford them should be paid. […]

We are convinced that among working women today there is a real hunger for knowledge, for a fuller, fairer life and a wider hoping than has been theirs in the past; and we make this appeal in sure confidence that all share in satisfying that hunger will bring its own reward. (Hony, 1982)

The words in this essay from 1912, echoed again in the 1970s and now in 2010, illustrate the way in which the radical needs to be continually re-imagined. Innovative ventures develop, flourish and fade, although always with some legacy of influence. There is little room for complacency. We need to look beyond what is to what *might be*. The Women's Education Programme and particularly the NOW courses, were the richest experience of my working life, existing as they did on the growing edge of a moment of cultural, social and intellectual change.

SOURCES CITED

Hony, I., 1982. *A Gift in our Hand* (A republication of a 1912 leaflet *Women in the WEA* with an essay by Eileen Aird and an introduction by Michael Standen). Newcastle: WEA Northern District.

Russell, Edward Lionel, 1973. *Adult education: a plan for development. Report by a Committee of Inquiry appointed by the Secretary of State for Education and Science under the Chairmanship of Sir Lionel Russell C.B.E.* London: HMSO.

WEA, 1984. *Making Our Future: Change in Women's Education. Newcastle:* WEA Northern District.

WEA, 1989. *Women's Education Past, Present and Future:* A WEA Policy Statement. London: WEA National Office.

A Commercial Traveller in Education:
Life as a Tutor Organiser in Cumberland[1]

Hilda Pickles

After one of his 'International Affairs' classes he [Dr Cobban] had said to me 'I think you would fit into adult education. Why not go down to the District Secretary of the Worker's Educational Association, and ask if he could give you a class. Say I sent you.'

So I set to work, entranced by the idea of studying history with those who, unlike school pupils, had some experience of life. I prepared a syllabus, and made an appointment with the Secretary of the Newcastle WEA.

After a long wait, I was shown into a small room where a dark man with a sharp nose looked me down[2] , down to my square-toed walking shoes, and up. 'Too young,' he said.

I was almost out of the room when he half-relented.

'Is that your syllabus? Show me it.' I laid it on the desk between us, thin and pathetic, a premature child.

'Huh,' he said with faint animation. 'Not bad … Come back in five years,' and there I was outside the door.

For quite two hours that night I raged inwardly. Not one whole sentence had I uttered! Only 'Good morning' (twice). Why had I never mentioned *someone* who, though young, had yet been trusted? Harry Hotspur? Mozart? Pitt? To glory such as theirs I did not aspire, but surely I could do something so insignificant as take a class? To and fro, with fretful repetition, went my recriminations, an inner stream of futile complaint, criticism and anger.

Superficially the episode was forgotten, amid all the preparation for evacuation, followed by war. Now, in 1943 it came upon me with a shock, that almost five years had already passed since my first ignominious effort to become a tutor. I would go back, and try again to find a minute place in the adult education movement.

So, the youth course ended, I sped to Newcastle, spent one night with a friend in edgy anticipation, and early next day made for the WEA office.

In five years, only a week had gone by there. The District Secretary looked me down as before, down — and up. 'Too late,' he said. 'We advertised five weeks ago. The university needs a Tutor-Organiser for the western area, Cumberland and south west Northumberland. We're interviewing a short list of six at the University this afternoon …'[3]

'But I was in Cambridge - never saw the advertisement,' I stammered.

'Too bad. You're just too late,' he reiterated, shuffling papers on his desk.

Perhaps it was his wintry negativity that did it. First 'too young' and now 'too late'. That little man with the nose jolted some mechanism that had been idling in my brain for thirteen years — in fact from my final day in high school as a pupil. 'Immature' I was called then. Was I going to waste my whole life being picked over and rejected like a damaged biscuit? That tutor-organiser's job in Cumberland was for me. The blood of all my Border ancestors, Redes, Halls, Charltons, Hawdons, thundered in my head, and a firm clear voice, unquestionably mine, said 'Can I not be interviewed as well?'

He was aghast; but recovering his best diplomatic, non-committal manner, he suggested perhaps … all things

---

[1] In the late 1930s the author attended an international affairs class where Dr Cobban was the tutor and he put this idea to her in 1938. This chapter is taken from Hilda Pickles' reminiscences (1993:172-89).

[2] The District Secretary was B. W. (Bertie) Abrahart who served from 1936 until 1947 when he was appointed as Director of Extra-Mural Studies at King's College, Newcastle.

[3] The WEA post was jointly funded by the Extra-Mural Department of King's College Newcastle and the WEA. Both organisations worked closely together during this period. H. E. R. Highton, Secretary of the Department, was a member of the WEA District Committee and District Chairman from 1945-48.

considered … since, in fact I had been interested in the past — and would have applied if I had not been in Cambridge — it might be arranged. Perhaps he would phone the Director of Extra-Mural Studies at the university …

I waited. My name was added to the list. I remember nothing of that long interview but the last two questions: Have you a car? Can you drive? I could get one. I could learn.

A week later I was in Cumbria, with a less than reliable second-hand Ford car, on which I had had five driving lessons. A new life began.

I had never dreamt of leaving school-teaching in Newcastle for good. Five or six years in Cumberland was the intention. I thought and hoped, that in learning the very different approach necessary for adult education I would at least begin to mature; and that the study and discussion of history, political thought and 'social problems' would be on a more detailed and worthwhile level than it could ever be in school. After five or six years of hard experience, I would go back to the Tyne.

But, having married, and since my husband's work was in Cumbria, there with our family, we remained, but that is another story.

A spell in adult education, however brief, has a bearing on what we try to do in school. My years as a tutor organiser were essentially a new attempt, let us hope with slightly more finesse, to link subjects and syllabuses so that knowledge might indeed be seen as a 'seamless web'. In Cumbria, as in those Walker schools in the early years of war, I was 'on my own' — a commercial traveller in education.

It was autumn, start of the new year, when, in theory, adult students chose their new subject of study. At various Branch opening meetings I was given opportunity to suggest to students that in genuine history, rather than in the then popular 'social problems' or 'post-war Reconstruction', they would find long-lasting food. And in Carlisle I did get one group to undertake a three year tutorial class in history. The aim of such a class is to reach university level; but, given the very different circumstances of undergraduates and our students, at work all day, this is always difficult, sometimes impossible.

'Not further back than Queen Elizabeth,' one man insisted, so we agreed to make a start on the explorers of the sixteenth century, with a little study of the way Hakluyt wrote his *Voyages.*

This modest man, who signed his great works simply 'Richard Hakluyt, Preacher,' was not, so far as we know, endowed with the more brilliant creative gifts. Nevertheless, his works directed the thoughts of adventurous scholars, statesmen and merchants, outwards across the oceans of the world. And upwards of three hundred years later, in one small provincial town, he inspired us to follow and learn from him. Through industry, he had, as he said,

> redeemed from obscurity and perishing, old records, patents, privileges, letters […]

In that frozen winter of 1943, sitting in the cold Carlisle library, we held communion with him.

> What heat, what cold I have endured […] how many famous libraries I have searched into […]

We felt we understood him well.

Since the subject matter of history embraces all human endeavour, and achievement; all successes, inventions and artistic creativity; all disasters nobly or ignobly born; all devastations of war and famine, it would take a very poor teacher not to move or thrill some of her students at least some of the time, and in Carlisle, it did not take us long to develop a comradeship of ideas.

Yet I still *talked* with our women students only in their own homes, among their household goods and children. In class, they sat gravely silent.

The stage has to be peopled with recognisable human beings, and a constant source of these is to be found in the paintings and writings of the seventeenth and eighteenth centuries. This is a period of particular attraction to a new group of adult students, who all know, vaguely, of the changes taking place in farming, transport, literature, justice, between the time of Defoe to the coming of the Georges. They can feel 'at home' because so many names are known to them, though what the famous people actually did, or wrote or intended; may be hazy in their minds. The tutor must make a provocatively ingenious and questioning syllabus, so that each term's work helps in the building of a gigantic jigsaw, bringing town and country life, with its changes, into focus.

Hogarth led the way

> My picture is my stage, and men and women my players [...] (*Hogarth*, World's Masters New Series, Intro.
> Antony Bertram)

He was both storyteller, and moralist. All our students knew of him, but none had thought about him or about his work.

A stranger to almost all of them was Thomas Bewick, born fifty years after Hogarth close to the Tyne, at Ovingham, where his father was a miner and small farmer. Apprenticed at fourteen, Bewick became one of the greatest of engravers, in his day or any other. He served seven years in Newcastle, then, because of his success was drawn to London. He enjoyed seeing the excellent work

> in every art and science — painting, statuary, engraving, carving [...] yet I did not like London [...] a world of
> extreme riches, extreme poverty, extreme grandeur and extreme wretchedness [...] The country of my old friends
> — the manners of the people of that day — the scenery of Tyneside — seemed altogether a paradise for me, and
> I longed to see it again ... (Memoir of Thomas Bewick, Frank Graham)

So, like many another before and since, he returned to the Tyne, never to leave it again.

I had never given a lesson on Bewick before, nor indeed ever talked about him, yet in quotation from that splendid man, in words and pictures, I was wholly carried away. Many of his tiny pictures brought back memories of our living, lively boys at Shields, for no one can have depicted boys and their impish pranks more amusingly and touchingly; nor country people at every task more exactly. Nor could he have described with less acrimony the constant 'whackings' that followed his own boyish escapades — 'the overflowings of an active, wild disposition.'

Here was a boy, by his own account, as often in trouble as any of our lads at the Ralph Gardner School, yet, aided only by his parents' commonsense, what a superb thing he made of life.

All our students had heard of, and a few had read, *The Vicar of Wakefield*, but although so near the Border, not one student knew John Galt, the long-suffering Scottish writer and 'man o'parts' whose *Annals of the Parish* is quite as enchanting as Goldsmith's 'Vicar', and probably even more valuable as a record of social life. It is an intimate portrait of Ayrshire during the rise of the cotton mills, not only one of the most vivid, enlightening and entertaining accounts of village life ever written, but certainly the most melodious to read.

One day, hunting in the Carlisle library for other books by John Galt for our students I found an ancient review of his *Tales of My Landlord* written by the Scottish Judge, Francis Jeffrey. In that review, written in the eighteen twenties, in a time of turmoil, shortages and hardship so like the one we ourselves were passing through in 1943 and '44, I came upon words of such good sense then that they have remained with me ever since.

> The quiet undercurrent of life keeps its deep and steady course [...] long tracts in the history of every country seem
> to be darkened with an oppressive cloud of unbroken misery, yet most of those who lived through the whole acts
> of the tragedy will have enjoyed a fair average share of felicity [...]

We seem now in a new stage of continuously oppressive world misery, but at the time of writing, Galt's words surely contained a sober truth?

Of felicity, I for one felt that I was enjoying more than my fair share. I was lodged with a middle aged, semi-retired farmer and his wife, and all through the golden autumn of my first term in Cumbria with the River Eden before us, sparkling through the tawny trees, I felt translated to the Forest of Arden. The Editor of the Arden edition of *As You Like It* says: 'Life in Arden is naturally happy and wholesome, good men flourish there, free from human malice.' Yes ... a great generalisation perhaps, though certainly true of the two I lived with, Mr and Mrs Fairish. Mr Fairish had Corin's homespun philosophy. One Sunday evening, taking a little walk together, we looked over a neighbour's wall at some rather weedy piglets. 'If them ever makes pigs, aa'll eat hay wid horse,' was his blunt dismissal of the little creatures. He was wrong in his judgment, (as we often are about our pupils), but he had the grace to admit it later.

I found endless delight in listening to him for his comments were always fresh and usually apt. One night, when I was off to a class in Carlisle, having promised to take Mrs Fairish with me to see a friend, I was fidgeting because she was not ready. 'Yu's nobbut good for a neet watchman. Aa nivver saw a body sae uneasy when she's barred oop — fizzling about, like cat on a griddle.'

Mrs F was her husband's equal in cheerful, unflustered moto perpetuum throughout the daylight hours. We all breakfasted together at 7.15, then he went out to his work while she continued her fifteen hour day: hens, chickens, baking, cleaning — wash (in the poss tub) iron, polish — '10 o'clocks' 3 o'clocks' and 'proper meals' in between. All she ever read was 'Births, Deaths and Marriages' on Friday night in the *Cumberland News,* and *The People's Friend* for perhaps an hour on Sunday afternoon. She, like her husband, was quite ready to see improvement for the poor and needy, but the idea of taking *thought* about it, of actually trying to do anything to change the future, would have seemed as absurd as the idea of walking round to Buckingham Palace for a rubber of whist with royalty.

While Mrs F busied herself in her clogs, in and out the dairy, the back kitchen and the stack yard, I busied myself on the kitchen table writing letters to Branch Secretaries, to existing or prospective tutors, and endlessly studying and preparing for five different weekly classes, as well as Saturday and week-end 'schools'. Though too polite to say so, it was clear they both thought my job probably pointless, and certainly very, very odd.

'Can't you just preach them summat you've preached afore?' Mrs F said wistfully one day; and one wild winter afternoon, as I was setting off twenty-five miles over Hartside to a class at Nenthead, Mr F, looking forward to a night by the fire, announced 'Aa's ganna clip cloots if aa had a bit shave first. 'Tisn't ivverybody as can clip cloots.' (cut rags into little pieces, to make a 'proggy mat') and he was right, I never had time even for that.

Over the years, Mr and Mrs Fairish gave a welcome to me as if to the daughter they had never had. But how like a changeling I must have seemed at first, an 'Organising-Tutor' being as far from their experience as a shogun from Japan. They themselves had attended one-teacher village schools, and very occasionally went to church 'to hear the sermon'.

In my studying by day and ranging the countryside at night, I must have seemed to them a kind of itinerant nocturnal preacher crossed with a Hammer-Headed bat. I could not make them understand that I was not there to *preach*. The only form of schooling they recognised was drawn from their own experience: Teacher talks; pupils repeat, repeat, repeat; and if 'successful', learn by heart. I had found, from visiting a variety of classes, that most tutors *did* talk continuously, though what the students recollected of all they 'listened' to, no one ever knew. But surely that great flow of exposition can never be the most important teaching function? It is the give and take between individual minds which is the source of life and learning. A teacher (so I thought, and think) must consciously and continuously *listen,* while students must talk as well as listen if they are ever to make new ideas of their own. There must be reciprocity.

Perhaps it was while studying the Bewick engravings so assiduously for Carlisle class that I began to understand that *listening* may be to teachers what *looking* is to artists. In addition to Bewick's autobiography, I had with me in Cumberland a book of Rembrandt drawings (pen and bistre wash) found long before in a Newcastle bookshop. Having no music in Cumberland, every Sunday I used to look at these superb drawings — *Interior of a kitchen, Study of a tree trunk, Trees and a river at dusk, Women in a doorway* and the wonderful *Lion lying down,* from the Boymans Museum in Rotterdam, and they gave the same kind of comfort that Beethoven used to give in those years of Mother's illness.

I remembered that Chardin used to say to pupils 'Hand and palette are needed to paint; but a painting is not made with the hand or the palette.' Would it not be equally true to say 'voice and chalk are needed by teachers: but a teacher is not made by the voice or the chalk'? How many times in the past, I had walked down that school corridor in Washington Road, seeing pupils in the back seats giggling and playing, while strident teacher-voices shrilled from every glass-framed cage; and not only were these hard-pressed teachers shouting, they waved their arms in frantic or despairing imprecation, ever and anon turning to write feverishly on the board.

    […] Not waving but drowning […]

I know the temptation, and had, at times, succumbed. Probably this irrational behaviour sprang from fear of several kinds: memories of our own school days, when we, too, tormented nervous teachers, perhaps now feeling that we suffered just reward; fear that the gifts we were so anxious to offer — of knowledge, of understanding — were not wanted; that the end of year, end of life itself would come and all that we tried to teach be wasted. Such fears, and others, can be felt, in every degree of exaggeration, if the teacher is tired, or despondent, and may produce that shouting at the class which is so destructive to teacher and demoralising to pupils.

When I first started the new job, it had seemed plain that such travesties of learning would be impossible in *adult* education! With twelve or fifteen in a class instead of forty, we would have genuine 'dialogue' each day. We would learn together. What a new-found opportunity to put all notions of 'good teaching' to the test!

So I imagined us, drawing up our chairs in a cosy circle, where, after an arresting introduction, we would launch into thoughtful and satisfying debate. What I found in practice, as a famous artist found in painting, was that 'there is no way to success in our art but to take off your coat, grind paint, and work like a digger on the railway all day and every day'. In every class, I was faced by a phalanx of silent women, all clearly intimidated by half-a-dozen men, mostly middle-aged.

Not that our men were a vintage year of former film stars either. Marianne Dashwood would not have given one of them a second glance, all but one being so obviously destined, before the course was over, for age, infirmity and flannel waistcoats. It could scarcely have been adoration which silenced our women — intelligent and strong-minded, managers of shops, schools, or homes with several children. No, it seemed an endemic female passivity in front of men; as if it was not seemly to speak except to one's consecrated husband and not always even then.

I saw this daily in my lodging, where Mrs Fairish behaved as if it were divinely ordained for her to work, and to suffer, if that were called for, in silence. If Mr Fairish had a cold he sat in the chair with his feet on the fender, murmuring in a wan voice, 'Aa's in sic a bad fettle — sic a bad fettle.' And if not enough sympathy ensued, he would grumble wistfully, 'Aa doan't think thou knaw's aa's as badly as aa is.' When Mrs Fairish was ill, on the contrary, she drooped about, martyr-like in her clogs, till I drove her to bed. All the women I knew then in rural Cumbria, however voluble to their own friends in their own kitchens, accepted their men's opinions on social or any other question with amazing docility.

I asked one farmer if his wife would come to the class I was running in the village. 'Nay, I doan't think it,' he said, shaking his head gloomily. 'I doan't like 'er to go t'Institute an' that. She gets wid a lot o' wimmin and gets gabby.' And the most macabre comment ever uttered in my hearing was made one morning when, on one of my journeys, I called, as asked, to leave a parcel at an isolated Pennine farm. I was shown into the kitchen only to be told that the farmer's wife had died the previous night. While trying to express sympathy to him, I found the sitting room door flung open, and myself staring at the corpse.

'Just luk at that' the farmer rasped. 'Luk at that, and sic a lot o' grand work in 'er yet.' Though perhaps sincerely sorry, he spoke in what sounded more like exasperation than remorse.

Oh yes, attitudes have changed in nearly fifty years; and among them attitudes to women. Yet not everywhere in rural Britain have attitudes to women (and women's thoughts about themselves) changed as much as people commonly suppose.

In our Carlisle class, when, by dint of carefully thought out questions, I did get nearly everyone to speak a little, the comments were more hesitant, more convoluted, more repetitive than those of our eleven or twelve-year-olds at Washington Road. The human mind tends to rotate, and its progress round a given subject often appears, during 'discussion', to be imperceptible. A new tutor (myself for instance) is *afraid* of this apparent stagnation: the anguished thoughts chase one another 'We are getting nowhere — everyone will be bored — the class will fold up,' and the temptation to interfere is fierce.

I did try to wait, patiently, as an artist must wait while concentrating on his subject; and, generally, someone would move the discussion forward an inch, and a comment of real illumination often followed.

In that wonderful extension of our adult classes, the Open University, I am delighted to see things that I was groping after in Cumbria in those war, and post-war years, now being done in a much more 'structured' way. What we strove for at varying levels in all our adult classes — through halting, unassertive exchange of opinion — was to reach individually and together a wider view of learning and of life.

But I am letting the tutoring side of my new enterprise run far ahead of the organising half. That unwelcome aspect loomed over me, part of the 'contract' I had agreed to in Newcastle so innocently and eagerly.

There may be a place for organisers in production or distribution of commodities. But in education? And if we decide, on balance, we should try having them, what should be their special skills? If there is any book where this topic is debated I had not read it. Perhaps the simple truth was that, in my hasty application, I had wanted *half* the job, honestly believing I could do that part. To the rest, I had shut my eyes, half wishing, half dreaming that magic would spirit it away.

In those first few weeks in Cumbria, when I imagined myself dispassionately observing how others conducted adult education, it was interesting to see how quickly roots of my own infantile behaviour were revealed! And not only once. In a matter of days, I had said and done things in an innocent, simple minded manner that brought untold trouble later. With foresight and experience could I have managed relations with the Carlisle Branch Chairman so that they would have been tranquil? The trouble is that foresight and experience are just what the novice has not got. I was unwary. And it is hard for anyone unwary to become a diplomat.

After the Extra-Mural Board meeting at which I had been selected for the job, the Chairman of the Carlisle Branch of the Workers' Educational Association told me to call upon him in his office when I arrived in Cumbria. This I duly did, and the whole interview was so reminiscent of that chapter in *Our Mutual Friend* where Mr Podsnap questions the 'foreign gentleman' at Georgina's birthday party, that it was hard not to laugh.

'How do you like Cumbria? You'll find it very different from Newcastle: more trees; more mountains; more space. People are individuals here you know.'

He gave me no time for comment.

'What you *ought* to do is watch a few classes taken by Plunkett. He's been tutoring for years. Very good man. Very sound. I'll fix that for you. Now let's see – there's Balderstone. He's another pal of mine: starting *his* classes next week, too. I could get you in to watch him. Then you'd have a notion how things should go on … '

'I've fixed you up with lodgings two doors away from me. You'll be all right there. Woman on her own; husband in the Army; just one child; about a year old. If you're there, I'll know what you're up to — see you're on right lines — sort out any difficulties.'

I murmured 'Very kind; but I think …' He waved me silent. Clearly it was not mine to reason why, anywhere on his battlefield. Like the original Mr Podsnap, he believed that what he put behind him was put out of his existence. What I thought did not signify.

From then on, every time we met, he went immediately into attack. I responded with deference first, but when he continually played authority, I took fright, as now.

Were even lodgings to be chosen for me? And by someone I hardly knew, and certainly did not respect. I evaded — 'I am thinking of living in the country.'

To this he gave snorting dismissal.

'You can't possibly do that.'

I had not, till that minute, made up my mind; but that decided me. He grew bitter and bullying: to be ten miles out of town, down rural lanes, would make night travelling that much worse. He *knew*. Oncomers should accept advice. Everything he said was sensible. I knew neither people in the district nor winter weather in mountainous terrain.

I had no reasoned answer, only intuition. I could not, and would not, live under his foot. To him, I was exploitable — as exploitable as Mozart's Susanna, though in a different way. While willing to be exploited for my own idea of education, *his* idea of education, so blatantly one of dominating authority, was not a cause for which I would die.

Should we have had a confrontation *then?* In the long run, perhaps that would have been wiser. But I pursued guerilla tactics, hoping that if I side-stepped often enough, he would finally tire of the pursuit. He never did.

When November drew on, with ceaseless rain and constant fog with nightly journeys in an aging Ford car with no heating and masked and minimal car head lights, few telephones and no sign posts anywhere, my allegiance to Arden almost failed. Then, without warning, would come once more a perfect day, with blue sky over gleaned harvest fields, and black-faced sheep higher up the fells. And beyond them the mountains, bronze and blue in sunset, with folds deeply marked in shadow, and white washed cottages at the foot of the slopes. Sometimes, journeying to see tutors or secretaries, I had to drive through the hills, to Cockermouth, or further, to Whitehaven and the sea. And alone in my car I would sing all the way, knowing I never wanted to live out of sight of the hills again. Getting to know that vast, mountainous and sparsely populated region — one quarter the size of Wales — provided problems that strained physique, as well as testing (and defeating) my small stock of car maintenance skill. But when the car broke down, I still had two good feet, and I learnt, in time, to know my district like a native. I do believe, moreover, that, living *like* a native in the country, I learnt more and belonged more quickly than I would ever have done if living even three times as long as a bourgeois 'oncomer' in a suburban 'semi' in Carlisle.

But let me not give any impression that I learnt to know this area *alone*. Only the quiet, unremitting kindness of students and Branch Secretaries, who gave me tea, or bed and breakfast, times without number, saved me from death by petrifaction long ago.

How often I have been asked 'What made you go into adult education? You could have stayed on in Newcastle and become a Head?' as if we were all expected to see the future in terms only of power and 'success'. In making any change in life the mind has conscious and unconscious motives. Consciously, as already noted, I wanted, for a time, to pursue the study of history with adults. But there was also a need — not identified until, in those years in Cumbria it was so richly satisfied, to strike off on my own; to do the unexpected; to venture up hills where every route was not marked by stone corridors and forty minute bells.

The contrast between the rich experiences of learning that my brothers and I shared in youth, and the years of war-time teaching on Tyneside was stark. In Cumbria too there was a rich store of local history dating back to prehistoric times.

I had been trying, over a period, to find a form of teaching in which pupils and staff could grow together. But neither the boys' school at Tynemouth, nor youth work in Cambridgeshire had offered scope for such experiment. War-time conditions forbade all out-of-school activities in the one, while benevolent dictatorship ossified all participants in the other. In adult education, however, restrictions and worries of the war proved an incentive to students. If there were rifts between officials, and occasional tiffs between the WEA organisation in Newcastle and the impetuous tutor 'in the field', at least our friction was fresh and productive, not a slow atrophy, as in my experience of the Cambridge youth world.

Above all this, Cumbria — if lacking in some of the cultural amenities thought necessary for salvation — offers always and everywhere, colour and space. Like drama, music, poetry, these free the imagination too. The Eden valley, the Pennine hills, trees by the old farmsteads, ferns in stone walls, all these brought back our years of walking holidays in Northumberland. Young and old, people sing when happy. And I sang as I had not sung for years. Certain things in life seem only obtainable obliquely — happiness certainly, and education at least in part. There are aspects of learning over which we can exert no direct control. That teacher at Ralph Gardner School, Miss Hislop who 'taught Roman Britain' by making her boys learn the dimensions of the wall (in feet and inches!) never knew what strange ships of fancy her class might embark upon while she talked.

Miss Hislop, most earnest of teachers, gave me her class 'examination paper', generously intending to help someone young and 'new'. Far from being a help, it was a horrifying glimpse of what anyone of us might come to after twenty years of continuous school teaching, if we never paused long enough to enter dry dock for a refit.

Cumbria was my dock — though even so incurable an optimist as I could scarcely call it 'dry'.

As an 'Organiser' in adult education the demands were great: time and energy were spent in constant travel; in efforts to promote goodwill between rival part-time tutors often jealous of each other; in efforts to promote classes in starved soil. But the rewards, as a tutor, far outweighed the distracting demands. It is enriching to be part of an educational movement where people come to classes purely for the joy of learning; a movement which exists for no other reason but that knowledge has value of its own. This, too, linked with some of our best school work in Walker when, in our great adversity in those early months of 1940, we had experienced the sustaining power of seeking knowledge for ourselves.

Without doubt, the search for knowledge sustained us yet again in the dark days of 1943 and 1944 in our adult classes. Yet we were not sombre about it, not at all. Many a time I was asked to give 'A little talk about education,' Church and Chapel organisations being particularly fond of filling up a weekly meeting in this decent, earnest fashion. I went to one such gathering called 'Women's Bright Hour' at Aspatria. Some twenty women sat on hard chairs, in a cold, dark, room avoiding my eye, but gazing at one another with expressions of self-lacerating misery. I told them I had been invited, the week before, to high tea at a farmhouse, where the ten year old daughter was bidden to 'Ask a blessing' before we began. She closed her eyes and said, without pause for breath,

'Forwhatweareaboutoreceivemakeustrulythankful — Mother what a little kipper you've given me.'

I thought that was how many people (especially women) felt about education. They looked forward to it so much in the beginning, but by the end, were so often disappointed.

Students were, in general, a more cheerful bunch than tutors for there was very little to attract anyone to part-time tutoring in those days. All of ours were middle-aged or elderly, mainly teachers from minor rural grammar schools who wanted to make a little extra money. They were amazingly cynical, and the few parsons included in our allotment, even more jaundiced.

To this there was one outstanding exception, an astronomer, T. L. MacDonald, who, after a distinguished academic career, because of his care for the deprived and the 'drop-outs', had become Youth Organiser for Carlisle and District. He was brilliant in science and unusually knowledgeable in literature and politics. He lived alone and had strange habits reminiscent of Dr Johnson. Officials like our Carlisle Branch Secretary, 'Mr Podsnap' used to laugh at him, but all his students were his devoted slaves, and would walk three miles in snow and tempest not to miss a class. I had listened to him in his office and talking informally at weekend schools, recalling always that splendid comment 'curiosity is, in great arid generous minds, the first passion and the last,' for he had that capacity, which Sir Isaiah Berlin has to so marked a degree, to fire his students with his own enthusiasm. Could we not make MacDonald's gifts available to tutors?

For the previous two years at least, I had felt that the best way to meet our problems was to keep a mental list of assets and drawbacks, trying to use one to minimise the other. T. L. MacDonald was one undoubted asset; our lovely countryside another. A major drawback was isolation from any university and consequent staleness and lack of intellectual stimulus and vitality; there was a total lack of 'bookshops' in the real sense, though four or five of the larger towns had a stationer with a handful of recent paperback novels.

To revive our less than buoyant tutorial spirits, I had started a branch of the Tutors' Association, but evening meetings were impossible for people twenty to forty miles apart, so we relied on Saturday and weekend schools for corporate inspiration. Weekends were always enjoyable, and tutors went away in a mildly more co-operative temper. We met several times in the Newlands Valley at the foot of Causey Pike, in a Holiday Fellowship guest house. At other times, we met at Dalston Hall, a Border pele tower with later additions, including mullioned turrets and pleasant grounds.

One of the best schools was at Maryport, a once-elegant little west coast town which had fallen on hard times by the nineteen forties, We stayed at the Golden Lion Hotel overlooking the tiny harbour, at a charge of 12/6d a day, dinner, bed and breakfast. (Can that 12/6d, 62p today — really have included *Bed* as well as Board?) We had some splendid speakers: Thomas Hodgkin of the Oxford Extra-Mural Delegacy; an HMI for Adult Education; Thomas Balogh (later Lord Balogh) then Director of the Oxford Institute of Statistics; Dennis Chapman who had been Director of the War Time Social Survey.

In arranging these Schools I was supported always by my 'boss', Herbert Highton, Director of Extra-Mural Studies at Newcastle upon Tyne, a gruff but fatherly Glaswegian. At the Maryport school, T. L. MacDonald spoke on 'The Lost years: bridging the gap between the youth service and adult education'. Since he was peculiarly fitted for this subject, and we had all experienced the problem, both talk and discussion were unwontedly successful, stirring even our reserved members to applause.

Speaking about this afterward with Mr Highton, I learned that he and Mr MacDonald had been students in Glasgow University together and that he had known and admired him then. He added casually, in one of the dry asides in which he always made his useful comments, 'He gave the Ford lectures once, you know.'

This put a match to a small fire I had been unobtrusively preparing in the background, intending it to be lighted perhaps several months ahead. It seemed as if the only way to build up something lasting and productive between tutors — a constant mental stimulus rather than the agreeable but evanescent exchanges at weekends — would be to run a weekly class for tutors. At the same time, I was disturbed by the lack, in Cumbria, of classes in science subjects, by lack of teachers trained to take such classes, and by what seemed a general lack of interest in the matter. Would it be possible to tackle both these drawbacks together? I had at that time a predilection for trying to do two things at once. Experience has shown this to be a short cut only to disaster, but *then* in roseate youth, a science class for tutors seemed a happy thought. We had no idea of converting arts graduates into scientists through a ten-week course; but hoped that tutors might stir the interest of students in the natural sciences if their own curiosity were aroused.

But if we *had* such a class, who could be the lecturer?

Would our tutors be willing, even flattered, to be taught by a Ford lecturer? Especially when they had just heard him speak with such success?

Mr Highton thought they might. Soundings were taken: most were mildly warm, a few were enthusiastic: Mr MacDonald was invited, and agreed. It was roses all the way. In a matter of weeks, T. L. MacDonald sent his title and syllabus, and I felt my first qualms:

> Scientific Method: with an outline of the history of science and the development of the scientific outlook; some discussion of how science works and its application and relationship to other subjects; with a sketch of the present position of important branches of science today.

It all sounded strangely like 'The World and Its Workings in Ten Easy Lessons'. But who was I to argue? Besides, the bureaucratic work was almost complete, firm promises of attendance had been given, and when, where and how had been arranged. A hundred other matters claimed attention, and I left this tutors' class to be picked up at New Year.

How I would love to say the course was the triumph of the season. Alas, it was not so. In the County Hotel, at Carlisle station, we met at 2.30 for ten Sundays, starting the first bleak Sunday of the year. To my perturbation (for as instigator, I felt myself to blame) I knew from the first meeting that the class would never flourish.

Why did it fail? The place was wrong. Windows looked out on a drab, dusty, station forecourt, with no relief from gloom — no flowers, no grass, only rubbish blowing in the January wind. The time was wrong. The men missed their snooze, smoke, and Sunday papers. For me, Sunday afternoons had been, from childhood, looked forward to, denoting freedom from household chores, school work, or other peoples' demands. We had all *agreed* to sacrifice our Sundays, there being no other way to meet, yet, in practice perhaps we resented it?

All this being admitted, the uncongeniality of time and place were really incidental scapegoats for something deeper. Our lecturer, in eagerness to give his best, treated us weekly to ninety or one hundred minutes of close-packed discourse on scientific matters as if we were an audience of learned dons. Theoretically, everyone attending that class *wanted* to learn: but we were all students of the humanities. It was too much, too late, too abstract, and too remote from anything we had ever done before. The more we struggled to hide our yawns of incomprehension and exhaustion, the more he strove to give a complete history of the known universe. With true Scots fairness, he wanted to give value for our fees.

Could we not have told him simply that we needed to be *taught,* not lectured at? But that would have been a criticism of his whole technique. There was he, clearly striving to give the most impressive course of lectures on scientific principles ever delivered north of Watford; and there were we, trying to glean a mite here, a mite there amid the alien corn. We could not meet.

We continued to the end of term but it was through iron determination and respect for our lecturer rather than involvement or delight. We learnt — at least negatively — that teachers must listen themselves as well as spout, and that if pupils don't discuss, they seldom learn. It was a brave try, but an object lesson in how to take the horse to water without enabling it to drink.

Twenty five years later, what I had had in mind for that tutors' class was done with superb success by Dr

Bronowski in his television series *The Ascent of Man.* Bronowski had for his lectures everything that T. L. MacDonald lacked: sound, colour, continuous illustration, opportunity to involve his audience through their ears as well as eyes, and so in imagination, through every other sense. Had we, too, been able to *read* Macdonald's lectures afterwards, as later we could read Bronowski's, our undersanding would have been so much enhanced.

So, back to the Carlisle Branch of the Workers' Educational Association, some hundred and thirty souls, a more diverse and individualistic lot altogether than our thirty tutors. With all their idiosyncrasies and varied tones of voice, they often reminded me, (especially when we held socials or Christmas parties,) of the characters in Brueghel's *Battle between Carnival and Lent* — some plump, smiling, buxom as if still nourished with the hearty fare of Carnival, while the more sober — in the main, those who attended history and economics classes — preferring the quiet life of Lent.

Among these contemplative persons was a young, silent, Yorkshire man, a member of our history class for three years. Courteous in attention to other members when they spoke, he himself was heard only when he murmured an occasional dry joke. Quite suddenly it appeared that this dedicated listener intended to marry that other dedicated listener, myself. And if he specialised in practice and I in theory, that might assist domestic harmony.

So, in a summer of phenomenal rain even for the north country, just two days after the Tyne had washed away a bridge that had stood for four hundred years, we were married. We had a perfect day, and were attended by a host of well-wishers from adult education, as well as friends from earlier times. We found a small flat in Carlisle in which to live.

I continued as a tutor, but was glad to give up all the organising side.

SOURCE CITED

Pickles, H., 1993. *Crooked sixpences among the chalk: seventy-five years of schooling.* Hawes: Leading Edge Press and Publishing.

Opening New Branches in Northumberland in the 1980s

Freda Tallantyre

In 1982 I was appointed as Tutor Organiser for Northumberland, after a six-year apprenticeship as a part-time tutor for the WEA, specifically within the Women's Education programme.[1] It was both a daunting and delightful prospect — daunting as my second and last child had a year to go before entering school, and delightful because the role was so flexible and varied. I remember being asked at interview by the local authority representative on the panel if it were not too early in my family's life to be returning to full-time employment, a question that would not even then have been asked by WEA employees, and would now be on the borders of legality. I gave a robust response, which probably sounded much more confident than I felt.

When I travelled up to Hexham to receive the files from Skeff Vaughan, the former Tutor Organiser, it all seemed rather staid, though orderly, after my part-time experiences of young WEA women students. In truth there was little branch activity in Northumberland, and what existed seemed caught in a time warp. Small local groups were dedicated to their ornithology and local history classes, and even more dedicated to their tutors, who seemed to have been leading them for years. Where were all the political roots of the WEA and the radical life transforming adult education?

I had to tread with care around these groups, since branches were the supposed powerhouse of the WEA, and the Tutor Organiser their mere servant. However, there were spare resources and with a bit of creativity I felt we might be able to get something more dynamic going.

Actually there were a few more interesting things happening, with the contemporary battles between Peace and War Studies, reinvigorated by the Falklands War, and the tiny Bardon Mill Branch requested some interesting day schools and evening classes around this theme. They attracted impressive tutors from Newcastle University including, I believe, Mo Mowlam. However, the scale of these activities was never going to be great in the rural districts of Northumberland.

It was in the early Thatcher years, and unemployment was rising. Parts of the rural county suffered the deprivation associated with remoteness from urban activity, and parts the deprivation associated with poverty, and for some, like the former coalmining areas, both at once. Needless to say, these were the parts that had least injection of WEA resources, even though if you dug back into the archives you could find remarkable stories of miners seeking to learn Latin in their spare time, in order to rise above the constraints of their daily lives. This phenomenon was revived vividly in my mind last year by seeing 'The Pitman Painters' play at the National Theatre in London about the Ashington Group of artists, described above in Chapter 8. They were the archetypal WEA students, seeking erudition associated with gentlemen, yet reluctant to leave their roots behind, and reflecting the rawness of their daily lives so powerfully through their painting.

It was also the era of flourishing feminism, and women were beginning to assert their rights to work alongside their families and to reach their full potential. I had already had six years of inspiration from such students in my part-time role, and had created new classes for women in the large conurbation of Tynemouth, branching out from the programme already flourishing in the neighbouring city of Newcastle. We worked with John Harris, a sympathetic adult education manager in a local authority centre there, who welcomed our contribution to his varied programme, the arrival of new kinds of students, and above all the experiment of offering a crèche alongside the class. The Pre-School Playgroups Association (PPA) had helped us set up a crèche, which was a very new endeavour and not surrounded by all the red tape which would make it so formidable today. It had been a lifeline for many women who could not otherwise have participated, and a liberation for tutors like myself who struggled to find the kind of childcare we needed to allow us to work. Other parts of this publication chart the way classes such as this led to significant career developments for many women and the forming of lifelong friendships.

This was to be my personal starting point for creating new work in Northumberland, since it was what I understood best, and I knew there was a huge untapped market amongst women in their middle years. We began two quite different groups, one in the rural and relatively conservative Tyne Valley at Hexham, in the

---

[1] See Eileen Aird's account of the WEP in Chapter 9.

grounds of the old grammar school I had attended as a girl, and the other in the bleak and unemployment-riven town of Ashington. Both had seen former WEA activity but had struggled to keep a branch going, so there was no contest to our new activities. We ran some small classes such as literature as testers in the local libraries first, and got up the courage to launch a full-scale New Opportunities for Women course in each setting. Recruitment was vibrant for several years.

Hexham drew in some women who might have been seen as living relatively luxurious lives as the home-based wives of successful businessmen or professionals. However, that concealed the suppressed desires of many for self-realisation and the frustrations of a limited domestic context. These women may have been careful about the concept of feminism, but they demonstrated all the desires associated with it. It was perhaps indicative of their caution that they chose to style their new branch as the Tynedale Branch, without reference to its Women's Education roots, but they fought hard to bring it into being against some resistance at regional level. Out of it came some remarkable success stories — a senior academic whose career only started in her late thirties; a now well known and published poetess, who acquired her confidence in one of our creative writing classes. When Bea Campbell was researching her book on women under Thatcherism (Campbell 1987), she asked permission to come and interview some of our Tynedale students, because they demonstrated so well the creativity, flair and energy of women who provided the backbone to any political party, but were usually in the background and often at odds with many of the values their party represented.

In a strange way, this provided a link to the very different ethos of the New Opportunities class we started in Ashington, which recruited from the wives of miners, who were then in the midst of the cruellest battle of all times between government and unions. These women had little status and little money, and desperately needed to be able to get jobs to compensate for the increasingly unemployed cohort of men who were their partners. The branch they became part of was much more overtly political, as both men and women got stuck into their contest with Thatcher, and the women backing the picket lines were often as fierce opponents as the men. They did the donkey work behind the scenes, raised money, eked out food, looked after each other's bairns, and supported their men to the point of exhaustion. Then came the awful split in the community when, after months of striking and dire poverty, the pits in Ashington and Newbiggin, three miles apart, came to different conclusions about going back to work. Not only was the community split but whole families were rent ausunder.

This agony was the undercurrent of our classes, and it is probably not coincidental that the subjects pursued here were more likely to be of a social science nature than arts or humanities. Our women students carved their way through their division with courage and tenacity, united in frustration again when, at the end of the strike, they felt so betrayed by their men and the unions who refused to acknowledge fully the roles they had played.

As usual in these contexts, the Tutor Organiser had to become utterly parasitical and beg, borrow, if not steal, from the local authorities in terms of premises, facilities and support. Relations with Northumberland councils were excellent, and schools, libraries and other centres could not have been more helpful, recognising the educational capital that the WEA would bring into their areas, to complement the rather blander forms of adult education they could offer. In rural settings, you have to be extremely creative to support a small class, and I well remember holding classes in an old lady's house in Corbridge with the precious book box delivered from the local library kept under her table from week to week. After the class I would drive her round to the local teashop to meet her friends. Another class was held in the early evening in the upstairs room of a working men's club. At the end, the largely male group would say to me, 'Eh, thanks hinny. It's a pity you can't join us downstairs for a drink'. It was still the days when the bar in the club was an entirely male enclave, which seemed somewhat contradictory to the education we were delivering.

In the case of Hexham and Ashington, it was the local high schools which were accommodating, before the concept of community high schools had really taken off. In Hexham, we used the old dining-hall for our class, and in Ashington we used a portacabin in the school yard. Luxurious it was not, but our spirits were high. In Ashington it was essential to provide a crèche, or most women could not have attended and indeed some respite from motherhood was probably as welcome as the class itself. Moreover, the students sometimes benefited from the wisdom of the crèche workers in tackling the problems of the kids, as well as from the wisdom of their class tutors. I recall a three-year-old whose behaviour was completely transformed when a crèche worker delicately pointed out to a mum that his hyperactivity could be connected to his diet.

Once he had all the crisps and other e-filled foods removed, he became a charming and sociable child, rather than a whirling dervish.

The Ashington Branch was bifurcated into the women's division, described above, and the largely unemployed men's division which was based at the local unemployment centre. My colleague, Simon Henderson, Tutor Organiser for the unemployed was of enormous assistance in setting up this arm, which would have challenged my credibility as a middle-class woman. We talked over together with the men what they might benefit from, and they were first cautiously, then later enthusiastically interested in acquiring a degree of literacy and political understanding to enable them to manage their lives and their campaigns better in their straitened circumstances. The men's courses were usually shorter and more pragmatic than the women's, but the fact that it got them talking and sharing their frustration was in itself a medicine. Often they were shy and embarrassed about their lack of schooling, as their forefather miners had been earlier in the century, but once their tongues were loosened, they began to see ways to work together to rebuild their tortured communities and lives. They became champions for regeneration, lobbyists and bid writers, and Bill, their leader, became one of the most powerful and articulate regional volunteers in the WEA District. It was heartening to see them take control of their own environments and refuse to be beaten down by governments many hundreds of miles away geographically, and even more psychologically, from their dilemmas.

These two communities, each about twenty-five miles away from the nearest city, were large enough to sustain a branch of their own, and to draw in people from the immediate surrounding area. However, many others were too small, and had poor local transport, so residents were unable either to travel to study or sustain a branch of their own. In these cases, we had to ignore the branch structure and direct some resource to stimulating more modest efforts.

In Prudhoe, trading unashamedly on the local knowledge and contacts of my sister, I managed to start a women's day class which began with Yoga and Alternative Medicine, and gravitated towards more academic studies. This was a regular recipe, on the spectrum of Maslow's (1954) hierarchy of needs, to tackle health and well-being first, and then provide food for the mind. I well remember a meeting with a few local women in Cramlington when they struggled to grasp the concept of the negotiated curriculum, so the conversation can be caricatured as 'What would you like?' 'Well, what can we have?' However, we did get a class established, which moved along a similar spectrum.

This is a conversation I have had many times since in higher education, especially in the context of those at work, or employers whose needs we negotiate to meet. They show the same kind of disbelief that higher education can provide in this way, and indeed the WEA was doing it decades before HE got the message.

It was an object lesson to me how much could be done with so little, and many years later the Chief Executive Officer of the Council for Industry and Higher Education asked me with gaping jaw where I got such ideas from when funding small projects in HE as part of the Enterprise in Higher Education initiative, and getting big returns. With pride I told him a little about adult education and its ways of operating.

Every year the resource situation seemed to get tighter and tighter, and classes in the summer were constrained. However, when working in tentative communities, you cannot afford to let momentum stop for six months of the year or you lose your hard-won students. Somehow we managed to scrape together summer schools, or six-morning classes, and get students through to the summer holidays when children's needs took over anyway. We also did what we could to offer progression to those who were not yet ready to move on into higher education. An extra year was often all it took. The one thing I was resolved was that our precious resources would not become the funds of exclusive, self-perpetuating clubs.

This might seem a tension in a democratic organisation where the people's wishes are meant to be the deciding factor. However, I have learned in my subsequent career as a middle, then a senior manager, that one has to find ways to enable all the people to participate and not just the few who might wish to be seen as their representatives. I know our work touched lives and in some cases transformed them for ever. This, for me, justifies sticking my neck out on numerous occasions and risking some of our resources in a new community.

My whole career after the WEA has been spent ensuring that those who were not best served by the school system, but had the courage to take the first steps as adults, do not get blocked further in the system in seeking to fulfil their wildest dreams. Moreover, I have learned more about pedagogy, the negotiated curriculum and the power of formative assessment in adult education than in any other branch of education, having now worked across the broad spectrums of schools, further and higher education.

SOURCES CITED

Campbell, Beatrix, 1987. *Iron Ladies: Why do women vote Tory?* London: Virago.

Maslow, Abraham, 1954. *Motivation and Personality.* New York: Harper and

Educate, Agitate, Organise:
Reflections on Trade Union Education

Tom Nesbit

In 1980 I was appointed as the Education Officer for the Northern region of the Transport & General Workers' Union (T&G) and worked there for most of the following decade. At that time the T&G was Britain's largest and most influential union and arguably one of its most politically progressive, at least to those of us with a radical stripe. With a newly-minted degree from the Open University and a decade of union activity behind me, I felt pretty capable of handling my new responsibilities. These involved developing and arranging a range of courses for union members, shop stewards and other activists in an area that stretched from the Scottish border south as far as, and including, North Yorkshire and Cumbria: pretty much the same region as the WEA's Northern District at the time.

However, I felt much less sure of just how the union's educational activities were or might be better located within the broader provision of adult and workers' education, especially those in Northern England. This was an area with a rich tradition of independent, working-class activity and education: the Chartists, the Co-operative Movement, mechanics institutes, workmen's libraries, university extra-mural education and the people's colleges had all been developed or thrived there. Moreover, while the WEA itself might have begun in London, it had in its eighty odd years grown into an energetic national organisation with considerable organisational and professional experience. It also had maintained close ties to the union movement and had developed its systems of local branch organisation, democratic decision-making and the tutorial class model as a consequence of such links. So, as a brand new union official with a large mandate I was somewhat in awe of this vibrant historical and political context — just how was my work expected to fit in or match up?

I needn't have worried. The Northern District was one of most vital of the WEA's regions. It had worked in close partnership with the regional union movement and local workers' organisations since its inception. For decades it had organised courses for the area's unions — most notably the Northumberland and Durham Federations of the National Union of Mineworkers but several other major unions (including the T&G) as well. It was a central part of the TUC's regional education system of day-release courses for union representatives. It provided courses on cultural, social and political issues for working people in the region's industrial and urban centres as well as the smaller, but no less active, rural towns and villages. It formed close ties with voluntary organisations and providers of workers' education both at home and abroad. It organised study tours for workers to visit other European countries. It provided opportunities for local branch representatives to discuss and decide upon the sort of courses to offer. And, it had a dedicated Industrial Studies Tutor Organiser, Tom Ellison, whose job it was to promote and co-ordinate all this activity. He, together with District Secretary Michael Standen, could not have been more welcoming to me and supportive of the District's ongoing attempts to provide and lobby for a broad range of workers and adult education in a national political climate that was less than sympathetic, (these were the Thatcher years). As a relative neophyte in this astonishingly rich world of adult and workers' education, I could not have landed in a better place.

Thinking on those times brings back fond memories of people I met (several of whom have remained close friends), and the network of contacts, colleagues and comrades we developed, the activities and approaches we imagined and debated, often in the Crown Posada and other bars close to the WEA office in central Newcastle, and then put to the test. This was a time of intensive energy and activity for me, and the contacts I made helped shaped the ideas and approaches to adult and workers' education that I have been lucky enough to pursue in my professional life ever since. Of course, ten years of intense and committed activity is far too much to capture here. Instead, I will reflect on a few of the outstanding memories that typify what I think of as the essential essence of the WEA Northern District and the ways that it informed and shaped trade union education and one trade union educator in particular. As 'think globally, act locally' is now a common organising slogan, I'll follow it here. I'll start internationally and work back to the local and then the personal.

International

The WEA had been co-ordinating international study tours for a number of years prior to my arrival. In the early 1980s, Tom Ellison led a visit of twenty trade union officials and representatives, including me, to the Hamburg region of *Arbeit und Leben,* the German adult educational organisation that sought to promote workers' education and the democratic reconstruction of post-war Germany through principles of social justice, equal opportunity, and solidarity. *Arbeit und Leben* ('work and life') was the model of a successful collaboration between two organisations that had not always seen eye to eye: the German trade union and the *Volkshochschule* movements (roughly equivalent to our old Technical Colleges, which had long been regarded by the union movement as too decentralized and bourgeois). Its basic goals were to provide political education for democracy through supplementing the German unions' basic trade union training with opportunities to consider political, historical and social questions in much greater depth. Through an imaginative approach to linking vocational and political education in a residential setting, *Arbeit und Leben* had been able to attract a number of young workers to their courses and introduce perspectives that were not covered in the curricula of more conventional educational institutions such as local technical colleges.

The twenty of us stayed in *Arbeit und Leben*'s residential facilities with the students, sat in on their courses, talked with them and their tutors, played football with them (they won, repeatedly!), visited other vocational and adult educational providers and explored our various perspectives on workers' education. As might be expected, finding common cause was high on our agenda and the visit cemented relationships between countries and people who, within living memory, had been fighting a bitter war with one another. One of my fondest memories is of a miner's union official from Blyth with a most pronounced local accent, (even those of us from the North-East had a hard time understanding him at best), deep in conversation with a German counterpart who spoke no English whatsoever. As the steins of lager arrived and were quickly emptied, their debates seemed to grow both more serious and more uproarious at the same time. Eventually with a mighty crack, both they and their table all collapsed onto the floor into a jumble of legs, arms, splintered wood, beer glasses and laughter. It would be hard to imagine a better physical example of the interdependence and essential solidarity of the international working class!

A couple of years later, the Northern District became interested in fostering closer links with *Arbetarnas Bildningsförbund* (ABF), the WEA's Swedish counterpart. ABF's Östergötland District in south-eastern Sweden was particularly receptive to the possibility of an exchange and sent Janet Ericsson and a couple of other officials on a study tour of north-eastern England. After several days full of meetings and discussions, it was felt that visiting a couple of the region's more scenic cultural and industrial sites might also be advantageous. One particular rainy day we resisted Janet's request to check out the Metrocentre, then Europe's largest shopping mall, and Michael Standen and I made the group climb up to Penshaw Monument where we all got thoroughly soaked. Having missed out on the possibility of a pub lunch (much to Michael's chagrin), we decided to move on to Beamish Hall, the former National Coal Board offices, which was then being run as an adult education centre and had a café of some renown. Outside the Hall was a small market with stalls selling the produce and handicrafts recently made by some of the local jam-making and art groups. After she bought the requisite gooseberry preserve, woolly hat and a bizarre three inch replica of a shepherd's crook, Janet found an audiotape (this was long before CDs) of traditional north-eastern music. It had started to rain heavily again and we repaired to my car for shelter. The strains of Billy Pigg's Northumbrian smallpipes streamed out in counterpoint to the rain washing down the windscreen. For me, it was an ideal Durham day, but I'm not sure the Swedes fully grasped that some of the region's significant labour shrines can only be truly appreciated in a downpour.

Despite this rather inauspicious start, the WEA/ABF links prospered and later that year, Vic Cadaxa, Tutor Organiser for Sunderland and Wearside, and I went to Sweden to plan a study exchange of trades unionists, adult educators and leaders of something called 'study circles', a term with which I was then unfamiliar. We met with national and regional trade union education officials, were plied with education materials (much of it written in English!), visited the newly refurbished Folkets Hus in Central Stockholm, got our photographs taken next to the statue of Master Palm, an early agitator for trade union and socialist ideas, and learned more about Sweden's 'study circle democracy' and the role of ABF. Although ABF was a politically independent organisation, it shared the labour movement's values of democracy, diversity, justice and equality and its philosophy was based on a deliberately socialist perspective of wanting to provide most to those who received the least. Its educational approach provided for people to study together and form their own opinions on key social issues; everyone should have the opportunity to gain the knowledge to influence their own situations and be able to shape both local and global developments. In fact, the ABF had been particularly successful generating international collaborations—especially around such issues as union rights, human rights and fair trade—that contributed to democratic development in other countries. ABF educators had worked extensively with the anti-apartheid movements in Southern Africa and had actively supported the then illegal African National Congress and various other South African trades union educational endeavours.

Although the planned tour never came about — I forget why — the links prospered and there were a series of staff exchanges between the WEA and ABF in succeeding years. I did eventually learn more about study circles — even introducing them to a reluctant T&G — and, together with my wife Adrienne, ran a weekend course on aspects of North American culture and society for Swedish study circle leaders who were planning a study tour of the USA. Through these links I was also able to visit and be a keynote speaker one year at the Nordic Adult Education Association's annual conference. This was by far the best adult education conference I have ever been to, bar none. Sixty delegates from Norway, Sweden, Denmark, Iceland, Finland and Latvia kept me occupied, entertained and never truly sober for three straight days. We started the first day at one folk high school, spent the second day cruising the Swedish Archipelago and finished the third at another folk high school, totally exhausted. I think I learned more — probably by osmosis — about Nordic approaches to adult and workers' education than I could have ever gleaned from months of reading. My personal friendship with Janet Ericsson, a truly dedicated adult educator, also prospered, and Adrienne and I were able to visit her in Sweden several times and host her and various family members when we later moved to San Francisco and then Vancouver.

Local

Although national political power lay with Margaret Thatcher's Conservative Party, North-East England was still Labour's heartland. Unfortunately, this did not really protect the region from the government's economic policies, which led to widespread closures, burgeoning unemployment, and industrial legislation that seriously eroded workers' rights and precipitated a steady decline in union membership. To counter these effects, unions became even more extensively engaged in most of the region's economic, social and political affairs. The T&G was especially deeply involved: the union's regional secretary chaired the regional Labour Party and other full-time and elected officials served as city and town councillors and were active in the TUC and local trades councils. Yet beyond the explicitly political realm, there was also much to do to advance the cause of working people. Because it was often so closely embedded in many of the region's progressive social and cultural activities, the WEA provided an invaluable entrée for me. I was quickly introduced to and began to form links with many of the region's more progressive and energetic organisations. For example, just in Tyneside alone were the independent and radical Trades Union Studies Information Unit (TUSIU, which the WEA had helped to found), then housed in NUPE's regional office in Jesmond, the Days of Hope bookstore on Westgate Road (one of the very few places in the North-East to buy trade union, socialist or alternative literature), Amber Films (the film and photography collective whose social documentary work was built around long-term engagement with the region's working class and marginalized communities), Tyneside Free Press, the Gateshead-based Trade Films, and the old Tyneside Cinema on Pilgrim St. (where the T&G sponsored a special showing of *Comrades*, Bill Douglas' film about the Tolpuddle Martyrs). Many of these organisations were within walking distance of the WEA District Offices and it would be rare to walk around central Newcastle without running into someone from a group with whom the union or the WEA were involved in some way.

Despite their commitment to working people and labour organisations, many of these groups did not have an explicitly educational mandate. Although making the conceptual links between working-class culture, politics and education has never been too difficult in Britain, especially after Raymond Williams' ground-breaking work, the greater struggle has been to see those links developed, supported and sustained in workers' organisations. Especially when union budgets are tight, anything that is not explicitly job- or workplace-related can be viewed as irrelevant or unnecessary and there is an in-built suspicion of anything that cannot be controlled or determined in advance. However, adopting a fairly broad mandate and with an approach of acting first and seeking permission later, I was able to find ways to introduce many of these groups into the T&G's educational endeavours. Here, the WEA could prove invaluable as an intermediary. I could usefully justify to the union's more reactionary elements that I wasn't wasting the members' money on some mysterious group of Marxist artists to introduce agit-prop theatre at a union weekend course but emphasize instead that, as they had been already 'sanctioned' in some way by the WEA, any questions or concerns might properly be best raised with them first. Of course, by the time that happened (if it ever did), it was far too late to reschedule any course activities. This might not have been the most direct way to introduce and support different understandings of the class struggle but it was certainly quite effective!

Despite such mischievousness though, the 1980s were a difficult decade for union educators. Recruitment to traditional union courses fell overall, and in some cases by up to 50%, within five years. However, it also spurred on some unions — and the T&G was clearly in the vanguard — to develop new areas and new approaches to education for its officials and representatives. Special courses for women representatives, courses on topics such as anti-racism, pensions, sexual harassment, the media and new technology, and courses based on models of distance learning and popular education flourished. Unions also began to target new groups, such as union members or young workers, and to provide courses in educational methods (often based on study circle principles) for 'lay tutors', experienced union representatives who wanted to become discussion leaders or instructors themselves.

Most of the T&G's conventional educational courses were held during the day, either at the workplace training facilities of local companies or the various union offices around the region, and they tended to be taught by me and other officials. However, the more original or innovative courses — or where we didn't want any employer interference — were organised on a residential basis over a weekend. For these I drew heavily on the WEA's experience and advice for suitable instructors and locations. For example, the Rex Hotel in Whitley Bay had long been a venue for union education. Whitley Bay was by then fading as a preferred summer holiday destination for workers and their families but it still suggested memories of time away from home and the anticipation of sea, sand, fish and chips and cheap beer. The Rex Hotel had seen better days but it offered preferential weekend rates, copious portions of food and, if you could put up with its archaic approach to plumbing (it was said that all its rooms had hot and cold running water but never both at the same time), it was convenient, cost-effective and adequately comfortable. One of its highlights was the lounge bar: huge, semi-circular and extensively mirrored where, to the sounds of two ancient sisters who played the piano, you could work your way around the amazing array of whiskies displayed behind the bar — some of which were rumoured to be as old as the pianists. No one in living memory had ever completed the whisky trail of starting at one end and reaching the other in one sitting. Frequent course-goers knew to place markers indicating where they had reached and where to take up again at their next visit.

Longer residential courses were also a feature of the T&G's educational provision. Each Easter during the 1980s, the union ran a week-long school in collaboration with the WEA at Durham University's Hatfield College. It was a large and complex undertaking: anywhere between a hundred and a hundred and fifty union members from every part of Northern England studied one of a variety of courses that developed their knowledge and skills to be effective union representatives. Those who lived locally travelled in each day, but about three-quarters of the group stayed in the College's residential accommodation close to the city centre. Having such a large group on site with little to do on an evening provided a wonderful opportunity to introduce some extra-curricular educational activities before the serious carousing began. Of course, the industrial and other political struggles of the day were paramount: TUC officials and Labour Party members of parliament would visit and speechify; striking miners from the local coalfields or the unemployed workers movements would come and rally support. Yet it was also a time to introduce broader and less predictable perspectives: both Amber and Trade Films came and showed excerpts of their work and discussed radical film-making; someone even brought along Ken Loach one year. Sid Chaplin,[1] Keith Armstrong and other worker-writers would read stories and poetry about working-class people and associated issues. Folks from the North-East Labour History Society would speak about local examples of Labour history and discuss the importance of oral and working peoples' histories. Community theatre groups would come and perform excerpts from working-class plays that they had written themselves or drawn from the work of playwrights like C. P. Taylor, David Hare or Willy Russell.

The last night of the school was always the occasion for some extra frivolity, singing and dancing. One of the more memorable highlights was the socialist magician and ventriloquist Ian Saville, who had developed a relentlessly funny act that attempted to 'make international capitalism and exploitation disappear'. With the help of a giant 'talking' cardboard cut-out of Karl Marx (who revealed that he always wanted his theories performed as magic tricks and only consented to write books at Engels' insistence), Ian would perform stunts like 'the class struggle rope trick', in which three red cords explained class-relations before a

[1] See Chapter 17 for Sid Chaplin's reminiscences.

revolution or 'the great privatisation swindle', 'where public assets dissolve before your very eyes'! Also, the 1980s were a time when every left-wing group worth its salt seemed to have its own band or choir, and the good ones would be hired to coax and lead the assembled throng through some early rock-and-roll and Labour and revolutionary classics. It sounds hopelessly idealistic now, but to hear a group of a hundred and more trade unionists link arms and blast out 'The Internationale' or 'The Red Flag' at the end of a week-long union education course, you could almost believe that the revolution (or at least the demise of Margaret Thatcher) could not be too far away.

Apart from its specific trade union education work, the WEA Northern District was also active in other areas of educational provision that I and the T&G were always glad to promote and support. The District was notably involved in women's education and its explorations of feminist perspectives on education had a major effect. Though the notion that 'the personal is political' is now commonplace, at that time it was seen as ground-breaking in traditionally patriarchal Northern England and especially in its male-dominated trade unions. As a result of the WEA's initiatives and, in an attempt to increase women's participation in the union, the T&G began organising regional women-only courses in the mid-1980s which soon became established as a regular feature of the union's educational provision. The District also pioneered many other educational initiatives for disadvantaged or under-represented groups of adults. For example, first Simon Henderson (who had been a WEA Tutor Organiser in the West of Scotland), and then Mary Lewis developed educational opportunities for the unemployed and those who worked with them. Mary was Tutor Organiser for South Durham and Cleveland, then moving on to the Leeds area to hold a similar post with WEA Yorkshire North District. Simon, in particular, became a close friend and colleague and we later battled a ceaseless wind cycling the Outer Hebrides and, more sedately, co-authored an article on the politics of union education for the WEA's Trade Union Studies Journal. Although Simon left the WEA mid-decade to pursue more artistic endeavours, he and I have remained close and, in the true spirit of international collaboration, we were able to celebrate jointly our sixtieth birthdays on a Northumberland beach with many old friends and colleagues.

Personal

During the early 1980s — a time of increasing government restraint — trade union education in Britain grew from a fairly modest provision into one of adult education's largest sectors. Of course, it was not to last. Towards the end of the decade, the continuing decline in union membership and a shift in union emphasis towards more workplace related and service oriented functions combined with tighter restrictions on the use of public funding for union education to restrict the earlier educational innovations. Having initially become a union educator to expand the capacity of unions and their members as social and political actors and to be able to say 'yes' to initiatives rather than 'no' or 'later', I became increasingly disillusioned. The failure of the Labour Party to secure power in the 1987 election was a particularly bitter blow and led to increased polarisation between the left and right political factions within the union. The position of progressive union educators grew increasingly untenable and when a couple of family issues intervened, I left the T&G (and subsequently Britain) to see how these ideas might be better explored in North America.

In retrospect, my time spent involved with WEA taught me a great deal: mostly by the way it did things as much as anything it professed. It welcomed newcomers and provided myriad opportunities to become engaged on many levels. Indeed, not too long after I moved to Newcastle, I was asked to sit on the District Committee, attend several national and joint regional conferences and later represent the District on one of the WEA's National Committees. So, I learned the benefits of, and the necessity for, active participation: not just in committee work but for educational activities as well. In fact, perhaps my most important learning from this period was discovering that effective education is built upon learners' own experiences and interests, links them to a wider social and critical understanding and then encourages social and civic action and involvement. In later years, I would find this expressed more eloquently by writers like Paolo Freire, Myles Horton and C. Wright Mills, but it was in the WEA that I encountered those ideas firsthand.

The WEA also allowed me the space with which to view trade union education and my own work through a different and more reflective lens. Conventionally, unions are reactive organisations; their structure and approaches tend to follow changes in patterns of industrial employment and economic and political systems. In this, trade union education occupies a unique and sometimes troubling place: at once a major vehicle for unions to explain and promote their existing structures, policies and values and also a way of re-imagining them. That is, trade union education done well promises a key way of identifying and exploring potential changes to the existing order, a means of raising workers' consciousness and abilities to promote and fight for any changes, and a system through which future union activists and leaders can emerge and develop. The tensions engendered by such multiplicity of roles have been endemic to union education for over a century and have provided it, and workers' education more generally, with a great deal of vitality and ideological fervour.

Thus, trade union education becomes a site of often intense political struggle for knowledge and power. Indeed, the history of workers' education within the WEA provides a good example, just ask anyone who remembers the Plebs League or the National Council of Labour Colleges (McIlroy 1996).) This struggle usually revolves around a couple of key aspects. The first concerns the balance of collective versus individual characteristics of education. Here, some feel that union approaches to education and learning should focus on building collective capacity rather than, or instead of, merely promoting individual transformation or economic productivity. As with the best adult education, trade union education has always been grounded in the notion that no matter how bad situations may get, people can always intervene, usually collectively, to improve them.

A second aspect concerns the enduring tension between education and learning. Most trade union educators now accept that union approaches to education should adopt a learner-centred approach and focus largely on workers' own identification of their concerns and interests. However others feel that it should also adopt a critical role of extending this into questioning accepted orthodoxies. For many workers, union education is often the first place they systematically encounter ideas that challenge the mainstream. It is also a place where, contrary to much of their schooling, workers learn that their own way of seeing the world represents a valid place from which to start challenging accepted beliefs and tenets. Trade union education can facilitate the development of a critical consciousness that fosters worker's understandings of their past, present and future and encourages them to act to address inequalities.

Of course, such ideas did not come to me either overnight or fully-formed, but instead were developed through the WEA-sponsored visits to sister associations in other regions and countries and participating in long, long discussions with other union educators both abroad and at home. I learned that there can be no abstract, apolitical or universal approach to trade union education. So much depends on the economic and social environments within particular countries and contests, the extent to which public education systems have been developed, the state of class relations, and the nature of political attitudes within particular trade unions and their movements. And, if such diversity could be seen abroad, why did it not also exist at home?

I also learned the importance of what we now think of as critical pedagogy. At the outset, I naively assumed that teaching, unlike content, was acontextual and apolitical. How one taught was essentially neutral and secondary to, or disassociated from, what was being taught. Yet through discussions with union educators in the WEA and elsewhere, I began to explore how teaching practices shaped people's attitudes towards education, learning and society at large. Of course, it's now easy to accept that how we teach has a lot to do with what we expect and want people to become but at the time it was a relatively novel idea. So, I began to question dominant approaches to teaching in union education and to promote the capacity to unsettle and irritate complacency and passivity. I began to ask such questions as: What counts as knowledge? How is such knowledge produced and disseminated? Whose interests are served by different forms of knowledge? Do certain forms of knowledge legitimate or privilege one set of interests above another? How might alternate forms of knowledge production be generated? I began to see the importance of stimulating and provoking learners to ask their own questions rather than just adopt others. Instead of ironing out complexity, I began to celebrate it, problematise it, and make it critical.

I also slowly learned that pedagogical expertise is not in itself sufficient. At one WEA workshop I encountered one of the classic statements about the role of instructors in workers' education (written, I think by G. D. H. Cole in the 1920s):

> Unless the tutor feels his fellowship with the workers to be more important to his life than any professional loyalty […] he will not be a good tutor. Tutors are not merely instructors, but essentially participators with their students in a community social purpose — the strengthening of the working class for the intelligent mastery of its problems and the improvement of the quality of working life.

Relishing its somewhat archaic style, I used to keep this quotation pinned on my office notice-board to show to those we were potentially hiring as T&G course instructors. Anyone who argued with, or (more likely) worked against, its sentiments tended not to have too long a relationship with the union as a tutor.

But despite all the theories and the ideas, perhaps my most abiding memory of those times, and the deepest belief I feel I gained from involvement with the WEA, is the now obvious notion that people matter. Not some idealized or abstract notion of 'people' but the very people present in the room. And, perhaps as importantly, not to get too wrapped in the importance of what we were doing that we could not occasionally put it aside. My memories of the WEA Northern District recognise and celebrate its general collegiality and good humour. Although we had serious business to discuss at the District Council, I can't think of too many other adult education meetings where I've laughed so much. And so many WEA folks were influential in promoting and manifesting this spirit of good fellowship: Eileen Aird (Tutor Organiser for Women's Education),[2] Liz Armstrong (District Treasurer 1976-80), Janet Atkinson (District Chair 1984-88), Jonathan Brown (Senior Counsellor with the Open University and member of the District Committee 1977-93), Victor Cadaxa,[3] Gilbert Edwards (Tutor Organiser for North Cumbria), Tess Owens (District Chair 1981-84), Freda Tallantyre (Tutor Organiser for Northumberland)[4] and Jill Younger (Administrative Assistant in the District Office). In particular, Michael Standen (District Secretary 1976-95) quickly turned from a colleague into first a mentor and then one of my closest friends. We shared so much and I will always miss him deeply.

These feelings of solidarity, collegiality and generosity have stayed with me and sustained me for the past quarter of a century and I've tried to practice them wherever my work has taken me. To close, one example will have to suffice. Although his day-to-day work had little to do with trade union education, I always found Gilbert Edwards a particularly engaging colleague. He was an ex-railwayman who worked in Cumbria and his ability to glean food — "lunchboxing" he called it — was legendary. His jacket pockets seemed to grow pockets as he stowed away the sandwiches, buns and the odd apple he thought necessary for the long journey home from Newcastle after late evening Council meetings. 'Never know when you might break down and be caught short, lad' is a caution I've always remembered, and when I've not followed it, pretty much always lived to regret.

SOURCE CITED

McIlroy, J., 1996. 'Independent Working Class Education and Trade Union Education and Training' In: Fieldhouse, R. (ed.). *A History of Modern British Adult Education.* Leicester: NIACE.

---

[2] For Eileen Aird's recollections, see Chapter 9 above.
[3] See Chapter 15 for Victor's account of his work with the WEA.
[4] See Chapter 11 above.

An Uphill Drive: The Northern District 1976 to 1995[1]

Michael Standen

This section of the WEA's hundred and the Northern District's ninety-three years of existence is more in the nature of memoir than history as was the first part of the book. 'Memoir' might not be the right word either; it suggests what each of us remembers about parts of our lives, incidents or episodes lit by the subjective and essentially partial lamp of memory. We seem often to remember what we want to — often the good times, the vivid moments, sometimes darker, recurrent buried events. An institution so noble[2] — or not — has no memory but it does have records. Even records of course are to some degree shaped by the perceptions and wishes of the recorders. The Recording Angel is never sufficiently ethereal.

The following account is both a subjective and a retrospective view of the time when I acted as Secretary to the Northern District.

Getting to know you ...

My first knowledge of the District, almost my first acquaintance with the 'real' North. was being interviewed at Carlisle for the post of Tutor Organiser in West Cumberland. It was the late summer of 1964. Three years previously I had graduated and for that time lectured in Manchester colleges of Further Education. Interesting work but I felt a leaning towards adult education, bolstered by a two-week summer school in Oxford (1963). West Cumberland, called 'the jewel in the crown' by then-chairman, impressive, Shakespeare-quoting Scottish miner William Allan, turned out to be rather a bleared diamond and economically depressed.

But the County Director of Education for Cumberland, Gordon Bessey, was a leading light and had established Further Education Centres in each of the often newly-built, comprehensive schools. This was ten years before 'Cumbria' came on the map and my three there were happy and productive. I learnt to work with the new FE Tutors and with the old branches and also to tune in to the way the Cumbrian regards the rest of the world and the North-East in particular. It was a privilege to know pre-war WEA stalwarts and people of the calibre of poet Norman Nicholson. Thus in 1967 when District Secretary Charles Hocking transferred me to Durham, still as Tutor Organiser, I came with a semi-Cumbrian perspective.

... to know all about you.

In the mid seventies, with eleven years' WEA service now, I found myself in a quandary, with my wife having been offered a year as visiting professor at Fairbanks, University of Alaska. We had two boys, then aged six and nine. An exciting opportunity and after much effort to obtain unpaid leave I went. It was a difficult time for the District (as alluded to by Ivan Corbett, 2003) and in 1976, not without reluctance, I agreed to the role of Acting District Secretary. It is fair to say that morale was low and there were severe financial problems. Refreshed by Alaskan absence and grateful for much support at that time, I moved into Bank Chambers. The post (as 'Responsible Officer' of the designated 'Responsible Body') meant simply that its incumbent had to raise the money, manage the staff, support the voluntary movement and deliver an approved programme. I possessed by then quite a long background in tutoring and organising but a shallow understanding of what the presiding mysteries involved.

On my side were a wholehearted belief in the voluntary movement if actively and sensitively encouraged and a genuine respect for staff colleagues in whom one had to trust and to whom delegate as freely as possible. The District's recent history also suggested a working principle, to make all information widely available to all. That was where I found myself, at the beginning of what was to be almost twenty years at the helm, sharp end, or 'sticky end of the stick' — or in the driving seat.

The driving mirror

One of the first things done — understandably not an obvious priority to all — was to find out the history of the District. Governments have become ever fonder of moving the furniture and relabelling everything. The Government at that time had just created the Manpower Services Commission from bits of outworn Civil

---

[1] The WEA is grateful to Val and Guy Standen for permission to republish this chapter, which originally appeared in Standen (2003a:82-93). There has been minimal editing of the original paper and where there are changes these are explained in the footnotes.

[2] *'An institution so noble'* This refers back to Ivan Corbett's 1980 history of the Northern District which is republished in Standen (2003).

Service: it was our first opportunist funding grab and the upshot was Ivan Corbett and his 70th anniversary history (2003). Annual Reports (one or two early ones missing) were found in a cupboard and a quite rich archive hunted out (now properly conserved at Blandford House in the Tyne and Wear Archives). We kept to the 'octavo' format of the first reports (or A5 as it became) and the Annual Reports (1976-94) are the basis of the more 'objective' account of the period making up the rest of this section.

Speedometer

It was deemed necessary by the new District Committee of 1976-77 to reinstate the full class-lists in the Annual Reports showing place, duration, tutor and enrolment. This was a public record of provision and from it basic and comparable year-on-year statistics could be derived. The pocket calculator had arrived just in time! From the earlier history it is clear that the WEA put great emphasis on the three-year tutorial class; this was what first attracted funding (one of the founder Albert Mansbridge's greatest coups). The three-year tutorial also carried a freight of moral worth, a quite numerous membership, commitment to written work, in short almost an idealised version of the university degree. The 'average', or typical tutorial student in those early days was male, aged 28 and quite possibly a schoolteacher. It is interesting to note that the profile of the first OU student body in the early seventies was exactly the same. As Ivan Corbett shows, the shorter and more flexible course and the development of daytime provision had struggled into being over many years. By the late 1970s the three-year tutorial was part shibboleth, part fiction and the linkage with the universities was everywhere coming under strain. Because of our particular history and because of support from Ted Hughes of Newcastle and especially John Dixon of Durham, the two directors of the University 'Responsible Body' departments, Northern kept the old alliance longer than most Districts.

Our policy of showing in detail the educational and financial outcomes of the eighteen years from the autumn of 1976 to the summer of 1994 makes possible some generalisation. Activity was recorded in 'class meetings' rather than student hours. This was the traditional unit and comprised both the one and a half and the two-hour class. Thus, to take one year at random, 1983-4, we find a 'Grand Total' of class meetings given as 6,853; also shown are seventeen sub-totals of meetings under different length and type of course: for example 'Sessional', 'Joint (University)', 'Women's Education Programme — All-day', '2-day Residential'. From 1976 to 1982 there had also been printed percentages of provision under four 'DES' categories. The DES was the Department of Education and Science, a name-change of the Ministry of Education dating back to Harold Wilson in the 1960s. (There have been several subsequent changes of course.) These four categories were 'Academic and Liberal' (the branch programme), 'Industrial and TU', 'Social and Political' (the old WETUC scheme) and 'Educationally and Socially Disadvantaged' (under which we included, for example, Women's Education and work with people with physical disabilities). They stemmed from the Russell Report of 1973 and were essentially an attempt to shape WEA provision to help — in present-day parlance — the achievement of government targets. You can imagine the discussions all those years ago, but the Northern District (one of whose own, Alderman Mrs Ellen Mitchell of Northumberland County Council, had sat on the Russell Committee)[3] accepted the Russell Report and — with the structural unemployment of the 1080s and the groundswell of what had started as 'Women's Lib' in the early 1970s — the District led the WEA field in delivering the priority categories for many years.

The year 1983-4, then, yielded 6,853 class meetings, a figure which was slightly above the median or average of the eighteen recorded years which — with a low of 5,205 and a high of 7,563 — was remarkably constant.

A similar picture emerges from student enrolment figures. In the 1983-4 session 8,734 students are recorded. This happens to be the highest annual figure, the lowest being 6,472. The average is 7,350 and, from the occasional reference to such figures in *So Noble An Institution* (Corbett 2003), it is tempting to think that the 'natural constituency' of the District is some seven thousand people per year.

Fuel gauge (running on empty)

In 1976-77 District income was £100K; this rose steadily in a fairly manner over eighteen years to become £533K. Some years had a surplus of income over expenditure and some a deficit. The total spent during this period of the District's history was about six million and though no reserves were built up the balance at the end of the sheet was about one per cent of total spend. This continuing year-on-year achievement was owing to the close working between District Honorary Treasurers, the District Secretary and the Administrative Officer, Judy Champion, who put in nearly forty years' service from 1963. If we stick to our randomly chosen year 1983-84, we find an expenditure of £305,048 and an income of £301,661, meaning a deficit of

---

[3] Ellen Mitchell served on the Committee of Inquiry into non-vocational adult education in England and Wales. The Committee reported in 1973 sat under the Chairmanship of Sir Lionel Russell.

about one per cent and a tiny balance (which is what in accounting terms the organisation is worth at the end of the financial year) of just £519. This was a fairly typical year and income came two thirds from central government (DES) with student fees bringing 12 per cent and local authorities 11 per cent (the two next-biggest categories). Roughly a quarter of the money was spent paying part-time tutors, 45 per cent paying Tutor Organisers and about a fifth on administration.

Nearly ten years later (1992-93), on a total of £538K, central government grant had fallen from two-thirds to under half of income and now, instead of single grant-in-aid to the Responsible Body, it had four separate categories, all requiring jumping through hoops. Student fees had risen to 16 per cent of total income and local authority support had fallen by 3 per cent. Significantly, a tenth of income is now shown as 'EEC' (European Economic Community). Outgoings remain remarkably similar to those of ten years before (given in the paragraph above).

It is worth pointing out that the DES threatened to claw back any significant surplus or attempt to build up a reserve. The only choice open to the District (to switch metaphorical transport) was to sail as close as possible to the wind.

The road taken

The 67th Annual Report (1977) takes us back to a time of high inflation, of baling out by the DES and of changing arrangements by government to encourage the WEA to follow the 'Russell Categories'. But it is the people of the period, the spirit of it and the genuine democratic debate then which are so memorable. The real home of WEA decision-making and central to it was the District Council. This met three times a year plus once as Annual General Meeting; a cant phrase which rose and now has declined was 'We don't have to reinvent the wheel' but one of the WEA's main contributions over the century gone has been just that. People learn by experience to put on classes, to realise there is a financial element and to engage in *democratic* debate. The only way to make these quarterly Council meetings worth delegates' while was to engage them in a real way. The wish of the committee throughout the year has been to move towards a more active franchise for the governing body' (Annual Report 1976-77).

Looking back, the District Officers of that period brought enthusiasm and drive and a practical idealism to the District's proceedings. For example there were eight meetings per annum of staff and committee and these were on the same dates with papers issued together and visiting rights on both sides. The difficulties of 1976 were touched on by Ivan Corbett above and Professor Peter Kaim-Caudle did sterling service as Chair in the first year. He was followed by Lee Fairlie who had gained much experience in the Pre-school Playgroups' Association and had an American can-do approach. The Treasurer, Liz Armstrong of Newcastle branch, was another significant contributor to the crucial re-forming of the District. It was during their early time that a four-year limitation on office was brought in. Many others — Val Portass of Darlington, Professor Emeritus Teddy Allen, George Patterson, Jonathan Brown — had WEA experience to bring to bear. Various training days and other events came on stream.

As the District (and country!) entered the eighties the landscape began to change fundamentally. 1980 was the 70th year, when *So Noble An Institution* was published (Corbett 2003), along with an exhibition (which was seen in fifty places), an appeal — first contributor HM The Queen Mother — and a specially funded Women's Education Project. At the 1979 National Conference (Birmingham) the District's motion that there be inter-district regional conferences was carried. The Northern District played an active part nationally from then on and in later years internationally.

The experience of the 1980s in the South was very different from ours here and the various national WEA meetings — especially of the District Secretaries — highlighted the 'two nations' syndrome. Twenty years ago the Department of Education and Science took a very close interest in the 'establishment' of staff, essentially the number of Tutor Organisers.

With the quite sudden closing down of the North's industrial, base (e.g. Consett as early as 1980), the District stole a march (with the active support of Laurie Speak HMI), so that by 1981 we had six 'territorial' and three specialist Tutor Organisers (to work with trade unions, with the unemployed and in women's education). The nature of 'team working' was a debate which lasted a decade.

In modern business parlance, WEA staffing for many years was on the 'flat' model. Besides office staff, there were two types of post, the Tutor Organiser (usually working from home) and the District Secretary. The

Tutor Organiser was someone appointed to work with the branches and to feed in academic graduate advice. They had 'a patch' and were in a way a bit like C. of E. clergy. It is perhaps of interest to reflect that the more senior (older) District Secretaries were known as 'The Bishops'. Tutor organising after the Second World War was viewed as a staging post to higher things (e.g. University Staff Tutor appointment) but by the late 1970s there was very little 'moving on' in adult education. Staying on until retirement was to become the norm and it was therefore important to have career Tutor Organisers properly graded. This was an exercise early carried out by Jonathan Brown of the OU. The Tutor Organiser role (and those who soldiered on in it over the years) was of paramount importance until, in the later 1980s, it was eroded and the whole pattern of provision began rapidly to change.

With Tess Owens as our new Chair, the 72nd Annual Report (1982) says: 'We are right to value above anything else the District's RB status. We should look not only for funding but very carefully at any strings attached.' A new General Secretary (Robert Lochrie) came into post that year and 3 per cent of the Districts' grants was earmarked to national office. 'Districts are likely to take a keener interest in national management from now on.' With hindsight it can be seen that this was the very beginning of a shift of power away from the branches and districts and towards the centre. This now familiar pattern in our national life was scarcely visible then.

Programme and the branches kept up steadily as mentioned above. From the start subjects offered by the WEA had to cater for the market in a very real way - not a rigged market but a simple need to meet what the adult returner really wanted. Nothing mystical: if you put on a course and no one came, it 'closed' — as simple as that. It could be argued that fully fledged research of all WEA courses since 1903 would show the changing true concerns of serious folk. Certain topics — local history for example — have remained fairly constant but others — psychology, international affairs — have come and gone. From 1980 onwards the change — as in society — has been towards individual emphasis, reflecting perhaps a historical shift from *citizen* to *consumer*. During that period the nature of subjects studied in classes changed: literature giving some place to creative writing, public policy to aromatherapy. All this is reflected in the record of branch offerings but of course it is also true that much (in the leading reins of funding) was increasingly directed by government, often on a back-to-work basis. And yet, and yet ... the fundamental idea of the founders — that of a competent tutor and a sufficient body of students pursuing a topic through discussion — always holds good. The good adult class is a unique event; rather than a set component of learning progression it is essentially an exploration of our common humanity and genuine cultural experience. Many students who went on to Higher Education have continued in a way to remain 'WEA students' and it could be that those ideas of a fellowship of learning have influenced the practice of other providers. Many tutors have persisted over the years because, however wearily they make their way to 'the class', they come out of it refreshed. The adult student is the point of it all and the adult student is the biggest resource. Charles Hocking was once moved to tell me, 'If the WEA was done away with, it would have to be reinvented'.

By 1984 that once legendary date — a quasi-Victorian 'payment by results' was making a comeback. That year when Janet Atkinson took the Chair, the District was the first one to be selected for a full HMI inspection. This was the time of the miners' strike, perhaps the most significant single example of the growing hegemony of central state power. The District was to come out of the inspection smelling of roses but, even then, we did not fully see that Her Majesty's Inspectorate itself — once as autonomous as the Judiciary - was under exterminatory threat. To help the universities' adult education departments, the District agreed to remit 40 per cent of fees. Adult education in the universities was coming under 'friendly fire' and departments could no longer afford to give the students' fees to the WEA. The old dispensation was unravelling. Government, having sorted out old industry, was turning its regard towards the professions.

Now, in the mid 1980s, more 'stress' entered work relationships and various District advisory groups — e.g. for Women's and Trade Union education (WEAG and TUSAG) — were set up. A training group — TESCO — was founded and had the longest existence. The real watershed perhaps came in 1986 and the 76th Annual Report speaks (a familiar theme from the earliest days!) of a crisis in adult education and of another basis of grant as being 'a spurious competition for a fixed sum amongst districts operating very differently in very different economic and social climates'. We celebrated ten years in Bennet House and many other achievements but could no longer sustain a Women's Tutor Organiser post on the departure of Eileen Aird to join the national office.

There were perhaps 20 per cent fewer branches by 1987 than had been registered ten years before, a sign of the quiet erosion of the old structures, while the national conference of that year at the University of York was staring face to face at the GERBIL, the Great Education Reform Bill, a creature waiting in July of the following year to become Kenneth Baker's Education Act, replacing the 1944 settlement. Robert Jackson MP — briefly man-in-charge as junior minister — shifted grants into the Local Authority Revenue Support which meant that 'the District's eightieth year was its last as a RB, as far as we can ascertain' (80th Annual Report, 1989-90). The District Development plan was evolved, at the behest now of the *National* Executive Committee. Temple House in London was beginning to change into the centre of an *incorporated* organisation. The celebration of the eightieth year was more muted than ten years before but a commemorative mug or beaker was produced and went into several 'editions'. The grant arrangements dreamt up by Mr Jackson and weirdly known as 'ESG/GEST' came through largely because of active support by eight of the nine LEAs via the old Jesmond-based Northern Council for Further Education. In fact as change after change crashed down all the 'traditional' providers worked — or huddled — more closely together. Someone decided we had to change our financial year, so 1990-91 was an eight-month year (August/March). We had to change back again, so 1993-94 was a sixteen-month year (April/July).

The Annual Report for the short year (the 81st, 1990-91) is tinged with dark danger. The Southern District had folded and an industrial tribunal had found that the employer was no longer a WEA District but 'the WEA'. By the time of this ruling the Southern District had ceased and its work amalgamated with the old BBO (Berks, Bucks and Oxon District). The ruling flew in the face of realities and it is interesting that the WEA did not appeal it. In the 81st Annual Report we find: 'The history of the WEA, instead of being too often and too fondly recalled, was to become rather taboo'. And also:

> We learned that the Northern Region PPA (Pre-school Playgroups' Association) with whom we have had a fruitful collaboration for nearly twenty years — after experiencing the 'rationalisation' to which we are becoming prone — was shortly to be closed down by PPA national office, devastating a broad voluntary and democratic base.

In the spring of 1991 there was a White Paper on Higher and Further Education; Adult Education as a category seemed to have been 'overlooked' by the Department for Education and only got back into the frame through the support of the Women's Institutes. That autumn Districts had to discuss two models of a new WEA constitution. Either we decided to be *Integrated,* or *Discrete.* It was decided in December, in Manchester Town Hall. By the narrowest of (perhaps) majorities the WEA integrated itself. Soon the responsibility — formerly inherent in the post of District Secretary — would be nationally situated (the General Secretary and the National Executive Committee), but not quite as clear as that because by now the word and concept 'accountability' was generally becoming conflated with the stronger old word 'responsibility'. At the same time the concepts of 'training' and 'education' became blurred into one meaning by Government will.

The 83rd Annual Report warns that the following year will be sixteen months long and then avails itself of a crashing general statement; the formal dissolution of the Districts had been effected at the annual conference in April 1993 in storm-lashed Scarborough. District activists sold a record number of the 'updated' 1990 beaker (90th-year national anniversary) at a stall marked 'Get Mugged Here'. The general statement was, 'Recent changes reflect central government policy over nearly all aspects of public life [from] a landscape of institutions of all sorts with a range of aspirations, duties and expertise to a market place of stallholders bidding for contracts and thus the funding to carry out tasks'. The leopard was upskilling in spot-changing skills. Back at home volunteers and staff were still talking to each other and the continuing debate went on: how to deliver what was required and above that stay true to WEA ways, 'holding to basic principles in a period of continuous change'. This became known as the 'Shepherd's Dene process' from the Church of England, Newcastle diocesan venue of at least two annual such meetings.

The 84th Annual Report (the sixteen-month year of 1993-94) was to be the last in the old format and the last for which I was responsible. Now all components of the Association — thirteen English Districts and the national office — were audited by one firm, Hacker Young. The Northern District with a surplus of some 4 per cent of expenditure over income was the largest single constituent part of the audit. The shape of things to come is seen in the number of projects and the significant contribution of the ESF (European Social Fund) to income. Much else in the report follows the pattern of its predecessors which, looking at it now, perhaps gives a false sense of continuity. Wishing to take early retirement and — after thirty years with the District — to leave by the window of opportunity, as my final editorial act I inserted two extracts from excellent autobiographies which had appeared that year. One of these — *When the Leaf Was Green* — was by Arthur Appleton of Sunderland and gives an intriguing account of being a student in the 1930s. *Crooked Sixpences among the Chalk* by Hilda Pickles describes the author's wartime work as Tutor Organiser in Cumberland.[4] Crossed in love and out of work in 1938, Arthur Appleton writes that he:

> […] hurried home to Sunderland where I bought fourteen books and joined two WEA classes […] The two were English Literature and The Economics of International Relations. Nationalism was deplored as divisive, retrograde, out-of-date, needlessly competitive and emotionally dangerous. Imperialism was even worse. The classes were five shillings each per term, and joining the WEA for a fee of two shillings and sixpence meant that one could buy the *Manchester Guardian* for a penny instead of two pence […] The literature tutor was WR Niblett, the first academic I had heard. I was impressed by his vocabulary, accent and knowledge not only of writers but of their times […] Mrs Caldwell Brown, the Economics tutor had not the same elegance and refinement but she was more animated. She would pace about, a closed fist held against the top of her head. She read out the *Communist Manifesto* slowly and lovingly (adapted from Appleton 1993:131-135).

SOURCES CITED

Appleton, Arthur, 1993. *When the Leaf Was Green: autobiography: 1913-1939.* Sunderland: Black Cat Publications.

Corbett, Ivan, 2003. '"So noble an institution": A History of the Workers' Educational Association Northern District 1910-80'. In: Standen (2003a:5-81). [Originally published 1980.]

Pickles, Hilda, 1993. *Crooked sixpences among the chalk: seventy-five years of schooling.* Hawes: Leading Edge Press and Publishing.

Standen, Michael (ed.), 2003a. *A hunger to be more serious …: The Story of the WEA Northern District.* Newcastle upon Tyne: WEA Northern District.

---

[4] In the author's original paper he ends with a quotation from Hilda Pickles. As a fuller section, including the quoted passage appears in this book as Chapter 10, this version of Michael's paper ends instead with a quotation from Arthur Appleton.

The WEA and the 'White Hot Heat of the Scientific and Technological Revolution'

Nigel Todd

The central feature of our post-war capitalist society is the scientific revolution. Both its pace and its extent are beyond the dreams of previous generations. New discoveries and inventions now produce upheavals in five or ten years which previously took a century to complete. And the range of discovery is constantly widening. In the 1960s mankind is conquering nature, releasing new sources of energy and even voyaging out into space in ways which were still no more than schoolboy fantasies when the war ended. This scientific revolution has made it physically possible, for the first time in human history, to conquer poverty and disease, to move towards universal literacy and to achieve living standards for the masses far higher than those enjoyed by tiny privileged groups in previous epochs. The central issue of politics throughout the world today is not merely how the new riches shall be distributed within and between the nations but — just as important — how the new powers and energies now released by science shall be controlled. (Phillips 1960:5-6)

With a ringing declaration, Morgan Phillips opened a narrative that would colour the politics of change throughout much of the 1960s. Encapsulated in Harold Wilson's 1963 speech, often paraphrased as eulogising 'the white hot heat of the scientific and technological revolution', a concept sometimes attributed to the radical scientist Patrick Blackett, the theme of scientific modernism helped to edge Wilson into office as Labour Prime Minister in 1964. Within a short time, the organisation of government was reshaped to give substance to the vision. The Ministry of Education was renamed the Department of Education and Science (DES), a Ministry of Technology was created and a Department of Economic Affairs set to work preparing a National Plan that would apply science to industry. The same reforming zeal later led to the controversial founding of the Open University (OU) in 1969.

A 'scientific revolution' was an idea that caught a tide in popular imagination. It had been building for over a decade, but largely in quarters that felt ignored by government. The National Institute of Adult Education, for example, had been trying intermittently to make science more central to adult learning since the late 1940s and with little success. In 1956, a group of physicists went further in tentatively widening access to the realities of science by launching the *New Scientist* magazine in the wake of anxiety surrounding nuclear tests.

But a lot changed in the very early 1960s as Britain's sluggish economy was compared unfavourably with the technological achievements of the Soviet Union, the United States, and Western European and Japanese industries. Critiques of perceived 'old fashioned' political and commercial leadership forced a step-change in mood, reflected in the 1963 Robbins Report on the future of higher education that recommended new universities with strong scientific components. Science became a hot topic exemplified in a report produced by the Association of Scientific Workers (AScW) in 1963 (the forward was written by Asa Briggs, President of the WEA), and new energies were brought into the debate by science teachers who formed the Association for Science Education, also in 1963, bringing together older separate associations for male and female science teachers. The WEA fostered the growing ferment by publishing a *Science and Society* discussion paper in April 1964 that defined the Association's role as building 'bridges between science and other fields of human endeavour' (WEA 1964:4).

As it happened, the WEA had already been negotiating with the Ministry of Education in 1962, following publication of an HM Inspectors' report on science classes in adult education in 1960-61, to arrange a three-year project designed 'to evoke an interest and stimulate a demand for science subjects through W.E.A. branches and groups closely associated with the Movement.' The aim was to overcome:

a widening gap between the advanced knowledge of scientists and technicians, and the lagging understanding of ordinary people [which] is socially undesirable. (WEA Memorandum 1962:1)

Grant funding was agreed and would be paid by the WEA to the Northern District — it's not clear why the North was chosen — in four tranches of £260, £506, £443 and £250 from the 1962 session.

The 'Project for the Promotion of Science Courses' sought to deal with the problem identified in the AScW report:

> The 'scientific revolution' raises many problems which concern adult education. Yet, in the main, the generation that attends adult educational classes is culturally-without-science. Their schooling in the past failed to equip them for today's scientific world. (AScW 1963:4 and cited in Hocking, 1964:1)

The District advertised in the *New Scientist* for an organising tutor to start in the Tyneside area from the autumn of 1962. G. C. Scoffield, a scientist with an industrial electronics background, was appointed and began recruiting tutors from universities and colleges to join existing WEA science tutors, and talking with WEA branches to include more science courses in their plans. The project was buttressed by the formation of a steering committee, composed of university extra-mural and academic staff, the WEA and the principal of Hebburn Technical College, and the holding of a scoping conference at the Extra-Mural Department's Joseph Cowen House in March 1963.

Charles Hocking, the WEA District Secretary, noted that a 'really pioneering venture was undertaken with women's organisations' by offering a programme of six short lectures to 'young wives classes and Co-operative Guilds' on 'Science in the Home' (the Townswomen's Guild opted for 'Astronomy'). 'Science in the Home' covered electricity and its uses, the nature of light and modern methods of lighting, the elementary chemistry and role of new materials such as plastics, chemical relationships between soaps and detergents and their washing action, and 'with one group it was possible to discuss some of the fundamental ideas behind radio and television transmission.' These informative lectures nevertheless had their limitations because they were often 'fillers' in the agendas of the groups' routine meetings, and the lecturers were treated as merely visiting speakers:

> Mr. Scoffield [drew] attention to the difficulty experienced in being able to convince students that the next stage in scientific enquiry is both interesting and relatively easy to understand, and he is doubtful whether we can expect requests for more sustained courses from these groups. (Hocking 1964:3)

Hocking related the outcome to a comment made by the HMIs in their 1962 report, namely that some courses were 'intelligent entertainment, giving superficial acquaintance with science, but avoiding the hard effort'.

Although Tyneside was the focus for the project, a good deal of work was incorporated from Northumberland and Durham. From these areas, where WEA provision was well rehearsed, Hocking and Scoffield gathered detailed reports from tutors teaching geology, gardening, ornithology and other subjects. Ornithology was launched at a three-day lecture and field study residential course on Lindisfarne, attended by thirty-four students who logged sixty species of birds. It was followed up with shorter courses 'involving a detailed study of the ecology of the region' and one of these at Sunderland mapped the distribution of breeding birds on the Durham and Northumberland coasts.

Ornithology subsequently became a standard feature of WEA course provision in the North East, but at the beginning of the Science Project it was 'traditionally popular' geology that occupied 'a very important sector in the total class provision'. Some of the courses were simple introductions to the subject and others 'involved advanced work'. Evidently, the students' enthusiasm was considerable:

> For example, the class studying Swaledale covered the influence of glaciations on the scenery, economic life of the dale and the characteristics left by old agricultural farms. The tutor taking the class at Whickham reported that initially 'it was intended as an introduction to geological terminology and basic principles but this proved unrewarding, the students wanting to run before they were able to walk'. However, he must have been most successful in restraining their impetuosity because the group have asked for a sessional course in geology next session. (Hocking 1964:2)

Gardening and biology were other popular courses, and included analysis of plant biology, genetics and soil chemistry. At Lanchester, a course on 'The Living Soil' 'studied the earthworm and other useful rivals, bacteria, fungi and algae', whilst a class at Chester-le-Street had access to a laboratory. The HMI's report had found that biology was the 'most successful' area of science provision by the Responsible Bodies, drawing Hocking's confirmation:

> In Durham and the Tyneside area we have our share of success. At Darlington two terminal classes in field biology were held in the afternoons for young married women and attracted enrolments of eighteen and sixteen respectively. The tutor in her report said 'all the students went to the expense of obtaining suitable pocket magnifiers as soon as they found that these were desirable for the working of the class'. (Hocking 1964:2)

An innovation implemented by the Science Project aligned WEA teaching with a BBC television series called *The Science of Man.* Three linked weekend schools based on the series were tutored in 1963-64 by Victor Bell, a part-time tutor who was also Vice-Chairman of the WEA Northern District. Additionally, Bell took science courses for groups at Cramlington, Bedlington 'and for Co-operative Guilds at Gosforth and Cowgate', and provided single lectures for the Civil Service Union at the Ministry of Pensions in Newcastle, and for WEA branches at Earsdon, Hebburn, Gateshead and Seaham: 'In none of these projects has there been a failure to hold the interests of the students'.

Reflecting on his work, Bell identified the ingredients that made for success:

> It has been a pleasure and from the purely academic point most interesting to follow the reactions of non-scientific people to scientific subjects. The material is by no means too difficult for them and sub-consciously, they already know enough to provide a foundation upon which one can build. Once started they become quite fascinated as is shown by during the questions and discussion periods. The local HMI commented favourable on the quality of the questions and at one school entered into and was impressed by the discussion [...] By far the greatest, but not insuperable problem is to persuade people to take the first lecture. This calls for someone who is dedicated to the work with the personality, keenness and the necessary tact and enthusiasm to explore every conceivable avenue where work in this worthwhile field can be done.

Bell emphasised how science from physics to biology could be presented in an accessible format but without having to 'water down' the 'modern scientific outlook':

> Obviously it has to be presented in such a way that comprehension was both agreeable and possible. Much of the difficult sections, particularly those in the realm of the invisible, were given by the use of models, diagrams, and film illustrations, many being actual photographs of material under the electron microscope. Wherever it was possible to do so, simple experiments were devised and performed, even though they only served to clarify one point. On the biological side, fresh specimens were used to great advantage and the use of the microscope proved of much value to the students. (Bell cited in Hocking 1964:5-6)

Despite optimism, Bell found problems. One of these was the lack of up-to-date books and magazines in local libraries. Another was reaction within the WEA itself. Bell believed passionately that there was 'a need for urgency' to enable people 'outside of the scientific field to be in closer harmony with their present day environment' and to bring them up to speed with 'future trends.' He was worried, though, that there were those inside the WEA who:

> cover their antipathy to things scientific as something outside of our scope — something which contributes very little in the way of culture. Surely a view point which is stilted, erroneous and ridiculously absurd. (Bell cited in Hocking 1964:6)

Bell's sentiments, prompted by a debate at a WEA national conference, echoed C. P. Snow's interpretation of the disjuncture between humanities and science that he re-emphasised in his 1964 book, *The Two Cultures: And a Second Look.*

Hocking and Scoffield listed other obstacles. While there had been television coverage of the launch of the project, with 10,000 copies of a promotional leaflet distributed and the insertion of references in their local brochures by WEA branches, the publicity was nevertheless thought to be 'inadequate'. Courses had depended chiefly on tutors supplying their own equipment and the Ministry of Education had declined to provide £450 to buy basic equipment such as projectors. Hocking complained, too, that the national funding was insufficient to pay for publicity and administration. The WEA had struggled to find enough science tutors, laboratories had not been made available by schools and colleges unless their own staff were present, and:

> As was to be expected we have had our crop of casualties in the programme as projected in the Autumn of 1963. The tutor-organiser in science has probably had more disappointments than is the usual experience of full-time tutors. (Hocking 1964:1)

Actually, the picture was not all that bad. Sixty-five science courses had taken place in 1963-64 which represented 19% of the District's total courses, and over 20% of the District's longer courses had been in science. 851 students had enrolled in class sizes from six to thirty-six, and about twenty-eight tutors, including a young David Bellamy, had been involved. Ten courses were run in garden science, nine in ornithology, eight in geology, six in botany and six in general science.

Possibly, WEA expectations had been higher, but in any event Scoffield resigned in June 1964, returning to industry after only a year, apparently anxious that he was falling behind in his own rapidly changing specialist field. Hocking, in thanking Scoffield, wrote that 'science is a more difficult subject to evoke interest in ... [and this is] sometimes very disheartening' (Hocking to Scoffield, 16 June 1964, in Hocking, 1964).

Scoffield was replaced fairly quickly by Irene Leveridge who had a background in chemistry and botany as a recent Newcastle University graduate. Hocking, describing the appointment as welcome because Mrs. Leveridge's husband was a PhD student and this meant she was unlikely to move away from the area for three years, confirmed himself as a man of his time. But times were changing and it is not altogether certain that social attitudes in the WEA and elsewhere were keeping pace. Hocking's own correspondence with the DES, for instance, still retained the slightly 'fuddy-duddy' quaintness of an earlier era (the senior civil servant responsible for the project at the DES always began his letters 'Dear Hocking' and Hocking replied in kind).

Irene Leveridge built up the project from 15.1% of the District's course provision in 1962-63, to 17.2% in 1963-64 and reaching 18.2% in 1965-66 when a survey of 940 students revealed an interesting occupational profile compared with a similar survey for the HMIs' 1960-61 report:

WEA Northern District HMI Northern Area		
Occupations	1965-66	1960-61
Teachers	10.2%	23%
Professional	10.0%	31%
Manual	12.6%	3%
Non-manual, Technical or Supervisory	15.4%	?
Housewives	27.4%	6%
Not in paid work	11.1%	4%

Allowing for any difficulties in comparing data (though the WEA and HMI areas were geographically coterminous), the project broadened participation among non-professional occupational categories. Significantly, 47% of the students had not undertaken formal education after the age of sixteen, although 51% had attended grammar schools, 25% technical colleges, and 9% university. A team of HMIs who inspected the project in the 1965-66 session were not very interested in what eventually became known as 'widening participation'. They ignored the fact that the HMIs' 1962 report had said that science courses had 'limited appeal to semi skilled and unskilled workers' (Ministry of Education 1962:16), but that this had now been contradicted in some measure by the WEA. However, they did log that more than half of the students had not previously attended a WEA class.

The HMIs commented that resources had been used well and the proportion of science courses had doubled, concluding:

> Final judgements cannot yet be made, because the Science Project has tried out new themes and methods as the three-year period went on, and it is, near the end of the third session, still in the early stages of some of its experiments. Growing points will continue to show, as may be expected with this evidence of much enthusiastic teaching backed by lively administration from the office. (HM Inspectors 1966:8)

It was a broadly supportive conclusion, but one rooted in sharp observations. There was concern that so few courses met in laboratories and it was 'unfortunate that in some areas it had not been possible to agree arrangements for the use of secondary school laboratories'. Although several classes had used university facilities, a few met in primary schools. The availability of equipment largely depended on tutors:

> Most tutors had provided themselves with slide or strip projectors, often their own property, and had gone to pains to bring with them films, photographs or charts [...] In ornithology classes tutors and students brought in pictures and records of bird song. The tutors in geology usually brought specimens.

For many WEA tutors, this was not unusual since the poorly funded Association invariably called on their goodwill for teaching materials.

The quality of teaching posed queries in numbers of cases, and the absence of syllabuses and reading lists, combined with the lack of textbooks or book boxes that could be made available for students, was a more widespread issue. On the other hand, the forty-nine tutors visited included ten with doctorates and thirty-four graduates:

> Evidence that paper qualification is not related to teaching ability could be found; three of the best managed classes were run by tutors holding doctorates, and three more by non-graduate tutors. Nearly all the tutors had taken the trouble to prepare an effective lecture, and although not all of them had solved the problem of the students' contribution most of them were aware that this problem existed. Indeed, a promising factor for the future development of science courses in adult education was the acceptance by thoughtful tutors of the need for faculty discussion of content and method.

The 'problem' was that opportunities for students to do practical work could be inhibited by the limited facilities, and by timing courses at the wrong season in the year to arrange field trips: 'it is a matter to be discussed by the body of tutors whether a science course can be satisfactory without some individual practice by students'.

Evidently, the ornithology courses had fulfilled their early promise in stimulating demand for successor courses, building on accumulated knowledge and deepening students' understanding of the subject through fieldwork (a similar point was made about geology). By contrast, garden science was not generating requests for courses that could be sustained over two or three terms and was largely classroom-based or attracted already experienced gardeners.

The HMIs argued that the inclusion of practical and fieldwork, especially in geology, botany, biology and ornithology, was the factor that led students to continue with the subject following an initial course, though with the proviso:

> [...] that failure to establish a continuous science group in any place is not a condemnation of the effort. The essence of the project was to experiment, and much seed had to be sown in the knowledge that patches of the ground would prove unfertile. Moreover, if an experimental course in science created a group who in the next session chose to study some other subject, it would not be fair to regard the experiment as a failure.

The willingness of the project to try new locations and fresh approaches was applauded. In particular, the HMIs were impressed that 'in four centres, east and west of the Pennines' teams of three lecturers from three different science disciplines had been brought together to contribute to a common theme. So long as a single tutor took charge, 'such courses may benefit students who would not be attracted to study a single branch of science'.

The HMIs also judged that the project could have gained from more consistent staffing. Scoffield had left after only one year, but it emerged that Irene Leveridge, 'is now leaving after less than two years' contradicting Hocking's hope to the contrary (HMI 1966:1-8). Leveridge's departure and the HMI's report brought the project to a close. It was a strange goodbye. Missing from everyone's assessment of the effectiveness of the science project was an evaluation of whether students really had gained a level of scientific literacy equipping them to intervene in public debate, or influence policy-makers. Did any of the students use their scientific insights to join campaigns or organisations that met Morgan Philips's and the WEA's ambitions to determine 'how the new powers and energies now released by science shall be controlled'? That evidence was not recorded, and a link between acquiring scientific knowledge and political action may not have been a developed, overt aim of the project in any case. It's probable that simply gaining scientific knowledge was considered sufficient, and progressing to sustained and practical studies was felt to be a bonus. Maybe, in the end, the WEA's liberal adult education tradition enveloped the project into the joy of learning and no more, though that was no bad thing in so far as it went.

Hocking negotiated with the WEA nationally to publish a project report (Memorandum, 1966), although nothing appears to have been printed. His attempts to persuade the DES to add a summary of the exercise to one of their reports also came to grief amid layers of civil service protocols. The only faint recognition came in 1973 when Jack Taylor, the WEA's deputy general secretary, used the project's statistics in an appendix to a paper that he read at an international conference (1973b), and which he followed with a WEA pamphlet, *Science Education for Adults* (1973a). Yet the experience had not been wasted locally. WEA culture had shifted in the Northern District, albeit temporarily, and for several years afterwards there remained a Tutor Organiser post dedicated to science, lifting the District's science provision from 19.8% of courses in 1966-67 to 20.8% in 1969-70.

SOURCES CITED

AScW 1963. *Science and Adult Education: A Report by the Association of Scientific Workers.* London: Association of Scientific Workers.

Hocking, Charles, 1964. *Science Project   Progress Reports,* (Newcastle upon Tyne, WEA) in Tyne & Wear Museums and Archives (TWMA), F WEA1/15/141-44.

Ministry of Education (April 1962), *Report of HM Inspectors on Science and Adult Education; conclusions of a group of HM Inspectors after visiting science and mathematics classes provided by the Responsible Bodies in England during the 1960-1961 session,* (London, Ministry of Education)

HMI 1966. *The Project for Promotion of Science Courses by the Northern District Workers' Educational Association.* London: Department of Education and Science.

National Institute of Adult Education, 1949. *Science in Adult Education,* London: NIAE.

Philips, Morgan, 1960. *Labour in the Sixties.* London: Labour Party.

Taylor, Jack, 1973a. *Science Education for Adults.* London: WEA.

Taylor, Jack, 1973b. *The WEA and Science Education for Adults: Paper to 2nd International Institute of Science Adult and Continuing Education, 11 July 1973* in TWMA E.WEA1/15/141-44.

WEA, 1966. *Memorandum of Consultation between Mr. C.H. Hocking, Northern District Secretary, and the General Secretary, 24 June 1966,* in TWMA E.WEA1/15/141-44.

WEA, 1962. *Memorandum on Proposed Pilot Project for the Development of Courses in Science,* (London, WEA) in TWMA E.WEA1/15/141-44.

WEA, 1964. *Science and Society.* London: WEA.

Friends Abroad: International Work in the WEA Northern District

Victor Cadaxa

In the late 1970s, the mid-decade crises described in Chapter 6 were being resolved, enabling District Committee and staff to look to the future. One area for discussion was how the 'new' District could meaningfully work in an international context. We felt we could do good work, and we needed to develop innovative ways forward.

The WEA nationally was an active member of the International Federation of WEAs (IFWEA). This meant occasional attendance by members of District Committee, and sometimes staff, at International Committee meetings or even more occasional IFWEA events in London. These were not very relevant to the District or its 'natural' areas of educational work which were in current affairs and trade union studies.

Like other WEA districts, Northern District had organised group visits abroad, but these were not based on existing courses of study, and often cost too much for the majority of WEA course members.

So, our innovative international work followed two linked paths:

1. To develop contact visits based on course groups (existing or proposed) and in groups drawn from affiliated organisations. We found that trade unions were especially interested in international contact/visits and would often support members financially;

2. To seek contact with IFWEA members and in particular their Regional/District/local bodies. It was hoped this would give a degree of similarity in concerns and interests.

Trade Union Studies links are covered in Chapter 12 by Tom Nesbit, but it is important to note that the earliest practical successes came through contact with *Arbeit und Leben* (AuL), a West German federal organisation and IFWEA member. AuL worked with trade unions and social organisations to promote democracy — a priority just after the war — and international friendship and co-operation. By the 1980s, AuL Hamburg in particular was keen on exchange visits. Co-ordinated by Tom Ellison, Trade Union Studies Tutor Organiser, a good number of reciprocal study visits were organised over more than ten years, mainly with AuL Hamburg. Usually there were at least two visits per year, with financial support from the then West German government and also trade unions at both ends.

We tried with less success to link the strong programme of exchanges between AuL and the WEA with existing town-twinning arrangements. Most North-East cities, towns, Districts and Counties had twinning arrangements with German counterparts, almost all in Nordrhein-Westfalen. This region in North-West Germany was occupied by British forces after 1945, and was similarly engaged in coalmining and heavy industry. Contact with AuL in Nordrhein-Westfalen and elsewhere was less productive than with Hamburg, while North-East town-twinning committees were busy enough with their existing programmes. After Tom Ellison left the District's employment, the AuL programme limped along for a short while, but petered out without his direct involvement.

Scandinavian WEAs (Danish and Norwegian AOFs, Swedish ABF) were an obvious and intriguing target from 1980. 'Obvious' due to geography and air and ferry links with the North-East, 'intriguing' because of the shared name and the fact that their foundation was inspired by the early WEA, which we found out after a little research. After chasing dead ends, we sought help from the head offices of ABF and the AOFs, and they circulated our letters seeking contact from Regional, District or local WEAs. We initially targeted Bergen and Gothenburg (Göteborg), both twinned with Newcastle, but they did not respond initially so we widened the net. Early in 1982, a reply came from Janet Ericsson of ABF Norrköping in South-East Sweden: they were to be our best international contacts for the following twenty years or more. At that time, Sweden had not yet joined the Common Market, so finding areas for useful co-operation took time, especially as there were some real differences in funding and structure.

Early in 1983, a tentative reply also from AOF Stavanger in western Norway. Stavanger had a loose 'friendship' arrangement with Sunderland. The city of Stavanger provided huge trees for North-East Christmas events, and had twice weekly flights to Newcastle. A few letters were exchanged, then in April a sudden fax — three AOF colleagues would arrive in two weeks, two from Stavanger, and one from Rogaland (the province).

The three AOF members arrived at Newcastle Station one early evening. Odd was Stavanger AOF Chair and Labour Party Chair, Egil was senior AOF Stavanger staff member (a role less than District Secretary, but more than Tutor Organiser). The Rogaland representative was an ex-seaman, very keen to re-acquaint himself with British beer, more so as it was so much cheaper here than at home. The group was busy getting into Victor's car, just off Grainger Street, when along came part-time tutor Tony Corcoran and his eldest son dressed as Chicago Mafia gangsters, complete with violin cases.

Tony, now Chair of the Tyneside Irish Centre and main mover of the annual Tyneside Irish Festival, was a most inspiring WEA tutor. That autumn, he had taken over a dying class in South Shields, 'North East England 600–1,000' and renamed it 'The Golden Age of Northumbria'. Tony stepped up the cultural content, in music especially. Northumbrian tunes, Irish and French influences, links to later north-eastern folk tunes, were all played live on his fiddle. The course was also peppered with some saucy events of the period. By January, the class had a massive waiting list.

The violin cases carried by Tony and son contained fiddles of course, as they were off to meet other musicians at the nearby Bridge Hotel, and then play at a benefit *ceilidh* in the large upstairs room. The Norwegians were very keen to go along and watch.

Once in the Bridge Hotel, Egil asked Tony to give an example of Irish music, which he duly did and followed up. Other musicians then got their instruments out, and so a rehearsal took place in the lounge. The *ceilidh* upstairs was full, with people there joining energetically in the dancing. The Norwegians were wowed!

They never quite believed this was a once-ever coincidence and became very keen for the WEA to organise for a North-East group to take part in the Stavanger 'folk festival' in June 1984. Inspired by their recent exhibition of trade union banners and memorabilia, AOF wanted a younger, more popular event than the official Stavanger Festival, similar perhaps to the Edinburgh Fringe. Victor was to sound out WEA Northern District member organisations and contacts, and, given sufficient interest, to organise a return visit to AOF Stavanger

Youth clubs and community organisations working with the WEA were keen, especially in Sunderland, and the towns' 'friendship' status perhaps helped. A group quickly assembled for the visit, under Sunderland Trades Council's banner, to match in some way the AOF's strong trade union base.

The reception was great: visits to groups supporting the folk festival and to workplaces, such as Stavanger's shipyard, already starting to work for the oil and gas industry. The North-East group also addressed two large meetings. The Trades Council representative was a striking miner and many wanted to hear about the strike. Equally, Norway was then rather insular and there was much debate about whether Britain's problems — economic decline, unemployment, privatisation, strikes — could ever happen in Scandinavia. Odd and Egil thought they could and would and hoped the UK group would help inform and widen the debate.

During the visit, the AOF hosts proposed a joint AOF Stavanger and WEA Northern District venture to provide information technology classes either in or with English for Norwegian workers. Demand for both IT and English was booming in Norway, especially in the oil and gas industry. Odd and Egil were impressed with Durham as a venue and calculated that courses in the North-East would be significantly cheaper than at home, with the unbeatable advantage of an English language environment. It would also improve the finances of the English WEA and the Norwegian AOF, both of which were always short of funds.

Sadly, within a year both AOF and WEA initiatives failed. Stavanger Council pressured and conceded until the AOF Council agreed to drop the folk festival. The Norwegian Industrial Training Board liked the 'IT with English' proposal, but were unable to fund courses outside the Scandinavian Union. Soon afterwards, Egil left to pursue his first love, puppet theatre, and Odd gave up the AOF Chair.

As contact with AOF Stavanger faded away, relations with ABF Norrköping developed. ABF was much larger than the WEA — in relation to population, perhaps some ten times bigger — so larger branches in strong ABF areas like Norrköping were more like large Districts in WEA terms. ABF's membership was based on affiliated organisations, by then a fading feature of the WEA. The main ABF affiliates were the main Trade Union confederation Landsorganisationen i Sverige (LO), the Co-operative Movement and the Social Democratic Party. There were many smaller affiliated groups and organisations, particularly at local level.

ABF's learning philosophy had two central features, the study group and the study leader. Ideally, the study group was a more democratic version of the WEA class that might study a course. But the activities undertaken by the study group were not restricted to courses. They might also or instead do practical work e.g. arts and crafts or set itself a practical task or research a current issue. Ideally, the study leader was selected by the local ABF, an affiliated organisation or by a study group itself. The study leader was trained in adult teaching by ABF. With thousands of ABF study circles and an equal number perhaps in other study organisations, together with hundreds of thousands of members, Prime Minister Olof Palme commented that 'Sweden is to a large extent a study circle democracy'.

Despite such differences, there were several overlapping interests between ABF and the WEA, notably trade union studies. There was much to learn from each other. English language study was a major part of ABF's programme, so the WEA contributed in updating ABF materials, finding contacts and hosting ABF groups.

State funding of Swedish study organisations was very generous compared to British standards, allowing them to run courses on smaller numbers for instance. Yet ABF Norrköping saw that this might change, particularly with European Union membership. It was keen find out from the WEA Northern District how to survive on leaner budgets and later how to bid for European funding (the Social Fund, in particular).

As a consequence, exchanges were found to be useful and we had a number of reciprocal visits over nearly twenty years: individuals, small groups and large groups. A few were particularly interesting and productive:

- In 1987, Janet Ericsson brought some ninety English language study leaders and organisers over for a week. Highlights included an Elizabethan banquet packed out with the ABF group and their WEA hosts at Lumley Castle, though not all visitors could follow Geordie humour. The WEA Durham Branch hosted a farewell evening with music and song, where some of the ABF group noted that the English had become, in their eyes, 'more like continental Europeans'. Indeed, there was the Chair of WEA South Shields Branch wagging her finger just inches from the faces of the Mayor of Durham and the local MP. Unforgettable for the WEA members were the smoked elk meat smuggled in by ABF leaders and other delicacies such as cloudberry jam.

- Tom Nesbit, Northern District Committee member and T&GWU Education Officer, and Victor Cadaxa visited ABF for a week. Two days were spent at the ABF national office in Stockholm, then they then went to Norrköping and Linköping, a county town. We examined ABF's structure, its provision for trade unions, special groups such as immigrants, and the detailed working of study circles and study leaders. Study circles worked best and most democratically when set up jointly by ABF and an affiliated social organisation. Discussions and decisions were truly a collective affair. However, with less confident groups such as people with learning difficulties and immigrants, study circles were more often leader-led.

- In the summer of 1989, a week's WEA study visit to Norrköping was organised. Its eighteen members included Lesley Gillespie, the District Chair, Michael Standen, District Secretary, the District Committee and branch members, staff and three Northumberland miners. Prior to the visit, study meetings were held to study the ABF and prepare for the visit. As with Latin-American Study Group visits (described later in this Chapter), the visit was helped by fund-raising activities in the North-East. These included raffles and £10-a-head dinners. In addition, employed members paid 'cost-plus' to ensure that less well-off members could join the study visit.

In Norrköping, the WEA group stayed in the local *folksuniversitet* ('Folk High School'), a close ABF partner. It met study group members and leaders, ABF organisers and the ombudsmen (District Secretary equivalents) for Norrköping, Linköping and Östergötland (the county ABF). Small groups of four to five were shown a wide range of ABF work, from trade union studies to arts and craft, in many different locations. The high point was the ABF mega-barbeque for the WEA visitors, held beside one of the many lakes near Norrköping, a really quality affair despite the large numbers. The low point was being persuaded to swim in that same lake day before — despite the sunshine, it was absolutely freezing! On the last night, the WEA group held a show of sketches and traditional North-East songs — plus a few London numbers as Washington Branch's Secretary was keen to show off her Pearly Kings and Queens costume. Loudest applause was for the youngest miner as Cushy Butterfield with wig, dress and bra.

A few months later, Janet Ericsson brought over an enduring present, a tapestry which still hangs in the North-East Regional Office in Newcastle, made by an ABF craft group near Norrköping which was visited by WEA members. The piece shows typical scenes of the area in lively colours, and the group members' names. The tapestry is a lovely, mixed-ability piece, containing work ranging from highly skilled to appliqué roughly sewn on, reflecting ABF's belief that mixed groups could (and did) produce excellent work. This was at a time when the WEA was coming under pressure to show learners' 'upward progression'.

After 1990, ABF Norrköping's funding started to contract, as European Union integration speeded up. From the mid-1990s, ABF Norrköping experienced financial problems, with growing deficits in its Arts and Performing Arts programmes. The ABF-led Arts Centre was a particular problem. Other work, including new European Social Fund (ESF) projects, could not entirely fill the gap and so the study visits reduced, then dried up. The last exchange visit was by a small, self-funded WEA group in 2004.

We learned from our experience with ABF and from the mid-1980s, study visits were based on and fed into WEA Northern District policy concerns. Visits were prepared in detail, down to ensuring that enough gifts and North-East mementos were to hand for the hosts of any groups visited. The ABF study group experience led the WEA District to look more closely into its actual classroom practice, ensuring that classes became more learner-centred. Repeated contact with ABF Norrköping was also a useful spur to think bigger in the WEA and to try new ways of working (see also the comments on the Latin-American Study Group below).

In 1991, Daniel Fisher, projects manager and Karsten Jorgensen, Director of AOF Odense (Denmark) contacted the WEA Northern District. ABF Norrköping had spread the word about the District's international work, and as a result AOF Odense wished to cooperate with local and regional WEAs in Europe. With other WEAs, they hoped to obtain funding for transnational projects. After a number of visits, a four-country trade union study project entitled 'The Office Sector after 1992' was co-ordinated by AOF Odense and the WEA Northern District. This project would look at problems and opportunities for office workers in peripheral regions of Europe, outside the London–Frankfurt–Paris-Milan–Barcelona axis, where the bulk of European economic activity was concentrated.

The participating unions were: the large Danish union HK Odense, the Irish Services, Industrial, Professional and Technical Union (SIPTU), the Sindicato Unión General de Trabajadores (UGT) of Andalucía and the National Association of Local Government Officers (NALGO) North East. In addition, UGT Portugal were observers.

NALGO was then a large white-collar union in local government and public utilities (e.g. water). Three conferences were to be held, in Malaga, Dublin and Odense, each with a different core theme. Each trade union delegation was to prepare papers on each theme, outlining the situation in their country and region or locality. This involved a lot of study and preparatory work. The NALGO North-East study group met fortnightly to prepare for the Malaga event. In the immediate run-up, work groups were meeting weekly to finalise their section of NALGO's report. In the period between the Malaga and Dublin conferences, the NALGO–National Union of Public Employees (NUPE) merger was being finalised, which resulted in UNISON, the public sector and the National Health Service giant. In the process, NALGO decided it had to withdraw from the project, to concentrate on the merger. A new delegation took its place, from Britain's General Union (GMB) public sector branches. Unfortunately, given the short notice, they did not have the same study and preparation time as the NALGO study group. Even with meticulous planning, outside events can subvert the best intentions!

The highlights were the extremely positive interactions between delegations from very different regions, and the sophisticated reports from UGT and SIPTU. At the Malaga event, UGT detailed the problems of one of Western Europe's poorest regions and within it issues for white-collar workers in the public and health sectors. At the Dublin conference, SIPTU reported on new forms of office work, forecasting the subsequent growth of call centres and other forms of tele-working. The Irish Trade and Industry Minister and top officials came to SIPTU's presentation — on content and attendance, the bar was being raised! The low point was one of HK's leading members, who alleged a cold on arrival in Malaga, but was spotted the next morning on route to the beach. HK held a stormy meeting that evening and sent him home in disgrace.

There were other partnership initiatives between AOF Odense and the WEA, notably to assist the voluntary and Non Governmental Organisations (NGO) sector in Vilnius (Lithuania) to organise itself, no easy task after fifty years of Soviet rule. However, this project had limited impact on and relevance to the WEA so we participated for one year only.

From 1987 Victor Cadaxa had worked a three-day week in order to pursue international partnerships. However, in 1996 he returned to full-time work as County Durham Tutor Organiser. This left little time for international work. Soon afterwards, Karsten and Daniel left AOF Odense, so co-operation was placed on the back-burner.

Study groups and study visits were another feature of international work. The WEA Northern District ran regular courses on Latin-America with the Newcastle Branch tutored by Victor Cadaxa. But from 1980, interest rocketed due to dramatic new events, especially the successful 1979 Sandinista revolution in Nicaragua and the 1982 Falklands War. In the run-up to the war, the Northern District and Durham University ran a series of well-attended day schools, further boosting numbers in Newcastle and elsewhere.

The Argentine military dictatorship collapsed soon after its 1982 defeat. At much the same time the Uruguayan regime also collapsed. Huge demonstrations swept Brazil, calling for a return to democracy. By September 1983, numbers enrolling for the Newcastle class were unmanageable, but the group did not want to be split. Course members also wanted to do practical things alongside study. The result was similar to some the ABF's research-and-practical work programmes. Named the Latin-American Study Group (LASG), it became the largest and most enduring such group. Due to the numbers and the variety of interests, the group later split into three sub-groups focusing on three countries in particular: Nicaragua, Brazil and Chile.

The Nicaragua Children's Project was a noteworthy initiative. The Nicaragua group's research and contact work led to a project to support a remedial children's day centre-cum-school in Diriamba, the poorest province and the least fashionable location, as the uprising had occurred elsewhere. The children were mostly orphans cared for by relatives, and the centre lacked almost all resources. For almost ten years, the project raised funds to provide school materials and other equipment such as footballs, strips and a TV, to fund repairs and an extension, and finally to employ an additional teacher. Other sub-group members and new faces joined in the regular fundraising, ensuring its success. Members of the study group visited Diriamba, bringing back photos, examples of children's work and letters, which helped to maintain members' enthusiasm. In 1990, however, the Sandinistas lost the election; social programmes were given much less funding and so the Diriamba Centre closed.

Cuba was a constant topic of discussion, because of the ongoing conflict with the USA, its education and health systems, but also because of the lack of western democracy and its refugees. In 1984, a study visit was arranged to see the country first-hand. In the run-up to the visit, members worked on related topics and ran several day schools, the largest attended by some seventy-five people and addressed by the Cuban Ambassador. The Cuba Solidarity Campaign organised visits to Cuba at the time, but the study group itself set up this visit, with an independent stance in line with WEA practice. There was intensive fundraising, to enable less well-off or unemployed study group members to attend, including as before a surcharge for those employed. The visit was based initially in Santiago de Cuba, its second city, with under half a million people. Its manageable size and the coincidence of the annual regional music festival made it a favourite with the WEA group. The group then moved to the capital, Havana, where it visited hospitals and local social organisations, then some initiatives nearby. These included a boarding school, run on very different lines to the UK, with study in the morning and manual work in the fields or building/repairing premises in the afternoon. The visit did not resolve the issues about Cuba, but discussions became much more informed. Co-operation with the Santiago health service continues to this day, led by UNISON which provides practical help, for example, in providing reconditioned ambulances.

The Brazil group focused on pro-democracy campaigns and the new trade union movement. Assisted by the national WEA, it successfully applied for UNESCO (United Nations' Cultural body) funding, for an ambitious study programme, with a two-week visit to Brazil. Twelve people were selected from group members and other WEA people for this 1984 visit, with a rigorous scoring system to choose visit members. Preparation for the visit was intense, including Brazilian Portuguese lessons. The visit was based on three centres, starting initially in North-East Brazil, the poorest region in the country, hosted by Oxfam. Then, São Paulo, the main industrial and trade union centre, and finally Rio de Janeiro, the second-largest city and main cultural centre. In São Paulo and Rio the visits were hosted by social organisations that worked with Oxfam.

On return, the group published a report based on the visit's findings and subsequent research, very favourably reviewed in international development publications. Development charities and trade unions, notably NALGO, invited the group to address a number of meetings on its findings. From this activity, the group was key to the setting up of a national Brazil Network. Brazilian social and trade union organisations were especially interested in two areas of WEA members' work: confidence and capacity building for women members, and health and safety organisation, with safety representatives in particular being involved. Five group members returned in 1985 for six weeks with Brazilian organisations. Sadly, other Latin-American Study Group work, in Chile and El Salvador, for example, was less successful.

The District's last two study visits came in 1989 and 1991, both based on successful area study courses with the Newcastle and South Shields Branches. Current affairs classes in both areas requested that the theme for September 1987 be the USSR and Eastern Europe, where internal processes of *glasnost* (i.e. 'openness') and *perestroika* (i.e. 'restructuring or reform') were matched by improving relations with the West. Course numbers grew again in September 1988, so Jim Perry, the South Shields Branch Chair and course member, and also National Union of Mineworkers (NUM) Mechanics Secretary, proposed a WEA-NUM study visit, to be jointly led by Bill Etherington, NUM Mechanics senior official (later MP for Sunderland North) and Victor Cadaxa.

The June 1989 visit had three centres: Leningrad (later renamed St Petersburg), then Moscow and Kiev. Visits ranged from historical monuments and churches to old peoples' homes and a children's puppet theatre. With the old state travel agent Intourist defunct, small tourist firms sprang up everywhere, so standards varied hugely: visits and guides ranged from excellent (Kiev), to very poor (one of two in Moscow). The group saw for themselves evidence of the USSR's deep crisis: increasing crime and corruption in Moscow where bribes were asked even for seats in restaurants; empty river beaches despite temperatures of more than 25° C in Kiev which were the result, it emerged, of the River Dnieper having been poisoned by fallout from the Chernobyl disaster.

The most startling part of the visit was open conflict at a meeting with Ukraine's TUC Executive. The initial speech claimed, Soviet-style, that USSR living conditions were better than in Britain. Executive members shouted the speaker down as a Russian stooge. Several then sought meetings with the North-East group to explain the real, grim situation in the USSR, and the continuing Chernobyl disaster in particular. Members of the visiting party were not surprised at collapse of the Soviet Union's Eastern European 'empire' that very autumn. In the 1990s, the North-East NUM and Ukrainian miners staged a number of exchange visits, which became increasingly risky for the UK visitors as public order deteriorated.

The last study visit in May 1991 was to Andalucia, southern Spain. Courses on Spain and Portugal were well attended, due partly to interest in the democratic process in both countries, as well as the history from the Islamic conquest to the Spanish Civil War, and partly to a wish to see the interior, beyond the tourist 'Costas'. Links were developing with Andalucia, helped by Newcastle University's partnership with Malaga University. The WEA Northern District had recently contacted the region's Adult Education Service (AES), and discussions with the trade union confederation UGT Andalucia were progressing well in advance of the 'Office Sector' project with AOF Odense described above. Due to the UGT link, trade union members joined the visit after two study day schools.

Andalucia fascinated course members, with its long Islamic past and legacy, especially in architecture. The cheapest way to travel was to join a Thomson two-week tour of Malaga, Seville, Cordoba and Granada, with group side visits to meet WEA contacts. The low point was the heat wave inland: members found daytime temperatures of 35° C with no sea breezes very hard to cope with. High points included the visit around Granada's hilltop Albaicín, with its crooked alleys and tiny hidden squares, guided by local head of AES, Matias Bedmar. Matias also invited the group to the inaugural fiesta of a new town council, just outside Malaga. After an evening of excellent local food and wine, the new Mayor and Bill Etherington were photographed together standing in mutual support, with wide grins, summing up the group's feelings.

The visit led to a few exchanges with the Andalucian AES. An AES group visited the North-East during Adult

Learners' Week in May 1992, with a stall in Sunderland's main ALW event. A small WEA Northern District group then visited Malaga in the summer, also to finalise details for the first 'Office Sector' conference. The group witnessed a marvellous end of year graduation fiesta in a hilltop village near Estepona organised by AES head Ana Mora. Adult learners, most from literacy and post-literacy courses, showed their talents in front of a large audience with traditional songs and dances.

Arrangements for the Malaga 1992 'Office Sector' conference were successfully concluded during this visit: arrangements much helped by face-to-face meetings and visits to premises. Relations with Andalucian AES faded in subsequent years, mostly because they largely worked in literacy and post-literacy, which then formed only a minute part of WEA work. Attempts to involve North-East Local Authority Adult and Community Education Services in the contact, in view of their sizeable literacy and post-literacy programmes, were not successful.

In conclusion, twenty years of international contact and visits demanded much enthusiasm and hard work, not easy to sustain. Yet, the Northern District's leadership was far-sighted in supporting and taking part in such contacts. It broadened the experience of course members, affiliated organisations, staff and WEA activists and brought much pleasure. It widened the District's outlook, made us friends abroad and helped make this a special, adventurous time and place to be in the WEA.

Memories of a Tutor, 1950 to 1976

J. R. (Roger) Till

(Compiled and edited by Ruth Tanner in February 2010)

In the *Annual Report* for 1950-51, Roger's first address is given as: The Hare and Hounds, Frosterley, 'and thereby hangs a tale' writes Roger.

I was living at the Hare and Hounds simply because that was the only accommodation I could find. It was a condition of my appointment that in the first instance I should live in Weardale, where besides teaching as an extra-mural staff tutor my duties would include some organising. I happened to go to a WEA day school somewhere in Teesdale, and one of the people there was a Mr W. A. Clear, a full-time WEA Organiser. (After many years' service with the WEA, Mr. Clear, a staunch member of the Church of England, lived happily in his retirement in a local authority old peoples' home in Ferryhill. His Christian name was Arthur but I never heard anyone call him by that name — it was always 'Mr Clear'. That shows a big social change since I came to Durham in the last months of 1950.) He had a great dome of a head and a rather old-world manner of speaking. He was indeed a memorable character. For years he used to go to summer schools that the university and the WEA held at one or other of the colleges, such as Hatfield or St. Mary's. He made it his job to see that all those attending and choosing to go out in the evening should be back by a certain time. Woe betide anyone who wasn't! There were times when not everyone took him seriously, but Charles Hocking, for many years District Secretary of the WEA, said to me 'He'd do anything for the WEA'.

Another person I met was the late Denis Coggins who told me of a cottage adjoining a small farm. A few months later, Margaret and I went to live there at a rent of seven shillings per week.

Roger recalls taking the first of many literature classes, both tutorial (usually three years in length, though sometimes four), one-yearly, and 'terminal'.

I took my first class meeting in literature on a very cold evening at St. John's Chapel in Weardale at the beginning of December 1950. No buses were running above Stanhope, which made it necessary to travel back to Frosterley in a hired car. It was snowing. We sat round the fire to keep warm. That was in the local schoolroom, where in the freezing winter of 1946-47 I was told an inspector had visited a class. As the weather was so bad he wondered whether he could get through. He did, and stayed a week.

After a few years in Weardale I was moved to Durham where I could be sent more easily to take classes in West Hartlepool, Sunderland, Darlington and Spennymoor among other places, as well as Durham City itself.

Also in 1950, the Durham Extra-Mural Department appointed another staff tutor. This was Peter Kaim-Caudle, who was later (1976-79) Chair of the WEA Northern District and also a Vice-President. Peter and his wife Patricia and their children were to become much valued friends. To enable me to take a fairly early morning course that he had helped to organise for a group of trade unionists, on what would now be called communication skills ('The Written word and the Spoken'), he and his wife put me up for the night each week. Peter, who had been an immensely popular tutor during a spell of teaching in Africa, taught Economics when he came to Durham. He later became Professor of Social Policy. A deeply humane man, he was always acutely aware of the hard lives of a great many people in modern society. He had a most sincere determination to help them as much as possible. Even when I did not agree with him on some particular issue we remained very good friends as well as colleagues. In later years we used to go together to the AGM of the WEA Northern District. Peter always had something to say about the financial state of the District and searching questions to ask, sometimes with approval, sometimes critical, but never unimportant or merely destructive. No wonder he was so much appreciated by the many people he had helped.

I asked Roger to reflect on his tutoring styles as they developed through the years and the people who influenced him.

Not long after I started work in County Durham I was sent to Newbattle Abbey College of Adult Education near Edinburgh for a week to observe what was happening there and try to recruit potential students for our region. One day I accepted an invitation to give a talk on any subject I liked. Someone who was present told me that the college warden said to her later 'Did you notice how much more interesting he became when he got away from his notes?' I realised I should have been more confident, and that although a discriminating use of notes is sometime essential, this practice cannot take the place of spontaneity. The warden of the college who made the remark was that fine poet and critic Edwin Muir, a man of complete integrity, whose autobiography, telling of his early days of poverty and hardship in Scotland before his happy marriage and fame as a translator of Kafka, is one of the most outstanding books of its kind in our time. When I heard this man, sitting down informally, talking without a single note, his students, straight from the factory floor, listening with total attention, I saw that a tutor didn't need any gimmicks or showmanship to succeed

Although I was constantly trying to keep in contact with students in ways that would bring them regularly to classes, my approach was traditional rather than experimental. On some of the courses I attended we were split up into smaller groups and reported back afterwards to pool our resources and share our conclusions. Some probably found this helpful. I cannot say I got much from it, but that may have been because I was older than the others and was apt to distrust 'the latest thing'.

One way in which class members changed for the good was in their coming to see that it was possible — some might even say desirable — to hold views that were different from those of the tutor. That sounds obvious, but often those who had not done much serious reading since they left school found it difficult at first to see that it was possible for two people to have different and legitimate opinions about a book or an issue provided the judgement was based on good argument and not simply on prejudice. The usual way of testing these opinions was discussion, though students were also encouraged to do written work. Indeed, when I began it was officially a condition of coming to a class.

At Crook I started a custom that continued for years as 'members' evenings'. The word 'members' emphasised that it was their special chance to write or speak on their chosen subject. The following week I would give a summary of what each member had written the previous week. At first there were groans on the part of some members but once the custom had started it proved a success. Over several years the membership had risen to nearly twenty. True, it had its humorous side. At one class a member said she had been extremely nervous, but had been to the doctor's, taken a tablet or two and all was well. As light relief at the end of the session we would have a class supper at which I would read selections from some of the books we would be studying in the following year. A representative would usually be present from the WEA and members made a donation to the District. When Tom Daveney, the Extra-Mural Director who succeeded Jim Boyden, came to a class I was taking at Spennymoor, what he noticed was that every member took part in the discussion of the book we were studying.

One important change in methods of studying literature has been the substitution of close reading and practical criticism for surveys offering only a superficial view, the sort of thing parodied under the title 'English Literature from Beowulf to Virginia Woolf'. Richard Hoggart, author of a best-selling book *The Uses of Literacy* in the 1960s based on his disadvantaged childhood in Leeds, was himself a very successful tutor in his younger days, but he had less than a dozen in some of his classes. A man who had been to them paid tribute to the value of his deliberately slow and thorough treatment of only a few texts each session. Like any departure from long established conventions that kind of approach had its critics. Hoggart, however, combined a deep seriousness with a sense of humour. At a conference he read a sparkling paper on different types of tutor, for example, the 'Tired Titan' and the 'Visiting Olympian', just as an anonymous wag is said to have read a paper on 'The approach to the book box'.

On the whole, similar views to those of Hoggart were held by Raymond Williams, son of a railway signalman in the Welsh borders. At one summer school, he was kind enough to let me see him taking a group of students and applying his methods, which some found austere. Instead of telling them what his own views were or even asking students to comment on specific points in the passages he had handed out, he would wait for someone to speak, even risking embarrassment when there was silence. 'A bit grim, isn't it?' commented a newcomer! Yet from all accounts when people had got used to the new approach they got far more out of it than they had from the old type of study. At that time Williams was an adult education tutor working in Sussex. He later became professor of Drama at Cambridge where he had a great influence.

As an antidote to the old discredited method of skimming instead of reading with close attention and real understanding it has sometimes been said that a good tutor will be likely to have a small class and a bad tutor will have a big one. That seems to be disputable. I have had small classes and big ones. Neither extreme is really a criticism of the quality or otherwise of the course. It is true that a large class presents different problems. I think tutors should adapt their techniques accordingly. Here I may part company with some of my colleagues. I think there is a case for the formal type of lecture when students are more numerous. At one time there was a waiting list for new members in one of the Durham City classes. After the uphill struggle I and other tutors had had in teaching village classes, where one of our students was a shepherd, and therefore had seasonal duties, that was undeniably flattering, but also a warning not to think that in future everything in the garden would be lovely.

I also asked Roger to recall some of the people who came to his classes. With the aid of his exceptional memory and impeccable record-keeping, in addition to his customary concern and respect for his students, he took this task very seriously.

First, the word itself. 'Are we students?' said a middle-aged man in an extra-mural class later inherited by the WEA. Now that schoolchildren, as they used to be called, are described as 'students', I wonder how he would have liked to be bracketed with them. I know that there is a lingering feeling in some quarters that 'teachers' and 'housewives' are not what the pioneers of the WEA had in mind when the movement was formed, as though society had not changed since then. Many of those labelled 'teachers' and 'housewives' had similar ideals to our early members.

There was certainly plenty of variety in the students' occupations. For example, a housing manager, Joe Coleman, who had won the Military Medal at the Battle of the Somme; two ICI welders; a fitter's mate, Peter Murray, with a library of several hundred books, who once to his delight found that a fellow passenger in a train was the original of G. K. Chesterton's Father Brown; a miner; a prison governor; three doctors; a vicar; some teachers; a Methodist minister and a girls' grammar school headmistress. I did teach selected groups of industrial workers. I lectured to miners recruited through the Northumberland branch of the NUM at a hotel on the seafront at Whitley Bay. I should also mention some of the outstanding individual students I taught.

First, there was Norman Beevers, a Water Board labourer who came to live in Upper Weardale just as the depression in the 1930s started. He came to a literature class I was teaching in St John's Chapel simply to occupy his fine mind. He had several children, nearly all of whom went on from local schools to university and gained degrees with first class honours.

Another student, Frank Webster, a railway signalman, used to attend a literature class I took at Witton-le-Wear. We used to meet after the class each week. Like me he had been in the Navy. He was so keen on reading and discussing good literature that he came to the class in his working clothes after having been on a turn since four o'clock in the morning. The class, he said, had made a tremendous difference to him. He became one of the best friends I ever had.

The third outstanding student who comes to mind was James McFarlane. Like Norman Beevers, he knew what the prolonged effects of unemployment were. His chief interest was economics but he joined a class on literature I held in Sunderland. I remember taking him to the new County Hall in Durham when it was being built. He was out of work for some time before joining the class. He had an exceptionally good brain. He went to school at Sunderland in 1907 in a class of 107 children.

One more outstanding student should be mentioned, John Brennan of Crook. When he was fourteen he was put to work in the pits at Roddymoor. His parents thought that as he was not going to be a teacher, he should work there. Like me, he was a great admirer of Dickens' novels, which he read by the light of a candle. Determined to leave his cramping environment, he did so, and secured a job locally. For years he came to the Crook class regularly. When I was travelling to North America in 1965 to teach and examine in a university, I had the good fortune to meet a son of his who had prospered in business. He took me in his car to one of the big open-air theatres in Canada. He was full of admiration for his father's courage and determination.

I confess to having one general disappointment — that there were usually fewer men than women and that, except in specially selected courses, there were not more really young people. This was (and is!) true of more parts of the country than the WEA Northern District. In my experience as a tutor there was one exception to the usual preponderance of women members. That was the class I was sent to take early in the

1950s at Billingham — a class that had been built up by the WEA.

Roger also saw the class outing as an active approach to publicity.
In the summer months, it was our custom at Crook to visit places of literary interest such as the Brontës' Old Parsonage at Haworth in Yorkshire and Scott's home at Abbotsford. That was a good way of getting the class known. Even so, we found that in spite of publicity in libraries and newspapers the most effective way of getting new members was by word of mouth. When I passed a notebook round asking people to say how they had heard about the class many of them wrote: 'From a friend'. I am glad to say no-one wrote: 'From an enemy'.

Similarly, for a time we held summer schools at Alnwick Castle, meeting for meals in what used to be the servants' quarters, a contrast to the Duke of Northumberland's fine library in another part of the grounds. That provided a contrast also to present day attitudes and the part that the WEA among other bodies have played in the progress towards more social equality since the time of 'upstairs, downstairs'.

Roger was always aware of the reading needs of students and this was usually provided via the 'Book Box'.
We had a good supply of books from the county library and the library of the Extra-Mural Department (later re-named the Adult and Continuing Education Department and finally Lifelong Learning), containing sets of books representing different forms of writing — not only novels and short stories, but also poetry, drama, biography, diaries and letters. These were provided not for examination but for the satisfaction and often the delight resulting from systematic reading and a good-humoured exchange of views with the tutor. I always regarded myself as a fellow-student, not the voice of authority and I hoped that this was the attitude of our part-time tutors too. Although there were times when I felt I had been tolerably successful, I hardly ever felt I had done as well as possible. Perhaps that was just as well. I distrust people who tell you they have never made mistakes. We all do. We should learn from them, just as we should learn from our students. I still remember some of the comments that this or that person has made in a class thirty, forty and fifty years earlier.

Not all the classes I took were of the same length. After several years taking tutorial classes in Durham, shorter sessions were introduced which were intended, partly at any rate, for busy housewives, mothers and others whose domestic commitments were considerable, and for whom afternoon sessions were more convenient. I made it clear that no-one hesitating to come to a class should be deterred because they had not read everything. No doubt it is good to be well read. It is even better to read well! I think of the Teesside housewife who, in spite of busy domesticity put aside two hours every evening for reading.

Finally, Roger has memories of 'exponents of the Arts' and recalls some of these practitioners.
Now and again someone new made a reputation as an exponent of one of the Arts, and did so after a hard apprenticeship, as it were. One of these was Sid Chaplin, one of whose articles is reprinted as Chapter 17, once a blacksmith in a coalmine, who made his name as a short story writer and novelist. In one of his books he paid tribute to a class he attended at Ferryhill, where the tutor was Clifford Leech, a deservedly popular Durham academic. I had the good fortune to know Sid for many years before his death. He was a delightful man, modest and companionable without any affectation. It was always a pleasure to meet him by chance or to receive a letter or telephone call from him. He was not only a creative writer but a keen reader of literature.

The same was true of Michael Standen, the former District Secretary of the WEA Northern District, whose reminiscences are reprinted as Chapter 13. Besides being a novelist of distinction, he was also a poet and painter, whose untimely death at the age of seventy was regretted by many people. It is interesting to recall one occasion when he and Sid Chaplin were together. That was when the poet W. H. Auden wanted to do some sightseeing in Northumberland. It was arranged that Michael should act as chauffeur and Sid should be a passenger. It would have been fascinating to have had a tape recording of the conversation in that car! I feel sure that the action and interest of such people as Michael in the arts as well as teaching and administration had a helpful influence on people's tastes and interests in the region.

On the subject of controversial topics I would sometimes have to remind students that the purpose of our classes was not to teach people what to think, but *how* to think. In general, I would say this about the experience I had as a tutor of adult classes: I learned not to expect too much of students. I also learned not to expect too little.

"Work Cums Fust"[1]

Sid Chaplin

'There's a time and a place for iverything, but work cums fust,' said my Grandma the night she sent Grandpa in search of one of her lads who had threatened 'to lose a shift'. Grandpa walked into the dance, and tapping my Uncle on the shoulder said, 'Howway, lad — tha' must get to work'. And the lad came away like a lamb. I can see him now, pulling on his pit-duds and pulling down his mouth. But sharper still is the memory of my Grandma's words that portrayed a world still to come for me, words that echoed through many aching hours of labour — 'Work cums fust'.

When for the first time I leapt out of bed at the summons to work it was the first — and the last — time of leaping. Wearing my father's pit-boots and a pair of old overalls, an old yellow gansy and a bright red muffler, I must have looked like some gay, daft bird of paradise, as I stepped into the street. My tea can jingled inside my bucket, answering the jingle of other buckets in other streets. It was tatie-picking week and, at two bob a day, I would soon be as good as any working man.

Shire-horses blew into the brittle air and their bells and brasses danced and made wild music as the great hooves lifted and plunged along the furrows, steel cleaving through earth to uncover rolled gold roots and nests of round nuggets. Unaccustomed muscles made sharp argument in the small of your back but if you knelt the farmer shouted, 'Dost need a bed, lad?' So you bent to it, picking hard, with the cold snapping at your face and fingers. Toes curled inside hard, unfriendly boots in an effort to find warmth, and it was a relief to carry your full pail to the man holding the sack. But then you saw how long the furrow was: straight and immovable it stretched to a dyke at the other end of the world. All of twelve years of age, you were beyond weeping from either cold or despair, so you wept within yourself. Such is the nature of work to the worker — buckling into it with despair at an infinity of furrows. This is the 'sign and token of their sufferings', as Simone Weil so aptly put it.

What I came to hate about the pit was its enduring repetitiveness. But the smithy had its compensations. Sometimes, very rarely, there crept in a kind of magic, not unlike the magic of the fields when the sun shone bright and you grew conscious of something around you. The tremendous horses and the hissing man following them, the cart coming and going for the sacks, the man with a red face and a ready joke as you took up your full pail. And attacking the upturned furrows was an army of children, and you one of them. Not just two hands, but many.

This was the second great lesson of work: that it could be a sharing rather than an enduring.[2] In the smithy a craft had to be won, and work narrowed to a fire, anvil, and a piece of obdurate metal. There was a great art in slowly mastering the heat and hammer, and the mastery was three parts heritage. The craftsman whose working life you shared had in times past watched other craftsmen. So a trick of tempering steel had been carried maybe from a country shop, or a turn of the wrist in a particular job from Tyneside, and the older craftsmen I knew — ponderous George Campbell, silent Bill Henderson, and mercurial Alex Sylie — lads they taught.

In the smithy men worked within sight of each other. The finished product lay in full view of a dozen critical eyes and the botched job was a shameful twisted thing that stung your pride more than the foreman's sharp reproof. A shaft-key badly case-hardened could cost two hundred tons of coal as well as good men's wages. So a craftsman's pride was a sharper incentive than six shillings and sixpence ha'penny a shift. Yours was the mastery, and if mastery slept a moment yours was the shame. It sounds lovely — excepting that craftsmanship was far from being the real driving force. What counted far more was a last lingering remnant of Victorian work-discipline ('Work cums fust') which put the smooth functioning of the pit above all else; and the constant pressure of sheer economic necessity. The wages were so nicely adjusted that overtime was needed to top them up; so it suited the men to work endless overtime. In effect the pit became a prison,

[1] This chapter was first published in WEA Northern District *Annual Report* (1976-77). The WEA is grateful to Mrs Irene Chaplin for permission to republish. The original footnotes are retained with full references added. Typographical errors have been silently corrected.

[2] For a similar experience, see the fine biography of a WEA-educated poet: Clark, Leonard, 1945. *Alfred Williams: his life and work*. Oxford: Blackwell (republished Newton Abbott: David and Charles, 1969).

leaving no time for leisure and enjoyment, let alone for pause. I grew inevitably to hate the sight, sound and especially the smell of the place — an all-pervading stench of pit pony and human ordure which rifted everywhere along with the dust.

At least there had been a comforting feeling of certainty about tattie-picking — since tatie-picking lasted only a week. But the pit went on for ever. Neither before nor since have I felt so hopelessly and inexorably exiled as in the cage, first of the pit-screens (a suffocating jungle of noise, dust and Darwinian relationships), and later in the smithy during the first few weeks of my apprenticeship. Later, of course, I did manage to find along with other compensations an inner core of resilience which enabled me to get by. But the first reaction was to run away, if not physically then away inside myself. And that is how I joined the WEA in the first place, as an escapee blindly on the run.

One of the compensations was religion. Those were apocalyptic times. Unemployment spread like a plague. The old safe world was crashing in ruin about us. Half the pits in the country were 'laid in' and everywhere stark rusting hulks were accompanied by streets of boarded shops. Whole areas resembled nothing so much as an elephant's graveyard. I remember the elder of the tiny fundamental chapel I attended asserting quite seriously, 'We have come to the latter times'; and indeed there were days when I used to look up into the sky half expecting to see Christ return in glory. But he never did — and being a healthy young animal I was mostly thankful he didn't.

So by the queerest combination of folk and circumstances I set off and walked the couple of windy miles to Chilton Buildings one night and joined an extra-mural class in Old Testament History; Dr. Edwin Pace giving the blessing, with Arthur Clear (later to be WEA Assistant District Secretary but them employed as a cokeworker), James Rochester, a Quaker colliery manager and Tom Green, an ex-pitman, assisting in the kindest possible induction. If the shade of Pallas Athena were present she must have laughed up her sleeve. Not only was I the most unlikely Biblical scholar ever — but I promptly fell asleep and was only aroused when Tom Green got into a whopping great row with the Doctor on the correct meaning of a passage in the original Hebrew.

Tom Green was the first of many authentic scholars I was to meet in the WEA. Badly injured in a fall from one of the coaches which constituted the 'paddy mail' then used for transporting miners from Merrington Lane to old Westerton Colliery, he had set about teaching himself to read Greek and Hebrew. Short and stocky, he lived behind his pebble-thick glasses, with no other aim (so far as I could see) but the joy of disputation. Reading the texts was for him the equivalent of growing leeks or racing pigeons, and he brought to it the same hotly competitive spirit. But in a strange sort of way he was the catalyst of our class who, impervious and unchanging, invariably got all the rest of us on the boil. Joe Wedderburn was another such. Pure gold, both of them. In comparison I was only a butterfly; alighting and tasting, but never quite finding what I looked for — which was frankly a mixture of escape and replacement.

A passage I wrote more than a decade ago gives some idea of the kind of butterfly I was.

> To be fair, more than a couple of people were involved. I sniffed round every WEA class going, and in the end settled for an extra-mural class that had A.P. Rossitter and Clifford Leach in turn, both real men of letters … Then I discovered a pit-village university, the Spennymoor Settlement, founded to give unemployed men and women something to do. The top man there was Bill Farrell, actor, producer and painter. Thanks to him I saw all of Ibsen, and a lot of Sean O'Casey, Strindberg and Chekhov in a little gem of a theatre. His second in command was an ex-coal-hewer via Ruskin College called Jack Maddison who didn't believe in ivory towers. Oh, and there was a passionate cell of D. H. Lawrence followers at an Adult School five miles away; being a Primitive Methodist of sorts I recognised at once the source of all this blood-stuff and making marriage a mixture of class meeting, love feast and brawling for the sake of the soul. It was a great time, when you could keep awake, for on top of the sleep-walking which comes of the absence of the critical faculty I went to those intellectual exercises tired from the pit. It was only too easy to give in, especially after the five o'clock shift which involved a split sleep: you put your hand over your eyes and teetered deliciously between sleep and Jane Austen.[3]

It is only when you are running away that you take pause to think. I remember my last day before I left for Fircroft paid a final visit to the sand-house. Warm and secluded, it had been my own version of Coleridge's lime-tree bower. In its sanctuary I had read through all Benn's Sixpenny Classics, ignoring the richness about me. Now it was forced upon me: the audible sound of kernels of wisdom being cracked. When at last they presented me with my parting gift (the two volumes of Coleridge's *Biographia Literaria* which still occupy the place of honour on my shelves) I could only stammer my thanks and run. It had taken me all of

---

[3] Chaplin, Sid, 1972. *A Tree with Rosy Apples* (with illustrations by Norman Cornish). Newcastle upon Tyne: Frank Graham. [Originally published as "On the Poverty Line". In: Twentieth Century, Winter 1966.]

seven years to recognise in that ugly sprawl of buildings a human habitation and dwelling place. The next time I left, it was to be with a purpose other than running away.

What happened in the meantime was a tutor (true WEA model as well) who made no bones about taking my measure. His name was Bill Warburton, ex-potter, historian of the Potter's Trade Union and an ex-student at Fircroft College himself. His verdict related to one of my essays. 'Your economics may be inexact but they're jolly entertaining', he told me. 'You should be a writer'. He was the first person ever to tell me this. I had the freedom of a wonderful library, and for the first time in my life I was able to read nothing but the best. This is the only way to get your measure. I got it; I knew what kind of writer I wanted to be, and what I would write about. I would put into stories the life and landscape of home.

Not that it came quite as pat as that. Now that I was writing, everything and everybody seemed to be conspiring to stop me. At the same time I was readjusting to my job. I was no longer a blacksmith, but an underground mechanic — almost a miner. Although I never realised it, I was also serving my time as a writer.

The pit moulded men into objects that were subordinated not only to machines but to a system of work. Men trudged like ants to the coal-fronts, long trenches won daily from the narrow seam and the pincers of the strata. Day after day the fillers lay on their sides and shovelled coal, their only relief from the monotonous twist and sweep in putting up pit-props, and that grudged, for the cash was in the coal and not the niceties of roof-control.

Here was division of labour with a vengeance, for the fillers were only one group of several who ministered to the machines and to the cycle of coal-getting operations. The older men remembered the old hand methods. Then the physical demands were heavier, but men set their own pace and standards and (most important) were in full control of their working places. Remembering this, they reacted against the violence done against them with like violence. Faults, temporary failures in ventilation, the pressures and tearing apart of the strata, breakdowns in machinery — all these conspired to intensify the reciprocal violence. It was a world of fierce brawls in which the anger and anguish of men was only silenced by the mighty rending of the strata.

Despite this the coal was won. It was won because of the stubborn, cross-grained. undefeated spirit of mining men. Men were bigger than the system, especially when men were in jeopardy, and a sweating, dust-caked dwarf would squirm below a nightmare roof lowering an inch a minute aware of nothing but the props he placed and the mute but voluble hand of a trapped comrade. Five minutes before, perhaps, the pair had hurled bright blasphemies at each other.

In these moments the words of my grandmother would take on a deeper and more majestic meaning. Work does indeed come first, because work is man's life, and because it can challenge his body beyond the limit or hone his spirit to a true humility. But it would be untrue as well as vulgar to assert that I simply gathered material. The men taught me: I was penetrated by the heart of the matter. That I ventured to the nearest town and bought myself a second-hand typewriter was almost incidental. Writing is a way of coming to grips with the world; but there was one critical point where the present world inter-penetrated my past servitude. The elation of making a good story was at least equal to the mastery of the good blacksmith — something I had never really achieved. How to get it right — that was something I now had in common with the blacksmiths. This is the true meaning of labour. If it is to be satisfying a man must not be robbed of his birthright — the opportunity to give full play to skill and to judgement.

Work becomes most shameful when it is entirely subordinated to production. The triumphant industrial society — if ever it comes — will dare to encourage the interest and imagination of its workers 'in the act, as well as the end of labour', says Camus. It will give to its workers the dignity of creators. I got out, but the brand will always be on me. Happy in my calling — even, successful to a degree — I owe everything to my tutors; mural, extra-mural and informal. But I am in no doubt as to whom I am indebted most. It was the men of the smithy and the pit who made me. Perhaps my Grandma was right when she said that all things have their time and place — but work comes first.

The Right to Learn Today

Liz Armstrong

Adult learners treasure their right to learn and the best of that learning invariably produces independent thinkers. It is not surprising, therefore, that early in 2007 when it became apparent that government funding for adult education was under threat, a group of adult students got together to start a campaign to publicise the fact and to lobby against it.

Many of the students in the group had enjoyed years of WEA classes in the North-East; others were regular attendees at Sunderland University's Centre for Lifelong Learning (CLL) on the Newcastle University campus, or were students on local authority courses. All were strongly opposed to a government policy which had increased funding for work-based courses at the expense of wider adult education. One and a half million further places in education had already been lost, and subsidy for many adults on some part time higher education courses was due to be withdrawn. The threat to the type of education people undertake for their own interest or well-being was particularly serious.

So, what could be done? Most of the group had no previous experience of campaigning but there were some obvious starting points. First came the organisation of a public petition against the cuts which ultimately acquired over 1,000 signatures and was presented to Nick Brown, Minister for the North, in March 2008 when he attended the WEA Regional Spring Conference. There followed letters to MPs and local politicians, attendances at political surgeries, letters to the local and national press and radio interviews. Students across the North-East supported our work with enthusiasm — they too wrote letters and contacted politicians.

As the campaign gathered momentum it quickly became apparent that we needed to attract some funding to keep going. With the help of the Council for Voluntary Services (CVS) we agreed our own Memorandum of Understanding — a sort of informal constitution — which we were able to use to support a successful bid to the Co-operative Community Fund. Funding allowed us to produce an advertising leaflet and some posters to spread the word about our campaign.

All of this was happening against a background of national activity and we were pleased to be part of the national network Campaigning Alliance for Lifelong Learning (CALL), which lobbied parliament in February 2009. A group of twelve people from the Right to Learn Campaign joined with other students from across the country and met some of the region's MPs. They attended a meeting with John Denham who was then the minister with responsibility for adult education. We also contributed very fully to the consultation on John Denham's white paper *The Learning Revolution* which was finally published in April 2009.[1]

The proposals in *The Learning Revolution* are now embedded in government policy. There is some evidence that our contribution, together with that of other similar groups nationwide, had some influence. However, whilst perhaps more funding than expected has been directed at adult education, we still have concerns about the affordability of the type of courses undertaken primarily for interest as opposed to qualification — the sorts of courses that the WEA and others have been proud to offer to all for the last hundred years.

So, what now? In this, the centenary year of the WEA in the North and North-East, we faced a general election. With support from the WEA Regional Office the *Right To Learn Hustings* was organised in Newcastle-upon-Tyne. In April prospective parliamentary candidates were invited to a public meeting at the new City Library. The meeting focused on Labour, Conservative and Liberal Democrat policies for safeguarding the future of lifelong learning. Around one hundred people with a wide range of experience as tutors and students attended the meeting, giving our parliamentary candidates a clear impression of the importance of adult education. The hustings meeting was backed up with letter-writing and contacts with the press and media. Our overall message remains a demand for fairer funding for all types of adult education and we hope that students from all adult education centres will make their voices heard in this regard. This important message and our campaign will continue.

As far as the WEA North-East Region is concerned we are determined to play our part to ensure that it goes from strength to strength during its second century.

[1] URL: www.dius.gov.uk, accessed on 1 March 2010.

Notes on Contributors

Eileen Aird was Organising Tutor in Women's Education for the WEA Northern District from 1981 to 1985 and Assistant General Secretary, WEA National Office from 1985 to 1989. She was subsequently Principal of Hillcroft College for Women and Director of the Women's Therapy Centre. She now works as a psychoanalytic psychotherapist in private practice. Publications include *Sylvia Plath* (Oliver and Boyd, 1973) and chapters, articles and reviews on literature, education, counselling and psychotherapy.

Liz Armstrong has attended WEA classes and worked as a volunteer for the Newcastle-upon-Tyne WEA branch since 1971. She was elected to the Northern District Committee in 1975, was District Treasurer from 1976 to 1980 and served as a committee member until 2000. Currently she chairs the WEA Regional Curriculum and Quality Assurance Committee and the independent Right To Learn Campaign Group.

Jonathan Brown came to Tyneside in 1970 as Staff Tutor and Deputy Director of the Department of Adult Education (later Lifelong Learning) in the University of Newcastle-upon-Tyne. From 1977 until his retirement in 1999 he was a senior counsellor with the Open University in the North where he held a personal Chair in Educational Guidance. He was a member of the WEA Northern District Committee from 1977 to 1993 and District Vice-President from 1997 to 2003.

Victor Ricardo Cadaxa came to Britain in 1967 to study, first at Keele University (BA in economics, history and politics, 1971), then at London University (MA in Latin American history and sociology, 1973). After a period working in metal industries, Victor joined the WEA in August 1974 as Tutor Organiser for the brand-new Sunderland Metropolitan Borough and stayed with the WEA until his early retirement in December 2005. Victor's teaching was in history and current affairs (Europe, Latin America, Spain and Portugal) and trade union studies, in particular health and safety.

Sid Chaplin (1916-1986) was born in Shildon, County Durham. He was apprenticed to a colliery blacksmith but during the Second World War he worked as a miner at the coalface. After the war, Sid became a professional writer of novels, short stories and articles in magazine, local and national newspapers and lived in Newcastle-upon-Tyne. With the re-issue of two of his novels by Flambard Press, (2004a. *Day of the Sardine;* 2004b. *The Watchers and the Watched),* Sid's work remains in print to this day.

Robert Lyon (1894-1978) served as a private soldier with the King's Liverpool Regiment (the Liverpool 'Pals' Regiment) in the Great War. After the war he studied at Liverpool School of Art and the Royal College of Art, London and was awarded the Prix de Rome for painting in 1924. In 1932 Robert moved to Newcastle-upon-Tyne to become Master of Painting at what was then Armstrong College, now Newcastle University. In 1942 he become Principal of Edinburgh College of Art where he served until his retirement in 1960. Robert was also a mural painter and portraitist whose paintings include murals at Edinburgh Western General Hospital, King's College, London Dental School and Essex County Hall, Chelmsford. During his time at Newcastle in 1934, he was asked to tutor an art class for a group of miners in Ashington. The Pitmen Painters was probably the most famous WEA class ever held, whose history is recorded by William Feaver in *The Pitmen Painters: the Ashington Group* 1934-1984. More recently Feaver's book has been adapted for the stage by Lee Hall and his play, 'The Pitman Painters' was first produced at the Live Theatre in Newcastle from where it transferred to the National Theatre in London and subsequently to Broadway.

Tom Nesbit has worked in adult and trade union education in England, USA and Canada. He is currently Associate Dean of Continuing Studies at Simon Fraser University in Vancouver, British Columbia, and Editor of the Canadian Journal for the Study of Adult Education.

Hilda Pickles (1915-1995), née Dunn, was born and bred on Tyneside and worked in a variety of schools in the area before being appointed as Tutor Organiser for the WEA in North Cumberland in 1943. Hilda married in 1948 and remained in Cumbria for the rest of her life. She was a councillor with Eden District Council for seventeen years and also a member of the board of Northern Arts until 1992. She recounted her experiences of education and life in a very entertaining volume published in 1993, entitled *Crooked sixpences among the chalk: seventy-five years of schooling.*

Ian Roberts trained as an historian in London and subsequently obtained postgraduate degrees from Durham and Newcastle, where his PhD was in economic history. Ian has published widely in this and allied fields, notable recent books including *Telling Tales out of School* (with the Bellingham WEA, where he is a tutor) and *Drove Roads in Northumberland* (with Richard Carlton and Alan Rushworth). Ian is currently Deputy Chair of WEA North-East Region.

Michael Standen (1937-2008) was a poet, novelist and editor throughout his forty-four-year adult teaching career. He was appointed by the WEA in 1964 as Tutor Organiser in West Cumberland, moving to a similar post in Durham three years later. He was a very popular Northern District Secretary from 1976 until his retirement in 1995. Throughout the period from 1964 until 2008 Michael was a class tutor and viewed teaching literature as a central mission. Just before his untimely death in 2008, he was planning new courses in both Newcastle-upon-Tyne and in Darlington.

Freda Tallantyre obtained her first degree in English Language and Literature at London University in 1970, and her MLitt (on the works of Tom Stoppard) at Newcastle University in 1980. She worked in a girls' high school for five years, then as a part-time tutor for the WEA between 1976 and 1982, and a full-time Tutor Organiser for Northumberland between 1982 and 1986. Freda went on to various change management roles in the University of Northumbria and at the Higher Education Funding Council for England, before concluding her full-time career with eight years as Deputy Vice-Chancellor at the University of Derby.

Ruth Tanner studied history at university, and discovered the WEA while working as Training and Development Officer for the Pre-School Playgroups Association. She later returned to the WEA as a tutor in local history and became inextricably involved in its committee structure. She is currently Secretary of Durham Branch, a Regional Committee member, the North-East Region's representative on the National Association Committee, and a Trustee.

J. R. (Roger) Till joined what was to become the Durham University Extra-Mural Department as a staff tutor in 1950. He had previously worked as a journalist and at the BBC before serving in the navy during the Second World War. After the war, he went to Oxford to study for a degree in English: 'to equip myself for adult education work'. He continued to work in the department tutoring joint WEA tutorial, sessional and termly classes until his retirement in 1976 and continued to be a loyal supporter of the WEA for many more years.

Nigel Todd is North-East Regional Director of the WEA. He studied history at Ruskin College and Lancaster University and his previous books include *The Militant Democracy: Joseph Cowen and Victorian Radicalism* (1991) and *In Excited Times: The People Against the Blackshirts* (1995). Nigel has taught for the WEA and the Open University, and has an extensive involvement with the Co-operative Movement where he is a member of the Board of Governors of the Co-operative College.

Index

Arabic numerals refer to pages,
Roman numerals to the plates.